Illustrations
OF THE
Symbols of Masonry.

Yours with Fraternal Regard
Jacob Ernst

ILLUSTRATIONS OF THE SYMBOLS OF MASONRY

Scripturally and Morally Considered

By JACOB ERNST, K. T.

P. P. or CINCINNATI COMMANDERY, No, 3. KNIGHTS TEMPLARS,
P. H. P. or KILWINNING CHAPTER, No. 97, R. A. MASONS.

STONE GUILD PUBLISHING
PLANO, TEXAS
HTTP://WWW.STONEGUILDPUBLISHING.COM/

2009

Originally Published By:
JACOB ERNST & COMPANY
1868

This Edition Copyright © 2008
Stone Guild Publishing, Inc.
Plano, Texas
http://www.stoneguildpublishing.com/

First Paperback Edition 2009

ISBN-13 978-1-60532-053-3
ISBN-10 1-60532-053-6

10 9 8 7 6 5 4 3 2

To the

Masonic Fraternity,

A Brotherhood whose principles inculcate pure
benevolence, and comprehend a charity circumscribed only
by the limits of the universe; and to which
I bear a cherished and devoted attachment,
with a degree of
sincere respect,

This Work is Affectionately Dedicated:

And if the perusal of its pages will lead my
Brethren to the pleasant pursuits of a more thorough
cultivation and exemplification of the principles
embraced within its sphere, I shall feel
myself amply rewarded for
my labors.

THE AUTHOR.

AUGUST, A. D. 1868, A. L. 5868.

CORRESPONDENCE.

KILWINNING HALL, ANCIENT YORK MASONS,
CINCINNATI, Nov. 27, A. L. 5867, A. D. 1867.

To the W. master, Wardens, and Brethren of
  —lodge, no.—,F. & A. Masons.

The undersigned Committee have made arrangements with Brother Jacob Ernst, for a course of Lectures to be delivered at Kilwinning Hall, during the coming winter. Subject: "The Symbols of Masonry, Scripturally and Morally considered."

You are most cordially and earnestly invited to attend. Lectures free.

E. P. BRADSTREET, *Chairman,*
GEO. W. BROWN, *Secretary,*
WM. WINTERS,
T. C. THORP,
} COMMITTEE.

The following Resolutions were subsequently passed:

BRO. Jacob Ernst, Cincinnati, Ohio,—

Dear Sir and Bro.: At a stated communication of Vattier lodge, No. 386, F. and A. M., held March 19th, 1868, the following Resolutions were presented, and unanimously adopted:

"*Resolved*, That Vattier Lodge, No. 386, F. and A. M., deem it their duty, as well as great pleasure, to congratulate and express their thanks to our worthy Bro, Jacob Ernst, for the very valuable course of Lectures delivered by him on Symbolic Masonry, during the past winter.

"*Resolved*, That in full and earnest appreciation of the same, we would most respectfully request their publication for the benefit of the Craft."

W. STEELE, *Sec.*

CORRESPONDANCE.

HALL OF KILWINNING CHAPTER, No. 97, R. A. MASONS.

"*Resolved,* That Kilwinning Chapter fully appreciates the system of Lectures on the Emblems of Masonry, prepared and delivered before them by Bro, Jacob Ernst; and they earnestly request him to publish the same for the good of the Craft generally, and pledge themselves to give him all reasonable aid and support in so doing."

HALL OF KILWINNING COUNCIL U. D. R. & S. M.,
CINCINNATI, MARCH 10th, 1868.

JACOB ERNST, ESQ.—

Dear Sir and Companion: At a stated communication of Kilwinning Council, held this evening, the following Resolutions were offered, and, on motion, were *unanimously adopted:*

"*Resolved,* That Kilwinning Council U. D. R. & S. M. tender their thanks to Comp. Jacob Ernst, for the able course of Lectures he has delivered at Kilwinning Hall, during the past winter, on *'The Symbols of Masonry, Scripturally and Morally considered.'*

"*Resolved,* That Comp. Jacob Ernst be requested to prepare said Lectures for publication, in book form, for the benefit of the Craft."

Fraternally, yours,
GEO, W. BROWN, *Recorder.*

BRO. JACOB ERNST,   SHELBYVILLE, IND., Aug. 29, 1868.

Dear Sir: I have carefully read the proof sheets of your lectures, "The Symbols of Masonry, Scripturally and Morally considered," which you were pleased to place in my hands, and I am much pleased with of our Order, in giving a better understanding of the moral teachings of Masonry, and the objects of our institution.

The enterprise is praiseworthy, and whatever my influence may avail, shall certainly be exerted for its extension

Truly and Fraternally yours,
WILLIAM HACKER,
Past Grand Master of Indiana.

CONTENTS.

Dedication,	5.
Correspondence,	7—8.
Preface,	13—14.
Introduction,	15—20.

THE DEGREE OF ENTERED APPRENTICE,	21—24.

LECTURE I.

The Altar,	27—50.

LECTURE II.

The Badge of a Mason,	51—64.

LECTURE III.

The Working Tools of an Entered Apprentice,	65—78.

LECTURE IV.

Humility, fidelity, and innocence, ... 79—94.

LECTURE V.

The Highest Hills and Lowest Vales, ... 95—108.

LECTURE VI.

Wisdom, Strength, and Beauty, ... 109—122.

LECTURE VII.

Faith, Hope, and Charity, ... 123—134.

LECTURE VIII.

Book of the Law, ... 135—146.

LECTURE IX.

The Ornaments and Lights of a Lodge, ... 147—166.

LECTURE X.

The Jewels of a Lodge, ... 167—180.

LECTURE XI.

Dedication, ... 181—194.

LECTURE XII.

The Tenets, ... 195—214.

LECTURE XIII.

The Cardinal Virtues, ... 215—242.

The Fellow-Craft's Degree, ... 243—250.

LECTURE XIV.

The Working Tools of a Fellow-Craft, ... 251—260.

LECTURE XV.

The Globes and Pillars, ... 261—276.

LECTURE XVI.

The Orders of Architecture, and the Five Senses
   of Human Nature, ... 277—290.

LECTURE XVII.

The Seven Liberal Arts and Sciences, ... 291—308.

THE MASTER MASON'S DEGREE, ... 309—312.

LECTURE XVIII.

The Working Tool of a Master Mason, ... 313—316.

LECTURE XIX.

The Five Points of Fellowship, ... 317—336.

LECTURE XX.

Emblems of Consideration, ... 337—346.

OUR SYMBOLS, ... 347—356.

PREFACE.

THE following lectures, which we have dedicated to the Masonic Fraternity, were prepared under somewhat peculiar circumstances, and were not originally intended for publication. I had, during the past summer, an unusual amount of unemployed time, which seemed to pass wearily away, unproductive to myself and to others, and for which my conscience condemned me, Yet I was unable to relieve myself from the undesirable position in which circumstances had placed me.

To pass away these unemployed and tedious hours, and feeling a realization of responsibility for the waste of time, I devoted my idle time to writing short pencil sketches, illustrative of our Symbols, and which I found at first somewhat of a difficult task to perform, as I had never before given any attention to writing essays or literary compositions. But I had learned, from the useful instructions portrayed by our symbols, that it was only through application, industry, and perseverance in the pursuit of our object, that we were able to attain our desires. And although we might not fully realize them, yet we might approximate some what thereto. And when we had done all that we could, with such appliances as we were able to command, we would as least enjoy the consolation that we had done the best. that our feeble efforts and abilities allowed.

We can not all expect to become skillful and proficient masters in our work; for this would not meet. the great end and purposes of life. Some, by superior endowments, are intended to give the designs

designs of their genius upon the trestle-board, while others are adapted to execute and carry out those designs. Hence, it is a combination of genius and industry by which we design, prepare, and execute, Neither ought we to feel discouraged because we can not all arrive at an equal degree of eminence. Nor should we be envious of our superiors.

With these reflections and considerations, after having devoted some time to this enterprise, and taking the great Light of Truth as the foundation upon which to erect my edifice, and this being also the corner-stone and foundation upon which our superstructure is erected, I applied myself with diligence to my task, and the more I labored, the more my thoughts became expanded and developed.

Some of these productions, with considerable diffidence, I submitted to the inspection of several of my confidential brethren, and it was by their encouraging assurance and desire that I was prevailed upon to prepare and put them in a series of lectures; and which, at the request of the brethren of Vattier Lodge and Kilwinning Chapter, were delivered before the Fraternity during the past winter, and subsequently requested to be published.

This is my apology in appearing before my brethren in the character of an author and lecturer. And if my labors in this enterprise will be productive of good to my brethren of the Mystic Tie, in putting more fully into practice, in their daily intercourse with one another and their fellow-men, the sublime principles inculcated in our noble and time-honored institution, it will be the happiest labor that I have performed in life.

AUTHOR.

CINCINNATI, March, A. L. 5868-A. D. 1868.

INTRODUCTION.

THE following lectures are devoted exclusively to the first three degrees in Masonry, denominated the Symbolic Degrees. And, as the principles of morality inculcated therein are illustrated by the various emblems pertaining to the operative Mason, so they create within us an observance of those duties we owe to our God and each other, and likewise produce the reflections which impress the mind with man's earthly pilgrimage, his mortality, and of the innate principle of immortality. No human institution has yet been conceived or brought into being that, for harmony, consistency, and beauty of order, is its parallel, It stands unrivaled as a venerable monument of exalted excellence, surrounded and hallowed by ages of antiquity, and leads the van of all human associations for man's general good. As the pillar of cloud that attended the children of Israel when journeying to the land of promise, so stands our time-honored institution, a pillar of light to the brotherhood, illumed by the rays shed abroad from the center where rests its great light.

Those who may anticipate any thing in these lectures, relative to the origin of our institution, will be disappointed in realizing their expectations, as we do not propose entering that field; for that is a subject more especially for the exploration of the antiquarian. And it is really of but little moment to as, in our present time, as to what particular period of the world it is indebted to for its origin. Whether we trace it back to the antediluvian period, the Mysteries of Egypt, the building of King Solomon's Temple, the schools of those ancient sages and philosophers, Pythagoras, Socrates, or Zoroaster, does not concern our present undertaking. It is mainly for our present consideration and purpose that we treat what its purposes and uses are.

That our institution is of great antiquity, cannot be denied, nor doubted. That it is, and always has been, religious and moral in its principles and nature, cannot be controverted, for this is the testimony of our best informed writers.

We have stated that our object was not to enter into the misty ages of antiquity to seek out the origin of our institution. Yet, if we were permitted to venture an opinion of our own, we would trace it far anterior to the building of the first Temple. It existed with the Patriarchs and Prophets of old, for their system of instruction was imparted by symbols. Hence, those eminent pagan philosophers, who were cotemporary with many of those holy men to whom the Almighty was pleased to reveal himself as the instruments to proclaim his will from time to time, and thereby perpetuate his name and preserve it from being lost through the idolatrous worship of the nations surrounding his chosen people, it was from them and from their teachings they derived their knowledge of the supreme being. And the schools formed by these philosophers were based upon the truths proclaimed by them. But the prevailing idolatry and vulgar prejudices of the nations with which they dwelt, forbade the public proclamation thereof. These truths were too far advanced and sublime for the conception of ordinary minds. They ran counter to the prevailing interests of those engaged in the handicraft of idolatry. Hence they were only imparted in their esoteric departments, and only to such minds as were qualified and prepared for their reception.

When the alliance was formed between King Solomon and Hiram, king of Tyre, for the building of the Temple—the house to be dedicated to the pure worship of the only true and living God—then the connection and union was formed between operative and speculative Masonry. A solemn covenant was entered into between those two royal personages, in bonds of sincere and mutual ties of amity in commerce and friendship.

King Hiram furnished the timbers from the forests of Lebanon, and the stones from the quarries of Zeredathah, for the building, and bands of artificers as workmen, and the skillful architect and superintendent of the work, and for which he received, in return, corn, wine, and oil. And these three, Solomon of Israel, Hiram of Tyre, and Hiram the architect, were the original three Grand Masters of the Craft, and formed a trio, or union, wherein were blended the religious, the moral, and the operative principles of Masonry.

The principal architect of the building was also of Jewish and Tyrian parentage. Hence, in the character of this personage, were also blended the two then existing principles of the order, for he was as well known for his devoted piety to the true God, as for his superior excellence and unrivaled skill in architecture.

It is in no wise improbable, but very reasonable and consistent, to suppose that these bands of workmen, after the completion of the Temple, formed themselves into organized associations, for their mutual benefit and protection, whereby they were known and recognized by each other through the means of a language peculiar to themselves alone. And in this capacity they doubtlessly emigrated to other countries, and engaged themselves, under skillful masters, in the erection of religious and other edifices. Many of them, also, were doubtless retained in service at Jerusalem by King Solomon, who either gave them employment directly at home—as he was engaged in improving and beautifying the city—or were sent into other provinces, where he founded and built new cities.

Yet we can not reconcile the idea that these men were the real custodians of so sublime and sacred a trust; for, taking the age and existing times into consideration, the large masses of them were, without doubt, but poorly qualified to appreciate and enjoy so great a privilege. But that the better class of them, the master architects and superintendents, were the real repositories of the pure principles of Masonry, we think seems consistent and reasonable.

But the operative feature of Masonry has long since passed away, and it is only cherished and venerated for its past usefulness. Its implements are no longer applied by the operative in fitting, shaping, and preparing the material for the edifice, to give beauty and ornament to the structure. But their application with us, as speculative or philosophical Masons, is to rear and beautify our moral temple—make the affections the holy of holies, a sanctuary of purity. And this state still exists, and will continue so through time to come. Many are content with forms and ceremonies—a passive acquiescence and obedience—while others enter into the spirit and living principles of our most beautiful systems of science, explore its mines, and draw from them its precious jewels.

No institution has ever passed through the fiery ordeal of fanatical persecution with more fierce malignity, or bitter rancor, than that of Freemasonry; and it has found nestled within its own bosom some most venomous reptiles—actuated only by selfish and sordid motives. But its noblest feature has always been forbearance; no spirit of retaliation exists within it; it aims to harm no one, but rather pities the errors of frail humanity. And whilst, as a noble brotherhood, consistent to its professions, it lives in obedience to good order and harmony, as such it need never fear the ungenerous assaults or fulminating anathemas hurled against it, for they are as the refiner's fire—its purifying elements. Fidelity to honor, truth, and justice are its rallying points; and its strength is based upon obedience to God's law and will—charitable toward others, and just to all men.

These are the true and genuine principles inherent in Masonry and inculcated in its system of moral duty to man and reverential obedience to God. They are the cement of its union, the elements of its strength, and the enduring principles of its vitality.

The Mason who rightly understands the ground-work of our institution, and the nature of the duties and obligations resting upon him, will endeavor to live in accordance with the excellent precepts it inculcates, for, in so doing, he not only complies with its requirements, but with those he is also to observe for the government and well-being of society. In its benevolent operations we can truly say that we have often witnessed the most happy results flowing from the association.

Designing men have, at different periods, for sinister motives, endeavored to subvert the institution and use its influence for improper objects; but every attempt thus made to divert it from its legitimate channels and use it for unhallowed purposes has proved ephemeral in effort, and most signally failed in the base designs, and the institution has suffered in consequence of the evil effects proceeding from such improper motives.

But the attempts thus made to prostitute it, and make it the medium to sub serve selfish interests for any purpose whatever of an improper or unlawful nature, have always met the just and merited condemnation of the judicious and prudent members of the Fraternity; and, while foiled in the evil designs intended to make it serve, they have resulted in producing the strongest evidence of its usefulness to improve the moral condition of man.

That an institution which has enrolled within its brotherhood such eminent men as a Washington, a Warren, a Franklin, a Clinton, a Jackson, a Clay, and a La Fayette, the illustrious compeer of the immortal Washington, together with a numerous host who have stood prominent as jurists, divines, men of science, artisans, and in almost every capacity of life, respected and honored for their deportment and their usefulness, could possibly have loaned themselves to perpetuate, and with their presence give encouragement to continue the assembling of its members, if for any other than pure motives, benevolent in intentions, seems an inconsistency, incompatible with common sense and reason.

"Remove not the ancient landmarks which your fathers have set." —Prov. xxii: 28. This is a scriptural injunction, and it is also one of the fundamental laws of our institution. It is a maxim to which we rigidly adhere. "It is not in the power of any man, or any body of men, to make innovations in the body of Masonry." And while this principle is adhered to, the institution will continue, and it will remain preserved in its pristine purity. Masons who properly deport themselves need never fear of receiving just considerations at the hands of the brotherhood. And, while disposed to be liberal and indulgent to the wayward, it can not possibly, consistent to the principles of its own nature, give countenance to acts of wrong-doing in any manner whatever. It bears patiently with the infirmities of human nature until the last hope of reclamation has expired.

We have heard Masons express themselves that the lodge was good enough church for them, and the expression has given us pain, for it is not so regarded by Masons who correctly understand the principles of the institution. If it encourages morality and teaches reverence to God, it must necessarily lead to the sanctuary, the house devoted to his service; but, as to the particular form of service, we leave that to the brotherhood, as that is an individual matter between the creature and his Creator. Masons, however, on attending their lodges, should always observe that proper and becoming respect which its elevated character demands.

By information gained from reliable sources we learn that it is a requirement in some lodges that the admission of its members must be attended with cleanly and suitable attire. A brother, hailing from a lodge at Darmstadt, grand dukedom of Hessen Darmstadt, informed us that no member was admitted into the lodge unless cleanly in personal appearance of dress, and white gloves. A good example, we think, to imitate, and might be salutary to some of the lodges in this country. It would, at least. work to no detriment. And if brethren would be more observant of that dignified decorum their presence at the lodge demands. they would enjoy, to a much greater degree of satisfaction, the privileges it gives them, and its beautiful ceremony would be more highly appreciated.

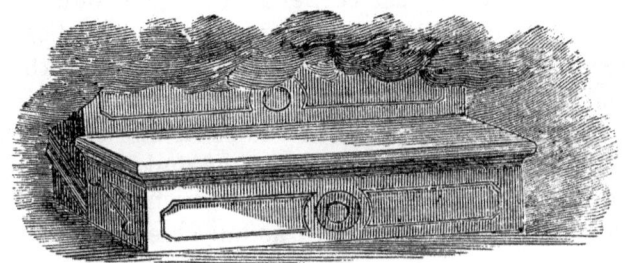

THE DEGREE OF ENTERED APPRENTICE.

THIS is the initiatory step in Masonry. It is that stage of our entrance when the mind should be properly divested of pride and selfish importance, of hauteur in our demeanor; but, in the spirit of sincere meekness and humility, seek the attainment of light and knowledge, whereby we become more useful to ourselves and to our fellow-beings, and learn to improve the virtues and social qualities inherent in our natures. It is here where we enter into a covenant to serve our Master for a given period of time, during which we receive that useful instruction necessary to our further advancement.

During this period of Apprenticeship, it is our duty to serve our Master with fidelity, fervency, and zeal; to apply ourselves with due diligence to our labors, cheerfully receive the instructions imparted to us, and render a respectful obedience to his just requirements.

It is here that we learn the use of the various implements presented for our consideration; their uses and purposes, as applied for their moral instruction; and, as the inexperienced novitiate, we are prepared and educated for more extensive labors and efficient usefulness.

Here it is that we lay the corner-stone of our foundation, upon which we are to erect our moral and Masonic edifice. And the instructions here imparted to us are impressed upon the mind by figures and illustrations well calculated to make their impression deep and lasting. We are presumed to be in that state of innocent simplicity, conscious of dependence, that makes us feel the need of a helping and befriending hand, and which we are taught is in god alone, whom we are to regard as our chief reliance in time of need.

It beautifully yet forcibly illustrates our dependence upon each other, and the great duties we owe to one another in life; that we are all dependent creatures, and that no rank or position in life can possibly render us independent of each other's aid and service; for in the great economy of human life we are so constituted, that, whatever our position may be, we have our sphere to occupy; whether it be in that of Apprentice or Master, our services are equally useful in the promotion of happiness.

Every virtue calculated to adorn and give luster to the moral character, is beautifully exemplified by hieroglyphic illustrations, and the intelligent mind can not but appreciate its beauties and participate in the enjoyments they afford; otherwise he is dull in comprehension, lacking in sensibility, and unfit for the precious boon.

To be entered, is to be admitted; and to apprentice, is to serve. Hence, too great care can not be observed in making a due and diligent inquiry into the merits and worth of the applicant; nor can too great a degree of decorum and propriety be observed in the proper preparation of the candidate, that his entrance be attended with the impressive solemnity the occasion demands, so that his service as Apprentice be faithfully observed to his Master.

No Degree is of greater importance, or should be more thoroughly studied and fully understood, to successfully convey and establish the principles inculcated therein, than that of the Entered Apprentice. Whilst forms and ceremonies are necessary and proper to be adhered to, the spirit should also be observed. Yet how few properly comprehend this! They haste to execute the work, without considering its real import and bearing, and thus, in a great measure, lessen the beauty and impressiveness of the ceremonies.

The mere illustration of emblems, forms, and ceremonies of initiation, are insipid and devoid of the force of their power and influence, when imparted without necessary qualifications to give effect. He who is called to the discharge of this important duty should not only be well skilled in his work, but he should possess the ability to illustrate and impart it with vigor and force to the mind of the neophyte. Tone of voice, distinctness of enunciation, power of inflection, deliberateness of address, gravity and dignity of deportment, are essential qualifications to a successful effort. And these are the distinguishing characteristics which will secure a respectful attention, a proper appreciation, and just consideration.

It is a matter of painful regret that we too often observe the want of these abilities in the discharge of the important duties which their nature requires. To witness a rapid and hasty execution of work shows a want of proper consideration; inarticulate enunciation is in bad taste, and want of decorum produces disgust. They are the contrasts of proper conception-a lack of beauty and elegance in delivery, a want of dignity, calmness, sobriety, and impressive solemnity.

If our forms and ceremonies are worthy of our attention, and lay a claim to our considerations, then they are equally worthy of a proper and respectful observance; and only in this light can they be fully appreciated, the necessity of their importance duly manifested, and their influence diffused in usefulness.

This first introduction into our Order most generally establishes the future Masonic character either for proper usefulness and devotion to the principles inculcated, or produces a listless indifference. So important are they, and so necessary that their importance be properly and decorously communicated, that the impression may be indelibly established upon the mind. It qualifies us for a better conception and enjoyment of the higher Degrees, and adapts us for the more faithful compliance of the duties and obligations we owe to each other and society in general, and strengthens the bonds and affections of brotherhood.

Masons owe obligations toward each other, but they are all honorable, affectionate, and endearing in their relations, and will be observed by all true and genuine brethren. They call forth every kind and tender sympathy for each other's welfare; they expel every thing obnoxious to the principles of genuine brotherhood, teach us to bear with charitable feeling each other's infirmities, compassionate the unfortunate, and give a helping hand to the needy. To emulate virtue, encourage industry, and regard the widow and fatherless, particularly of our own household, are duties we owe to each other. And these are the noble principles set forth in this Degree. Reverence to God, as the Great Master and Father of all.

From this brief sketch it will be observed that the obligations and duties as unfolded in this degree are not of a light or trifling nature, but every thing pertaining thereto is elevating to the affections, enlarging to the mind, and sublime in principle. To cultivate the virtues which beautify and adorn the character of man, develop his usefulness, and qualify him for the more full discharge of his duties, are the noblest pursuits in which he can be engaged. It curbs and softens the asperities of our ruder natures, animates our affections with tender sympathies, makes man more liberal and generous toward his fellow-man, and his power for usefulness more potent and efficient in its labors. Such objects and such pursuits are the acme that lead to his happiness, make life desirable, and prepare him for an inheritance in the eternal Temple.

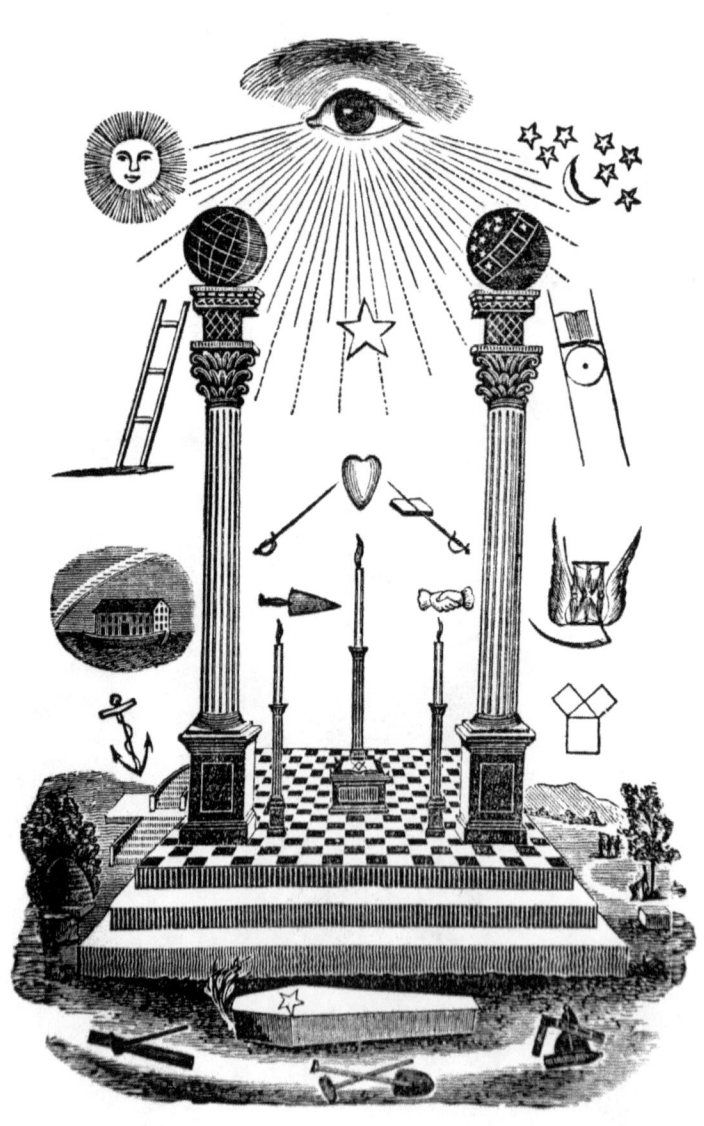

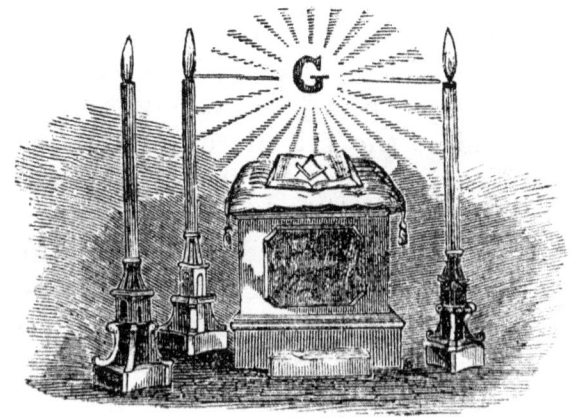

LECTURE I.

THE ALTAR.

AN altar of earth then shalt thou make unto me, and shalt sacrifice thereon thy burnt offering, and thy peace offering, thy sheep and thins oxen. And in all places where I record my name, I will come unto thee and I will bless thee.—Ex. xx: 24.

And thou shalt anoint the altar of burnt offering and all his vessels, and sanctify the altar, and it shall be an altar most holy.—Ex. XL: 10.

AS an indispensable piece of furniture, the altar is absolutely necessary in the lodge-room. It is the first object to which the attention is directed. Upon it rests the Holy Bible, Square, and Compasses, and without which no lodge could legally exist, nor would be recognized as such. Every Mason fully understands the great importance attached to these objects in the place they occupy in our rituals.

Altars were of two kinds: altars for burnt offerings and sacrifices, and altars of incense. The former have existed from the earliest periods of the world—almost coeval with the creation of man. We read in Gen. iv; 3, 4, that "Cain brought of the fruit of the ground, an offering to the Lord;" and "Abel brought of the firstling of his flock, and of the fat thereof; and the Lord had respect unto Abel and his offering." But Cain's offering was not accepted, "and he was wroth and his countenance fell. But the Lord said unto Cain, if thou dost well, shalt thou not be accepted?" Here we are not, however, informed whether these brothers erected altars or not, upon which they made their offerings, but presume they did so.

The first intimation we have of the erection of altars, was that erected by Noah, after the deluge, Gen. viii: 20: "And Noah built an altar unto the Lord, and took of every clean beast, and of every clean fowl, and offered burnt offerings upon the altar."

In the preceding Scriptural quotations, it will be seen that, whilst Abel's offering was acceptable unto the Lord, that of his brother was not. Cain did not come before the Lord with his offering in that meek and humble spirit which should characterize a true and needy suppliant seeking the favor of his God; hence, his offering was not, and could not be acceptable unto the Lord. Yet, "the Lord said unto him, if thou doest well, shalt thou not be accepted?" Here was a condescension manifested, of God's willingness to accept the offering of Cain; but it must be made in a spirit of becoming meekness and humility. God will not cast off, or be deaf to those who truly seek him.

So should it be with the candidate for the mysteries

of Masonry: presenting himself with a pure heart, as a voluntary and free will offering at our altar, "without spot or blemish," divested of the vices which defile and pollute the moral temple. A pare heart, voluntary and free-will offering —these are properly the qualifications essentially requisite, and nothing short of them will fully or truly meet the requirements. The offerings of Abel and Noah were thus typical of that purity of heart and sincerity of purpose which should be the motives that actuate those who seek admission to the altar of Masonry. Unsought and unsolicited, the petitioner comes, voluntarily, and of his own free-will and accord, and asks permission to be admitted to our altar; he declares that he is unbiased and uninfluenced by any improper motives; that his desire is to do good, his intentions pure and sincere; and as such he seeks this favor. How beautifully does this accord in harmony with man's better nature, when be comes with his offering to the altar of his God, seeking his divine favor. His trust is in God. It is typical of the requirements essential to an acceptable offering. Man may be a dissembler to his fellow-man, but he can not be so to God, for He only knows the secret workings of the heart.

The first information we have of any direct instructions in reference to the erection of altars, is that given by the Lord to Moses, Ex. xx: 24, 25. Here the Lord gives special directions how, and of what, the altar for burnt offerings should be constructed. A more minute and detailed description, with the various instruments and vessels pertaining thereto, is also given in Ex. xxvii: 48.

And in Ex. xxx: 1-5, we have a description of the form, size, and materials for the altar of incense.

The altars erected for the use of the first Temple, were on a much larger scale, and more imposing in their appearance than any former ones. They were constructed of brass, and filled in with rough stones. An account of them, with the accompanying utensils used in the daily sacrifices, will be found in Second Chronicles.

In the early periods of the world, previous to the construction of temples, altars were erected in or near groves, as they were deemed most appropriate to religious worship. But, in consequence of the prevailing idolatry, and the increasing propensity to worship false deities, the Jewish people were strictly forbidden to erect altars in or near groves. For God could not permit altars erected and dedicated to his service, to be profaned and prostituted to the degraded worship of idols.

"Thou shalt have no other gods before me; thou shalt not make unto thee any graven image, or any likeness of any thing that is in heaven above, or that is in the earth beneath, or that is in the water under the earth. Thou shalt not bow down thyself to them, nor serve them: for I the Lord thy God am a jealous God, visiting the iniquities of the fathers upon the children unto the third and fourth generations of them that hate me."—Ex. xx: 3—5. Here is a direct command against idolatry, and the punishment entailed therefore; and this we may observe in every day's experience in life.

> He who reigns on high,
> Upholds the smith, and spreads above the skies;
> With none his name and power will he divide,
> For he is God, and there is none beside. —*Montgomery.*

The Apostle Paul, on his visit to Athens, was importuned and requested to explain the mysteries of this new doctrine he was promulgating to the world. He told the Athenians that, in all things, they were too superstitious. He said, "As I was passing by, and beheld your devotions, I found an altar with this inscription, 'To THE UNKNOWN GOD;' whom, therefore, ye ignorantly worship, Him declare I unto you." From this it is very reasonable to conclude that the Athenians worshiped a deity of whom they must have possessed some limited knowledge, and considered as being superior to their other deities, yet worshiped him through ignorance.

How truly applicable is this case of the Athenians, in many instances, to Masons. How many worship at the altar of Masonry, and yet remain ignorant in knowledge as to the true and genuine principles inculcated in our rituals? They perceive a momentary glow of light and beauty, but it soon vanishes from their vision, and is lost in obscurity. They perceive beauties, but have not the inclination to pursue and enjoy them. The proper appliances are not brought into requisition to examine, investigate, and explore the arcana that reveals the hidden beauties of our Temple, and there seek to obtain the treasure. They perceive, but partake lightly of the pleasures. They enjoy the shadow, but have not the substance. Such material will never add much ornament or beauty to the edifice; but, like the rough ashler, be unfit for the builder's use, until the proper appliances are brought into requisition to give it shape and form, suitably adapted to its proper place. A benighted and darkened mind ill becomes a true and genuine Mason—who, in his unenlightened state, like the Athenians, worships a god of whom he has no knowledge.

No field of operation in which the human faculties can be employed. presents a larger scope or greater latitude for their intellectual exercise than the study of philosophical Masonry, for man's general usefulness. Properly understood, and properly exemplified in life, its principles are sublime and elevating. It is man's paradise on earth, and his highest hope in the future. He who cultivates and improves his knowledge, and lives in obedience to the precepts of Masonry, will not likely be found among the rubbish of the Temple, as material unfit for use; but will be an ornament, not only for beauty, but for utility —a shining light —a pillar of wisdom, strength and beauty —a living support to the Temple.

The Mason's altar, with the LIGHT OF DIVINE TRUTH resting thereon, is dedicated to GOD—the GREAT I AM—and a constant recurrence to it is to remind the brother of the necessity of offering those sacrifices and atonements for the transgressions he daily and hourly commits. By nature, man is fallen and degraded —but immortality is pure.

Our altars may properly be said to partake of both forms, for a brother's consideration. The outpourings of a grateful heart, laid upon the altar of sacrifice, imploring relief from its manifold transgressions, acknowledging its entire dependence upon the GREAT I AM—seeking his aid in all our laudable undertakings—living in the daily practice of Brotherly Love, Relief, and Truth, is, and ever will be, an offering ascending to the Throne of Mercy as a sweet-smelling savor—an acceptable offering of Incense from off the altar of a pure heart.

> When gratitude overflows the swelling heart,
> And breathes in free and uncorrupted praise
> For benefits received, propitious Heaven
> Takes such acknowledgments as fragrant Incense,
> And doubles all its blessings.—*Lillo.*

The Altar, Holy Bible, Square, and Compasses. —No objects in the Lodge can lay a stronger claim to the consideration of our affections than these emblems justly demand of us. It is to them the mind is constantly directed, and brought to the reflection of those pious duties man owes to his Creator, and a faithful observance of which is the only true source of his peaceful happiness. The Divine Light of Truth, ever open to his view, is the source from whence he draws that invigorating nutriment which sustains and supports him with fortitude, nerves him with strength adequate to withstand the trials and vicissitudes he daily encounters in life, and devoid of which he is but poorly fortified to bear up against coming ills and adversities.

As the Holy Bible is the rule and guide of your faith and practice, the Square the symbol by which you learn to square your actions, the Compasses that by which you learn to circumscribe your desires —so is the Altar the symbol of devotion, to direct your thoughts to God; and as a Mason, if consistent in your profession, you will pay a due regard and veneration equally to all, as their association is intimately connected. Hence the Altar is symbolical of our devotional duties.

Man left to his own guidance would soon become estranged and forgetful of that Being upon whose all-sustaining Hand he is dependent, and without whose support he would be but a frail and feeble structure, poorly able to endure the trials of life. Withdraw from him the Divine influence, and he would soon wander astray from the paths of virtue, for, by nature, he is prone to err. Hence, then, the necessity of the mind being constantly warned by those useful monitors, which point out the way and lead to the path of virtue and happiness.

As the sacred volume is constantly open in every Lodge, and as we are under the most implicit obligations to make it the rule and guide of our faith and practice, we can not see how any Mason, who rightly understands the nature of his obligations, can remain ignorant of its injunctions or deaf to its requirements, without being seriously culpable in violating one of the first duties enjoined upon him.

No Mason can fully realize and enjoy the beauties of our ceremonies without a knowledge of the teachings put forth in the volume of Divine Truth. It is the arcana of man's earthly paradise. Through its revelation, he has faith that leads him through hope to Immortality. So intimately are the duties required of us to exemplify and practice in life, that they are inseparable in their association with the great and first light in Masonry —God's Divine Word.

As those claiming to be the Sons of Light, it is our duty to make ourselves familiar therewith, as the great light to guide and direct us, and without which our labors can not be productive of that usefulness we desire them to be. As the luminary whose rays, if shed abroad in the heart, it will lighten our path and will direct and lead us in the discharge of every good and virtuous duty, which, as Masons, we are enjoined to perform. Make it the man of your counsel. and you will not likely err, or depart from the Landmarks of our Institution. It is the germ from whence emanates every virtue and principle, inculcated and illustrated by the symbols which so forcibly impress your mind in the moral instructions they are intended to convey. Uprightness, justice, and integrity are virtues upon which to build your moral and spiritual edifice. Let the foundation-stone be laid true and firm-cemented in the bonds of brotherly love, and you will rear an edifice, useful to your fellow-man and honorable to yourself.

What, then, can be more worthy of your consideration? what more ennobling to your dignity as Masons? What more exalting and sublime in sentiment? What more conducive to your present state and welfare in life's journey? what more cheering and encouraging to your hope in future, than the study of the great. Book of Light—the greatest of luminaries—God's revealed gift to man —your great light.

On every step we advance in Masonry, the Altar, with its accompanying emblems, is the first object that arrests the attention and directs the mind to thoughts of meditation.

A frequent recurrence to it keeps within view the duties we are daily called upon to perform. When man was in his state of innocence, the Creator permitted him to hold converse with him in his Divine presence. But when he transgressed the Divine law and fell from his high estate, that especial favor was withdrawn from him; hence man sought GOD through intercession and supplication.

This emblem of devotion should be ever present to the mind of a Mason. Influenced by its sacred calling, his thoughts are constantly directed to those pious duties he owes to his God, his Creator, Benefactor, and Sustainer, the chief source of his happiness, the light of his life, the object claiming his highest and most constant regard, of gratitude and veneration.

The faithful performance of pious and virtuous actions surrounds and fortifies man with that divine influence which he needs as a shield to guard against and resist the temptations that waylay and estrange him from the paths of virtue and lead him in the downward way to vice. Man, in the rational exercise of his faculties, does not seek misery. Happiness is the great aim and object he seeks to attain, and, through faith, hopes for a realization thereof. But true and genuine happiness is only to be attained in a pious duty to God. A cheerful and obedient acquiescence, and willingness to his requirements, embrace and sum up the category of the noble precepts inculcated in our rituals.

Masons have a much higher responsibility resting upon them than they often conceive of. They claim to be the Sons of Light, yet, how often is it they do not merit the appellation, for it is too frequently the case with many that their light soon becomes obscured, enshrouded in mists of clouded darkness. Their light is hid under a bushel —it does not radiate forth with that brilliancy which should illuminate the pathway of the truly good and upright Son of Light who honors God, and lives in the daily practice of his precepts, and thereby ennobles and dignifies his own character, as becomes a true and worthy Son of Light, and as such, enjoys the highest favors bestowed upon him by his Creator. Such a Mason can truly and proudly claim to be a worthy Son of Light—an honor to the profession — a firm support to the Temple.

> God, who oft descends to visit men,
> Unseen, and through their habitations walks,
> To mark their doings. —*Paradise Lost.*

The principles of Masonry diffuse light and knowledge. When properly understood, fully appreciated, and exemplified by its votaries, it makes them true and worthy Sons of Light. GOD is LIGHT—the great and ineffable source of Light, and, as such, we are taught to adore and revere him as the fountain of light and life—for light is life, and this we desire to attain.

What objects can present themselves to the human mind more worthy of its attention, or that can have a higher claim to its just consideration than the study of the great works of nature? The productions of infinite and unfathomable wisdom—founded in strength of almighty and enduring power—clothed in robes of empyrean beauty—fragrant with joys and pleasures delightful to the senses—impressive to the mind, with pure, holy, and elevated sentiments—abounding in unrestrained love and adoration for their great Creator. Such were the themes of meditation that guided our ancient brethren in their pious duties. Such were the glimmering rays of light that led them to contemplate the wonderful works of creation, and inspired them with holy and elevated feelings of veneration for their great Creator. It was the Divine Light of Nature.

How much greater, then, are our obligations, as philosophical, or, more commonly termed, Speculative Masons, when we consider the highly favored privileges we enjoy by the additional light of Divine Revelation, as our guide and unerring rule of faith! Constantly to our view the sacred volume is ever open, and the mind continually directed to it. Every Mason at his initiation, expressly, openly, and unequivocally takes the Holy Bible as "the rule and guide of his faith and practice," solemnly engages to walk by its unerring precepts, and this he continues to do, as he progresses step by step, to the highest degree in Masonry. Every step he advances its beauties become more and more manifest, more fully opened and developed to his view— its light beaming more effulgent in brightness to his vision.

Humility, meekness and an entire dependence upon God, virtue, uprightness, integrity, love to God and his fellow-man, are ever constantly impressed upon the mind of a Mason, and enjoined upon him as duties to be observed. And these he draws from the greatest of our light—God's great gift to man.

SCRIPTURALLY AND MORALLY CONSIDERED. 39

The Altar, Holy Bible, Square and Compasses, as has been observed, are the first objects to arrest the attention on entering the Lodge. In every degree of Masonry, the mind is called to their consideration, and in intimate connection therewith is the badge of a Mason. In Symbolic Masonry these are closely associated. But the most important significance of the badge is illustrated in the Entered Apprentices' Degree, and when properly brought to the mind of the initiate, can not fail to make the impression it is intended to convey.

Our rules and regulations require that the strictest decorum be observed in the preparation of a candidate. Nothing light or trifling in its nature, or levity, ought, under any circumstances, to be indulged in, for thereby you may cast a blighting influence upon the mind of the candidate, and destroy the very object you desire to effect. It is here you lay the corner-stone—the foundation upon which the moral structure is to be erected—and too much care can not be observed in this first incipient step. It is no light or trifling matter. The requirements of Masonry are of too serious a nature to permit its ceremonies to be lightly indulged in. Hence, if not fully conformed to according to their nature, we trifle with serious and sober things, and fail to accomplish our object, which is to do good to our fellow-man and elevate our scale of happiness in rational and intellectual improvement.

It is the duty of the Master first to make known to the candidate the objects and purposes of our Institution, that he may fully understand its nature and importance, as it is proper he should first do so, to a correct understanding of the step he is about to take. Masonry requires nothing that is not rational and consistent in its purpose, and assigns a reason for all its acts; and if the candidate has any hesitancy or objections to proceeding, he is at full liberty to retire, for it seeks none but voluntary gifts to be offered at its shrine.

A Mason should ever regard the altar of devotion with feelings of sincere veneration and pious thoughts, to remind him of his insufficiency and dependence, the necessity of constant watchfulness and preparation, as he knows not the dangers constantly surrounding him. Its presence should ever remind him that it is his duty to IMITATE the example of the truly good and virtuous, the pious Brother, who daily knelt in devotion to his GOD.

The altar is a symbol of devotion. It elevates the thoughts to heavenly contemplations, and directs the mind to meditation and the performance of pious duties. Such is the position it occupies in our Lodges, and, like every other emblem within our temple, it has its significant application, its uses and purposes, to serve. Its accompanying emblems, the Holy Bible, Square and Compasses, lie constantly upon it, and are its inseparable companions. And, as the Altar is to us a symbol of devotion, so is the Holy Bible to us the symbol of our faith; and whilst the one directs the mind to devotional duties, the other directs it in the paths of faith; that faith which God requires of us—a belief in the promises he has been pleased to reveal to man for his guidance in life; the promises therein contained, that a faithful adherence to its precepts meets its just reward of the Divine favor, and a disregard thereof will meet a sure condemnation; for man can not, with impunity, disregard the declared will and law of God.

The Square and Compasses have their moral application, and with which, as Masons, you are perfectly familiar; and the moral precepts they illustrate are drawn from the Divine Record—our great light—and you can no more disregard the principles they inculcate than that of the latter, without incurring the consequences resulting in a departure from right to wrong. Every Divine or moral law you violate has its corresponding punishment, and it will be sure to come, sooner or later. And every good act performed has its reward of approval. So says the Book, which lies upon your altar, and which you have promised to make the rule and guide of your faith and practice, and all human experience proves its truth. How necessary, then, that we understand our duty, and live in obedience thereto.

If we could trace the cause of our trials in life to their true source and origin, we would find that we had, in some manner or form, either directly or indirectly, present or remotely, transgressed one of God's divine commands; that we have bowed down to false gods—that our affections have been estranged and centered upon some object, contrary to his divine law—our sacrifices made upon unholy altars—our offering to impure objects—our departure from the paths of duty, and the punishment therefore, according to his own declaration, will be visited upon us; and by our own transgressions, we often entail our punishments upon our posterity.

The altar, as our symbol of devotion,
Directs the mind from thoughts of earth to heaven,
Leads man his God to seek through supplication,
And converse with him hold, through humble prayer.

The Holy Bible, a symbol of our faith—
A Mason's guide and rule, whereby he walks,
Upright, and just, true before God and man,
As Masons should and ever ought to do.

The Holy Bible, Square and Compasses,
Inseparable on our altars lie,
The first as our great light and guide to truth,
The others as our moral instructors are.

At the Altar we our devotions pay,
Light Divine from the Holy Book we draw,
Our actions by the Square of truth adjust,
And virtues by the Compasses circumscribe.

Prayer is a proper consideration for a Mason; he is taught the necessity of it. It is enjoined upon him as an imperative duty he owes to his Creator, as an expression of his gratitude, as the recipient of the favors and bounties he daily receives from his hand. He owes it to him, as an acknowledgment of transgressions he commits, for by nature he is prone to err, and needs a guiding and directing influence. And an observance of this duty certainly qualifies a Mason for the better performance of the various duties he is daily called upon to discharge in life.

The mind guided and directed by prayer more fully realizes the affections of brotherly love. It draws the bonds of union more firmly in pure fellowship, and endears man more closely to his fellow-man. It opens more freely the tender affections of sympathy; causes them to flow in kindness, and makes us more solicitous in each other's interest and welfare, and leads us to more cheerfully perform the kind offices of relief to our less fortunate fellow-beings. It purifies the mind, elevates the thoughts, strengthens the confidence, and makes man more regardful of truth.

Prayer is the aegis of man's faith, the cheering ray of his hope that stimulates and strengthens him with courage to battle the adversities of life. It is the balm that soothes its cares and sorrows, mitigates its griefs and trials, and inculcates within him the liberal virtue of charity—the noblest trait to adorn the character of a Mason.

It leads man to inculcate and observe the precepts of the cardinal virtue of Temperance, and thereby enjoy the blessings of life with becoming rationality and consistency. It strengthens him with that Fortitude which is essentially necessary to bear up against the ills and adversities of life with becoming resignation. It directs him ever in the paths of Prudence; guides him in a just and proper consideration of all things; and, with the power of his reasoning faculties, enables him to discriminate between good and evil, to judge between right and wrong. It inculcates the principles of Justice, directs man in the paths of integrity, to be just, upright, and true, faithful in the discharge of his duties. Such, my brethren, is the efficacy, the power, and influence of prayer.

It is not the multiplicity of words we use, not the choice phraseology of our expressions, not the high-sounding titles we lavishingly bestow upon Deity that constitutes true and sincere prayer; but it consists in that plain, unassuming, sincere, meek and humble attitude in which we come to the altar of mercy with our humble petition and supplication. It matters not how simple and unadorned it may be with glowing words of expression, for the more simple the more pure when from a grateful heart; or how plain and unpretending the locality; or whether on the highest hills or lowest vales; whether in the crowded throng or in the desert plain, unobserved by mortal eye; for God beholds the penitent, and hears the humble prayer.

It is the spirit, not the form, which constitutes its efficacy —the motive, not the place, which secures its favor. The mind, imbued with the spirit of prayer, will be constantly engaged therein, as it is the nourishment that sustains and imparts strength to the living principle of man. Its hallowed influence will be ever present with him, as the guarding aegis of his protection. It is the compass of man's hope, to guide him in the voyage of life, and lead him safely to the harbor of security; the anchor of his hope, sure and steadfast in his faith; the acknowledgment he offers from off the altar of his heart as a testimony of gratitude for the favors of which he is the recipient, a manifestation of his love to God, a recognition of his authority, an expression of obedience to his divine will.

Prayer is the inner emotion—the working of our affections —the affinities that assimilate good and virtuous principles—the artery through which the life-growing principles flow in unison between the Creator and the creature. It is a sacred spring of refreshing joy constantly flowing forth in streams of benevolence and gratitude. The ejaculations of the affections—when engaged in the exercise of this virtue are as the dewdrops of heaven, dispensing their sweet influences within the soul.

PRAYER.

Prayer, the soul's sincere desire,
Uttered or unexpressed, 'tis
The treasure of a hidden
Fire that slumbers in the breast;
Unobserved by man, but seen
And known to God's observing
Eye, which alone penetrates
The thoughts of man's designs.

God knows the heart of man,
Whether in good or evil
Intent inclined, no rankling
Elements can dwell therein
Unobserved, unseen, unknown,
Or hid from him. Purity
Within the heart is incense
Sweet that from its altar flows.

Man's affections, when sincere,
Pure, and holy in design,

> Like gentle streams from the fount,
> In unruffled rivulets flow,
> Shed their influence far and
> Wide in works of charity,
> Good-will to all, love to God,
> And earth a paradise to him.
>
> Prayer, the needy suppliant's
> Relief, humble petitioner's
> Balm, that soothes the troubled soul,
> Gives relief to the burdened
> Mind, disenthralls man from sin
> And vice, leads him in virtue's
> Ways to walk, upright and just,
> In the paths that lead to life.

No prayer ever uttered which, for its plain, unostentatious simplicity, equaled that given by the purest being that ever walked the earth; so broad, so liberal and catholic in sentiment, that no one governed by good desires could refuse its adoption, whether he be of the old or new dispensation. It is free from sectarian sentiment, and covers the broad virtue of charity in its most liberal view, and brings forth a response of approval from every heart.

It is such a prayer as a Mason can enshrine in the sanctuary of his affections, and offer from off the altar of his heart. It embraces every virtue and principle inculcated in our beautiful science and system, as taught in our esoteric schools.

It is affectionate in its address; unassuming, save in the endearing expression of "Our Father." What can be more tender in affection than the name of father! It is the symbol of affection.

"Thy kingdom come: thy will be done on earth as in heaven." It asks not for worldly power, honor, or distinction, but simply that that principle may prevail on earth which exists in heaven—charity, that charity enjoyed by the seraphs of heaven. Imitate that charity toward one another.

"Give us this day our daily bread." It asks not for wealth, but simply for our daily bread. For man's treasure is not of earth; he has a higher inheritance to seek for. The riches of this world, with all its glories and honors, will pass away, but his chief treasure— his soul—is for an inheritance of eternity, the treasury of God—the sanctuary of heavenly purity—a jewel for the diadem of eternal glory.

"Forgive us our trespasses, as we forgive those who trespass against us." It asks not for an unforgiving, unrelenting disposition; but, as we expect pardon and forgiveness ourselves, so we must exercise this principle toward others. We should be governed by a kind and forgiving disposition; always be liberal in the formation of our views as regards the acts of others; not be prematurely harsh or overhasty in our judgment, but, as man is prone to err, and needs forgiveness, so should he exercise that virtue toward others.

"Lead us not into temptation, but deliver us from evil." It asks not to be led into temptation, but to be guided in the paths of virtue, that we may escape the evils of sin, shun the snares and temptations which surround us on every side, and thereby avoid the consequences resulting in a departure from right to wrong.

"For thine is the kingdom, the power, and the glory, forever. Amen." And it closes with the beautiful ascription of glory and honor to the Father on high, who rules and governs the kingdoms and powers of earth, and weights them in the scales of divine justice.

Surely, nothing can be more liberal, nothing more fully comprehend the principles inculcated in our Institution, and taught in the esoteric departments thereof, than is embraced in this simple prayer. And what can we ask for that is more consistent and more beautiful, in harmony with our duties as Masons, than an observance of the precepts put forth in this unassuming petition! It embraces the great duties of man, put forth in the most simple form language can convey. It is comprehensible to the most humble mind, as well as to the most exalted.

A Mason's lodge ought not to be opened without a suitable prayer, or closed without a benediction or an exhortation to the brethren; and this duty devolves upon the Master; yet he may waive this privilege to some suitable brother. Our ceremonies being religious in their nature, therefore it is proper this duty be observed. The beneficial effects resulting therefrom have a salutary influence upon the lodge. It affords a wholesome example; inculcates faith, hope, and charity; draws us more closely together in the bonds of brotherly love; ameliorates the affections, and makes them more susceptible and benevolent in the kind offices of relief; more sympathetic to the frailties and weakness of human nature;

to aid, by good counsel and advice, an erring brother, and, through good example and influence, endeavor to reclaim him from his evil ways. It establishes in us the principles of truth, and the practice of every good and commendable virtue.

WHAT IS PRAYER?

What is prayer? Not the great display of words,
High sounding in expression or of thought,
Or imaginations clothed in vain display,
Or gorgeous show, as though Almighty God
By poor, frail man need be told his power,
His strength, his knowledge, wisdom, or domain;
Or how the thunder-bolts of heaven within
His grasp he holds, stays the forked lightning's
Flash, stills the ocean's tempestuous billows'
Roar, or checks the furious tornado's
Course. These are his works, in wisdom infinite
Created, by strength almighty sustained,
And in harmonious beauty and concert
Move; incomprehensible to finite minds,
But comprehensible to him—God alone,
Who rules and governs all things well and just.

What is prayer? The supplication of the meek,
The humble petitioner's offering to God,
An outpouring of the heart, when sincerely
In affection's love, from the creature to the
Creator and Benefactor flows, like as
Incense fragrant, pure, and holy, offered does,
"T is the manna from heaven, life of the soul,

Communion of love with the Father on high,
Consoling friend in the dark hour of need.
'T is the germ of man's life, for celestial birth—
An imperial plant from heaven on high.

It matters not to him how plain or simple
It may be expressed, or how clothed in glowing
Eloquence, refined and chaste; how humble
Or how low the meek petitioner may be,
Who comes before his God; how, or where, or when,
If in the pure spirit of meekness he comes,
As humble and contrite sinner should before
Him come, conscious of his own unworthiness,
His need of consoling and succoring aid
From him who alone true relief can give,
And administer to man's most needful wants.

Its simplicity is its pure eloquence,
Its humility is its true dignity;
Such is the true spirit of prayer; such alone
Acceptable to him—to Jehovah God,
Father of mercies, who reigns supreme on high,
And ever hears the sincere and humble prayer.

LECTURE II.

THE BADGE OF A MASON.

THE *lamb-skin* or *white apron*, is an emblem of innocence and the badge of a Mason; more ancient than the golden fleece or Roman eagle; and when worthily worn, more honorable than the star and garter, or any other order that could be conferred upon the candidate at that or any future period.—*Craftsman.*

With the pure in heart thou wilt show thyself pure; and with the froward, thou wilt thou thyself unsavory.-2 Sam. XXII: 27.

If thou wert pure and upright, surely he would awake for thee, and make the habitation of thy righteousness prosperous.-Job VIII: 6.

A *Mason's Badge.*—This is presented as an emblem of innocence and purity, and as such is intended to impress upon the mind of a Mason the necessity of preserving a pure and spotless character, untainted and free from vice and its concomitant influences.

The white lamb-skin, as the badge of a Mason, is regarded and worn by the truly good and worthy brother without worldly ostentation, pride, or vanity. Its ornaments, simplicity, and innocence, and its spotless purity continually

(51)

reminds him of the necessity of preserving a pure and unsullied character. It is to him as a cherished talisman, a faithful sentinel, ever on duty to remind him of the time when first, as an Entered apprentice, he was presented with the lamb-skin as an emblem of innocence and the badge of a Mason. What emotions of pleasure and feelings of affection must have throbbed within his breast at the time when he accepted this symbol of innocence and purity, as the badge of a Mason, and received it in charge as such, to wear it with pleasure to himself and honor to the Fraternity!

The pleasure of wearing this emblem does not consist in that of vain and empty show, but it is in that of being a just and upright Mason that it imparts true dignity to the wearer, and as such a Mason wears it who reveres the badge, and thereby preserves unsullied the honor and reputation of the Fraternity by a virtuous, praiseworthy, and upright life. The great Architect of heaven and earth created man just and upright, and only in the character of such can he honor the author of his being; hence, Masons should be just and upright to all.

The great Pythagoras, whom we claim to have been a patron of our ancient institution, in his system of instruction, divided his pupils into two classes. His school was one of Philosophy, consisting of the exoteric and the esoteric mode of instruction. The exoteric was public, and given to all who desired to attend. The esoteric was private, and pupils admitted thereto were selected, with the greatest care for their probity and their attainments, to receive the instructions therein imparted, and which were communicated and conveyed to the mind by symbols.

None were permitted to enjoy these privileges excepting the most virtuous and pure in mind; for such were the prevailing prejudices existing in the minds of the masses, that they were unprepared for the reception of the principles and truth taught in these select and retired apartments.

Ordinary minds had not progressed to that state of intellectual and cultivated discipline—that serenity and purity of mind, as to enable them to comprehend and appreciate the more advanced and elevated branches of science here taught.

This illustrious philosopher taught the immortality of the soul, and the existence of a Supreme Being, creator and governor of the universe—the great first cause. The principles taught in these secluded apartments were too profound and metaphysical in their nature for the ordinary mind to grasp and comprehend. Hence, those favored with this especial privilege were but few in numbers, and they of the most confiding, trustworthy, and exemplary in life.

The candidate for admission to these honors first underwent the most rigid scrutiny of investigation. If he was found worthy, he then underwent a severe trial of probation and was obligated to secrecy. Previous to his admission he was robed in a white garment, to signify the purity of his heart and the sincerity of his profession.

How beautifully does the science of Masonry harmonize and comport with this system, when fully conformed to in its requirements! Purity of heart, sincerity of purpose, honesty of intention, a desire to do good and obtain knowledge, are the leading features of our institution, and these are the requirements, and should be the motives, of those who seek admission to our esoteric departments. A belief in God, an abiding faith in his all-supporting and sustaining hand, are principles inculcated to the mind of the initiate. It is a beautiful panorama, illustrative of the varied scenes of man's life, and inspires within him a hope of immortality.

No human system ever devised equaled it in harmony, consistency, and elevated sentiment. Properly comprehended, it impresses the mind with man's insufficient and dependent state. It inculcates a spirit of meekness and humility, and a reposing confidence in God. Its ethics are of the purest cast—congenial in sentiment, with every noble virtue that gives true dignity, worth, and eminence to man.

We have our exoteric system of instruction as well as our esoteric, and it consists in that of a Mason's deportment and walk in life; and he illustrates it by uprightness and integrity, honor and truth, brotherly love, and the practice of the precepts inculcated by the cardinal virtues of Temperance, Fortitude, Prudence, and Justice. Such are the illustrations and examples a true Mason observes in the exoteric department of our institution, and the Mason's badge is emblematic of these virtues.

What can be more in harmony with the finer feelings of our natures, or draw more largely upon our affections than the virtue of purity—purity of mind, purity of thought, purity of thought, purity of sentiment? It is angelic—heavenly—divine. And such should be the mind, the thoughts, the motives, and the desires of the candidate for the mysteries of Masonry. Such virtues will insure an appreciation and enjoyment of the beautiful lessons taught in the esoteric department of our Temple. And the Mason who rises to this standard will ever preserve unsullied his BADGE, and wear it with true nobleness and becoming dignity.

> Be purity of life the teat;
> Leave to the heart, to heaven the rest—*Sprague.*

The operative Mason wears his apron to preserve his garments from spot or stain; but we, as speculative Masons, are taught to wear it for a more noble and glorious purpose. We wear it as a memento, to remind us of the ever-watchful necessity of so governing our acts as to preserve a life of blameless purity and innocence, letting our light so shine as not to bring a reproach upon our profession; preparing ourselves as acceptable material fitted for the celestial temple, there to be robed in a garment of immortal white.

If, in the capacity of an operative, you wear that emblem to preserve your garments from spot or stain, how much more honorable and praiseworthy is it, then, to you, in your speculative character, to wear it as an emblem of a pure and spotless heart—plain, unassuming, unostentatious, unadorned, save for its heavenly parity?

> I hope to other hope; who bears a spotless breast
> Doth want no comfort, else howe'er distrest.—*Daubourns.*

My brethren, have you ever given this subject that careful and thoughtful consideration it merits at your hands? Have you ever thought of the beautiful lessons it morally intends to convey? If not, we ask you to pause and reflect. Your younger and weaker brother looks up to you, and as you walk in life, deporting your actions according to the plumb-line of rectitude and virtue, so will your example, to a greater or less extent, influence him. Remember, also, the eyes of the uninitiated and profane are ever-watchful of your acts, and according to your light and knowledge so rests your responsibility.

As a just and upright Mason, then, wear that sacred badge, typical of the robe of purity and innocence, with becoming and unalloyed pleasure to yourself, and unsullied and untarnished honor to the Fraternity, that the world at large will be convinced of the sincerity of your profession. The busy tongue of envy and slander will then spend its venom in vain to detract from your character of defame your good reputation. The malignant shafts of bigotry, fanaticism, and persecution, will fall, harmless in their efforts, and ineffectual, at your feet. You will be as a strong citadel, impregnable to assault. You will be as the wise man who laid the foundation of his house upon a rock, that when the whirlwinds came, it withstood the rage and fury of the elements. Having laid the foundation of your moral temple upon the rock of virtue and purity, justice and uprightness—armed with the panoply of divine truth— you need not fear the envy, hatred, malice—blind and infuriated bigotry—of ignorance and prejudice; they will be only as fulminating shafts, vain in their malignant efforts, and recoil upon their instigators.

> Virtue may be assailed, but never hurt;
> Surprised by unjust force, and not enthralled;
> Yea, even that which mischief meant most harm,
> Shall in the happy trial prove most glory,
> But evil on itself shall back recoil.—*Milton.*

A Mason who rightly comprehends this emblem in its proper application will always regard it as a symbol of purity and innocence. And as the operative wears it to preserve his garments from spot or stain, so should the speculative wear it as an emblem that be may be constantly reminded of the necessity of preserving a spotless character, pure from the stain of injustice, violence, fraud and corruption.

"The Lamb-Skin is an emblem of innocence, and the badge of a Mason." What is all the glittering show, the gorgeous paraphernalia we display to the world? These are all proper and suitable on particular occasions, and afford their momentary and imaginary pleasures; yet they are but frivolous ornaments, possessing no intrinsic value. They impart no moral or useful instruction of solid or substantial worth. No useful lessons are gleaned from them for moral edification or intellectual entertainment, and whilst they merely tend to gratify the vanity, the only ornament that gives true dignity to the Mason is his badge, the white Lamb-Skin—the emblem of purity and innocence. It is significant in its meaning.

"It is more ancient than the golden fleece or Roman

Eagle," for, while the former is but a fabulous myth, and the latter was but the emblem that heralded forth the victor's sanguinary conflicts, the virtues symbolized by the Lamb-Skin are primeval and celestial in their nature. They are the emanations of Deity. Purity and innocence surround the throne of mercy, and are the robes of empyrean beings.

"When worthily worn, it is more honorable than the star or garter." It illustrates the virtues characteristic of man in his primitive state, as he came from the hands of his Creator, and is prefigurative of what man must be to become purified and regenerated for the enjoyment of endless felicity. And while the star and garter and all other human distinctions must pass away, the virtues portrayed by this simple badge pertain to the cycle of Eternity, and are endless in duration.

"It has been worn by Kings, Princes and Potentates, who have ever deemed it an honor to wear it, and mingle with the Fraternity." Such are the potent influences inculcated by the precepts of our Order, that the monarch who sways the scepter and the humblest of his subjects meet on the level and pay a like veneration to this badge of a Mason. It has been honored by the most virtuous, exalted and eminent of men in our own country, and in all parts of the world wherever civilization has extended.

We here quote what an illustrious brother says of himself. The late Most Worshipful Grand Master of England, his Royal Highness the Duke of Sussex, says: "If brethren, when they enter into this society, do not reflect upon the principles upon which it is founded; if they do not act upon the obligation which they have taken upon themselves to discharge, all I can say is, that the sooner any such individuals retire from the Order, the better it will be for the Society, and the more creditable to themselves. When I first determined to link myself with this noble institution, it was a matter of very serious consideration with me; and I can assure the brethren it was at a period when, at least, I had the power of well considering the matter, for it was not in the boyish days of my youth, but at the more mature age of twenty-five or twenty-six years. I did not take it up as a light or trivial matter, but as a grave and serious concern of my life. I worked my way diligently, passing through all the different offices of Junior and Senior Warden, Master of a Lodge, then Deputy Grand Master, until I finally closed it by the proud station which I have now the honor to hold. Therefore, having studied it, having reflected upon it, I know the value of the institution; and I venture to say, that in all my transactions through life, the rules and principles laid down and prescribed by our Order have been, to the best of my faculties, strictly followed, And if I have been of any use to society at large, it must be attributed, in a great degree, to the impetus derived from Masonry."

What a noble example of an illustrious brother, of royal lineage, who entered the Fraternity from the purest motives—was a zealous and faithful laborer in our Mystic Temple—mingled in fellowship with the brotherhood, and worked his way through the several offices to the exalted station of Grand Master—an example worthy of all imitation! Such a brother stands as a golden pillar in the Temple, based upon a rock of adamant—a brilliant ornament, surrounded with a halo of Wisdom, Strength and Beauty.

The pure in mind and thought, elevated in moral sentiment, is not governed by low and groveling appetites, no impure or unholy desires to gratify, as these are incompatible and uncongenial in association with a pure heart and an upright and virtuous life. Such, my brother, are the moral lessons conveyed to the mind; such the elevated thoughts for contemplation; such the virtues portrayed and illustrated by this simple and unostentatious badge of a Mason. And, as such, every Mason ought to wear and honor it; then his deportment in life would be consistent with his profession.

As the Altar is the symbol that directs the mind to thoughts of meditation, the Holy Bible the symbol that inspires it with faith, the Square the symbol that inculcates the virtues of truth and justice, and the Compasses the symbol whereby we are taught to circumscribe our desires and passions and keep them within the bounds of moderation, so is the Lamb-Skin the symbol whereby we are reminded of the necessity of preserving a pure and virtuous life, untarnished and unstained with sin and vice.

So intimately is the Lamb-Skin in its connection with the former emblems—so closely allied in association— that their requirements are intimately interwoven and blended into each other, like the beautiful ornaments surmounting the Pillars in front of the Temple, entwined with wreaths of net-work and the Pomegranate, and encircled with those of lily-work—an emblem of purity, prefigured by the Lily.

Without a mind devoted to meditation and prayer, a firm and abiding faith in God, a full conformity to the precepts as portrayed in the moral application of the Square and Compasses, a Mason can not fully meet the requirements, as illustrated by the moral lessons conveyed by the Lamb-Skin, the badge he professes to honor.

An upright and virtuous life is not given to an indulgence of sensual gratification, for by so doing man prostitutes it to impure and unholy purposes, and thereby places a stain upon his moral character. And as a Mason, he is inconsistent with the profession he makes and of the duties required of him, and thereby dishonors his badge. The Lodge-room should always be regarded as a place devoted to the virtue of Purity. It should ever be entered with respectful and dignified decorum. It is the sanctuary where Masons meet to enjoy themselves in useful and profitable instruction, and good order and harmony must always prevail therein.

The Lamb-Skin is the appropriate badge to be worn on the occasion of the funeral obsequies of a brother It reminds and admonishes the wearer of his own mortality —that sooner or later, too, his mortal remains must repose in the bosom of our mother earth. It betokens purity. It is significant of the robe of purity and holiness with which the immortal soul—the living principle within the earthly tenement—will be clothed when disenrobed of its mortal garment.

Purity of mind and thought do not debar us from the social union and refreshing recuperations needful to our temporal comforts, conducive to our moments of recreative intercourse and relaxation from our labors, but fit us for their more rational enjoyments and improvement of happiness. Our festivities, intermingled with useful and profitable interchange of sentiment, are beneficial and instructive to each other, and for this object should they properly be considered. Man is constituted for mirthful recreation as well as for the more arduous cares and duties of life; and without the enjoyments afforded by the one, he is poorly fitted to sustain and endure the burdens of the other. They are the counterparts thereof, and go to make up the sum of his being, and serve as the equilibrium to adjust the varieties of life.

There is joy in heaven; rejoicing and gladness prevail in the regions of ethereal bliss; celestials have their felicitous enjoyments. Ambrosial food is the feast of the seraph, and the purity of love the spirit of its life; otherwise the Great Being—the great first cause, whom we are taught to reverence and adore—would not be an object of love, for love is the primary cause that begets within us a desire of companionship; and the more elevated and pure the affections, the more powerful the attractions, when purity is the basis of action. Celestial beings surround the Throne of Mercy, not depraved with low desires, but regenerated and purified, clothed with robes of empyreal purity—ever engaged as messengers of heavenly mission for man's good. Hence, man's great aim should be, to govern himself and control his desires with purity of purpose, that the bestowments of life may be to him a blessing and real enjoyment, for whatever his Creator has bestowed upon him, he has destined for that end, and has endowed him with the faculties of discrimination, which bring into play his powers of distinguishing, reasoning and judging.

Honor, probity and uprightness are the emanations of a pure and elevated mind. They are the characteristics which distinguish true nobleness, and give eminence to man; secure confidence, respect and esteem; give stability to his labors, and make them productive of usefulness; they distinguish true and genuine merit, command respectful consideration, and gain the plaudits of the good and virtuous.

The badge of a Mason, then—emblematic of purity and innocence—comprehends all of the virtues essential to man's duty and to his happiness in life; and while the practice of them does not prohibit the enjoyment they afford him, yet he is most religiously and strictly forbidden the abuse of them. Such is the moral instruction intended to be conveyed by the badge of a Mason; and as such, every good mason will honor and live in obedience to its precepts.

Love your God with all your soul, and it will beget love within your affection; serve him as your lawful Master, with Fidelity, Fervency and Zeal, and it will sustain you through the trials and tribulations of life; prepare you so, that when your allotted time of probation is filled, and your mortal remains return to repose in the bosom of its mother earth, your immortal spirit will be prepared to be robed in a spotless robe of enduring purity and innocence.

THE LAMB-SKIN.

The Lamb-Skin, a symbol of purity,
An ornament the brightest that adorns
A brother who in virtuous paths doth walk,
Conscious of spotless purity to God.

Who walks in innocence and purity,
Shuns the ways of vice and sin degraded,
Honors God and glorifies his name,
As Masons faithful will in duty do.

Who lives in obedience to God's law,
Conforming in all that is just and right,
Walks according to the precepts taught
In the School of our secret Mystic Art.

Purity and every noble virtue
Consistent with truth and integrity,
Honor, justice, and uprightness in man,
Are inculcated therein for his good.

Rectitude, by the Plumb-line symbolized
As the unerring rule of justice true,
Neither to the right or left inclining,
Is the true guide by which a Mason walks.

Who wears the Lamb-Skin as a Mason's badge—
Emblem of Purity and Innocence,
Should be free from vice and polluting sin,
Not stained or sullied by corruption foul.

LECTURE III.

THE WORKING TOOLS OF AN ENTERED APPRENTICE.

The *twenty-four-inch gauge* is an instrument made use of by operative Masons, to measure and lay out their work; but we, as free and accepted Masons are taught to make use of it for the more noble and glorious purpose of dividing our time. It, being divided into twenty-four equal parts, is emblematical of the twenty-four hours of the day, which we are taught to divide into *three* parts, whereby we find a portion for the service of God and the relief of a distressed worthy brother, a portion for our usual vocations, and a portion for refreshment and sleep. — *Craftsman.*

To every thing there is a season, and time to every purpose under the heaven.—Eccle. III: 1.

> Our time consumes like smoke, and posts away;
> Nor can we treasure up a month or day.
> The sand within the transitory glass
> Doth haste, and so our silent minutes pass.—*Watkins*

> Time, the prince minister of death,
>   There's naught can bribe his honest will;
> He stops the richest tyrant's breath
>   And lays his mischief still.—*Marvel.*

66   THE SYMBOLS OF MASONRY:

> To make daily progress in knowledge and virtue is our constant duty, and expressly required by our general laws.—*Ahiman Rezon.*

THE *Twenty-four-Inch Gauge.*—This instrument is used by the operative workman for the purpose of laying off and dividing his work. In speculative or moral Masonry, it constitutes one of the working tools of an Entered Apprentice, and its illustration as such is symbolically intended to convey to his mind a proper division of his time—how and to what purpose it should be employed.

Man is not placed here to be a useless or inactive being. He has his destiny to fill in the great drama of human life; and this he will do, for good or evil, as he employs his allotted time. Hence, how important for his present and future welfare and happiness, that a proper division be made of his time, and to each part be allotted its proper sphere of action. Time unprofitably employed benefits no one, and, to a greater or less extent, redounds to our injury; and it is a loss which can not be recalled. Hence, we can not be too careful in the employment thereof, either in our mental or physical engagements. The mind is so constituted as to be constantly exercised; inactivity is incompatible with its nature; it is the moving element of our actions.

The twenty-four-inch gauge emblematically represents the twenty-four hours of the day, which we are masonically taught to divide into three parts, thereby dividing our time, giving a portion to our daily vocations, a portion to the service of God and a distressed worthy brother, and a portion to refreshment and sleep. These are the duties we are called upon to perform in the arrangement of our time; and, according to our talents and abilities, are we required to labor; and a just account will be required by the Master, who will reward us according to our services.

> The man who consecrates his hours
> By vigorous efforts and an honest aim,
> At none he draws the string of life and death;
> He walks with nature and her paths are peace—*Young*.

Here the NOVITIATE is taught of what his labors shall consist. A portion of his time is allotted to that physical or mental employment, whereby he may obtain those necessary comforts essential to life—health and happiness— for himself and those dependent upon him; a portion of his time allotted to the service of God and the relief of a distressed worthy brother—to god, which is to keep him in continual remembrance of the many blessings and favors he daily receives from his hands as his Creator, and of his entire dependence upon his supporting arm of mercy, and ever to seek his divine aid and favor, in all laudable enterprises, through supplication by prayer.

The relief of a distressed worthy brother—to counsel, aid, advise, admonish, relieve, and administer to the wants of the needy and afflicted—is allotted in the discharge of those brotherly offices, as a portion of our time set apart to the service of God; and these are duties incumbent on all men, but particularly enjoined upon us as Masons. And what service can we perform or render more acceptable to God than the performance of those benevolent and truly charitable acts? They constitute a part of the services we render to God. It is not the amount we do, or the exhibition thereof, but the spirit in which the act is performed, that the reward is enjoyed; and as these constitute a part of our duty to God, he will reward us according to our just merits.

"Cast thy bread upon the waters, for thou shalt find it after many days."—Eccle. xi: 1.

> Who does the best his circumstance allows,
> Does well, acts nobly; angels could do no more—*Young*.

A portion allotted for intellectual improvement, refreshment and sleep.—If we desire the improvement to advance in the scale of intellectual enjoyment and happiness, we must employ our higher faculties in the pursuit of those rational amusements which furnish wholesome and invigorating nutriment to the mind, and which prepare us for the more advanced stages of society and usefulness. Intellectual improvement and cultivation of the mind are noble and praiseworthy pursuits. God endowed man with intellectual faculties and the power of reasoning, and as he seeks information and knowledge he reasons thereon; and the highest attribute of honor he can render God is to know himself, and then he will truly know and honor God. All minds are not created equal in capacity; some are of large and extended abilities, whilst others are less so; yet each, in its proper sphere, receives its adequate share of enjoyment. God does not require impossibilities; but he does require all to advance according to their measure; and whatever our pursuits may be, if laudable, they promote our interests and conduce to our happiness, and their influence has a salutary effect, beneficial to others.

> Through knowledge we behold the world's creation,
> How in his cradle first he fostered was;
> And Judge of nature a cunning operation,
> How things she formed of a formless mass;
> By knowledge we do learn ourselves to know,
> And what to man and what to God we owe.—*Spencer.*

Refreshments are those moments of relaxation when relieved from the toils and anxieties attendant on labor, we may be permitted to enjoy the society of friends, in those relations of innocent mirthfulness and amusement which afford us a pleasant respite from the daily cares and solicitudes of life, and enjoy our moments of retirement in the needful repose of slumber.

Such are the various duties enjoined upon us in the division of our time, and, as Masons, we should faithfully observe them as incumbent upon us to perform, that we may be able to look beak with the happy retrospect that our time has been well spent, and look forward, as we advance on the stage of life, with faith in the cheering hope of being called to partake of the refreshment of eternal joys as the reward of a well-spent life.

> Old time will end our story,
> But no time, if we end well, will end our glory.—Beaumont.

We learn from the sacred record of divine truth that the great Architect of the Universe took six days to accomplish his work, and rested from his labors on the seventh day. Six periods were allotted in the division of time, in creating the heaven and the earth, and all things therein contained; and the last of his great work was the creation of man; and he created man from the dust of the earth, in his own image, and after his own likeness, and breathed into his nostrils the breath of life, and man became a LIVING SOUL, endowed with eternal life. And God saw that his work was good, and he sanctified the seventh day, and rested from his labors.

> Here finished he, and all that he had made
> View'd, and behold all was entirely good;
> So even and morn accomplish'd the sixth day.—*paradise Lost.*

Here we have the highest authority as an exemplification of the necessity for a just distribution of our time, and the proper employment thereof, and, as rational beings, formed in the image of our Creator, destined for eternity, we should profit by his example, for our reward will be according as we have improved or neglected our privileges. How important is it, then, for us so to apply ourselves and improve our allotted probation, that when the Grand Master of heaven and earth calls us hence, we may be prepared to obey the summons, and admitted to enjoy that day of rest realized in the temple on high, where time will be no more, but lost in eternity, and our labors will be praise and glory to God the Most High!

TIME.

> Time—fleeting time—how swiftly it posts away,
> Nor lingers in idleness or wasteful play;
> Not a day, an hour, or moment's delay,
> But rapidly on wings ethereal hies;
> Hastily speeds its flight, unconcern'd of man;
> And unobserved by him, listless the moments
> Precious fly, as like the rustling winds whirling
> Hurriedly, ne'er recalled nor returned again
> To be—lost in the great ocean, limitless,
> Boundless, in the cycle of eternity.

Time, the repository of man's earthly
Estate, the treasury wherein he casts his
Mite, for good or evil, to be applied—
The garner wherein he gathers—stores the fruit
Of time employ'd—harvested for useful or
Unuseful purposes design'd, whether
In knowledge of intellectual culture
Pursued, or for gain of worldly wealth—menial
Sought—observ'd in servitude to mammon's god,
Or whether in heedless wastefulness consum'd,
Or giv'n for carnal desires to gratify—
Time, faithful monitor of man's destiny,
Still rolls on in its impelling onward way,
Till lost, absorb'd in endless duration's course.

Time is but as a grain upon the ocean's
Shore, but a span when with endless duration
Compar'd—a moment brief to eternity.
God alone is self-existing, infinite,
Eternity—man the creature, finite is;
His earthly frame a tenement, by nature
Mortal—but immortality dwells within,
And reflects the Creator, author of his
Being, when just and upright in virtue's paths
He walks, as design'd he should to honor him,
As man's first, great, and constant duty to do,
That when the mortal, material, to earth
Returns, then the pare, immortal part, the life
Eternal, to God on high again ascends—
A tenant in the celestial realms of love,
Where joy, peace and happiness forever reigns

Who wastes his time consumed in indolence—
In lingering dalliance, useless play,
Unproductive or unprofitable
To himself or fellow-man— in mental
Or physical employ of useful art,
Or science to pursue—does not employ
The faculties on him bestow'd, giv'n
By his Creator for useful purposes
To be employ'd; but a drone in nature's
Hive he is—unworthy, undeserving
Her great works, whose labors are constant
Praise and glory to his great holy name.
  Man, on earth here by his Creator placed,
In his own image form'd, endow'd with reason,
Wisdom, power, and capacity—
Superior to all his other
Animated works—lord and master
Thereof to be—has a higher, greater
Destiny to fill in evolutions—
Time—eternity his abode, when all
Things else, and the mortal clay, shall perish
And pass away—the soul, the living spark
Within, before the great eternal throne—
Tribunal of unbiased justice—must
Appear, disenthrall'd from the tenement
Of clay—this mundane sphere—judgment to receive
Of awards for works done, time spent, whether
Profitably or unprofitably
Employed—each according to his merits
Just—the Great Arbiter will reward
By the rule divine, the law by him decreed.

THE GAVEL

The *common gavel* is an instrument made use of by operation masons to break off the superfluous corners of rough stones, the better to fit them for the builder's use; but we, as free and accepted masons, are taught to make use of it for the more noble and glorious purpose of divesting our minds and consciences of all the vices and superfluities of life; thereby fitting us, as living stones, for that spiritual building—that house not made with hands—eternal in the heavens.—*craftsman.*

Hark! the sound of the Gavel; to duty it calls;
Come, brethren, assemble; our labors await us.
With pleasure responding, the summons obey;
The Master so wills it—obedience demands it.

The Common Gavel.—This instrument, made use of by the operative mason, is for the purpose of dressing rough stones, as brought from the quarries in a rude and natural state, and preparing them, by the hands of the workman, as suitable for the builder's use. From this we see how appropriately applicable it is in its symbolical illustration and moral application in the science of speculative Masonry.

This instrument, while presented as one of the working tools of an Entered Apprentice, is also placed in the hands of the Master, as the instrument of authority, by which he rules and governs his lodge; and any irregularity, improper or indecorous conduct, is instantly brought to a proper restraint under its influence.

But, as one of the working foots of an Entered Apprentice, its hieroglyphical illustration is intended to convey and impress upon the mind the cultivation and practice of moral precepts—to teach us of the important necessity of divesting the mind and conscience of all the vices and superfluities of human life pertaining to our rude and uncultivated natures, which enthrall as to vicious propensities. By its moral application we learn to divest ourselves of the asperities of a harsh and unpolished nature, of gross and improper sensualities —cultivate the finer elements of our higher and nobler qualities, which better adapt us for the bestowment and blessing of life, and fit us as living stones for the celestial Lodge on high.

Man by nature is rude and imperfect; left to his own guidance, he would soon become lost in the rubbish of the lowest walks of life, and buried in the grave of sin and pollution. Fierce and unrestrained in his nature, he needs a controlling influence; hence the necessity of having ever present to his view the moral application of the GAVEL, with the record of Divine Truth and Light, to guide and direct him in the paths of virtue, which alone leads to true happiness. Seek the Lord, and the Sun of Righteousness will beam brightly in your hearts, strew your pathway with fragrant flowers, and lead you safely through the trials of life.

The incense of a grateful heart is ever an acceptable offering to God; and Masons are taught to revere the Lord; and he who fails to do so falls far short of one of the most sacred duties enjoined upon him to perform. The dumb brute, who bath not reason, guided only by instinct, will manifest its gratitude for favors bestowed upon it. Can man do less?

The moral application of the GAVEL teaches the necessity of curbing the unruly passions of man's nature;

and, as the gem, when divested of its external covering, sparkles in its native brilliancy, so will the character of man shine forth in the luster of beauty when divested of corruption and vice.

My brother, make it your aim to profit by the useful instructions you have so often received; apply yourself diligently in the pursuit of your labors; live in the bonds of brotherly love; practice charity; have mercy; and walk humbly before your God. Seek, through the abounding favor of the Grand Master above, that aid which will enable you to divest your soul—that immortal part—from the vices and corruptions which sink it in the mire and slough of sin; prepare it, that when presented to the Master workman for inspection it may pass the ordeal, and be presented, as a pure and garnished GEM, shining in brilliant luster, fitted for the diadem of eternal life, as your reward when you shall have accomplished your earthly mission.

> Rugged strength and radiant beauty—
> These were one in nature's plan;
> Humble toil and heavenward duty—
> These will form the perfect man.—*Mrs. Hale.*

The lodge is a figurative representation of the Temple; and the individual members thereof, in the same figurative light, represent the stones of the Temple divested of their roughness, properly fitted and adjusted to their place. The Temple also figuratively represents man, as he should be, in his perfect state, as he came from the hands of his Creator, pure and free from all the contaminating vices of sin which pollute and degrade his nature. Just and upright he stands before God; and, as the divine light of the Shekinah was visible in the Most Holy of Holies of the Temple, and continued so as long as the children of Israel were true and faithful to God's divine law, so does the heavenly light of the divine influence illuminate the heart of man while he is just and upright and true to his God. It will continue to shine in beauty and illuminate his pathway in life.

What is man but a moral temple, and the affections but the Holy of Holies! where the indwelling influence of Divine Love should ever beam in rays of glowing light—devoted to love and gratitude, animated with the virtues that give excellence to his character, and which alone constitutes his real greatness. His aspirations are only useful when disseminated for good, and directed in the pursuit of objects consistent with his divine and moral duties; but, when perverted to selfish considerations, disqualify the affections for the abode of Divine favor. Divine Love can not dwell with impurity.

When God's chosen people departed from his Divine Law—when they forsook the worship of the True and Living God—when the Holy of Holies of the Temple was desecrated and polluted by idolatry—then the light of the Divine Shekinah ascended, and ceased longer to dwell therein—the glory of the Temple departed, and darkness surrounded its once hallowed shrine; so, man, when he departs from a line of rectitude and obedience to God, his moral and spiritual temple becomes darkened, obscured, and lost to the Divine Light, and God ceases to dwell therein.

The twenty-four inch gauge and the common gavel, as the instruments presented to the Entered Apprentice as his working tools, are the most appropriate and proper for that purpose, and are best adapted to his then present state. Coming as he does from the outer world, to be prepared for a new and more extended field of enterprise, where the better qualities of his human nature are to be developed and brought into requisition for usefulness, he needs the necessary training to prepare and fit him for this new state of his being—his entrance upon servitude. Hence the moral illustrations and precepts, as inculcated by these instruments, are here presented as best adapted to secure that object, to give shape and form to his mind, purify it from the external dross which surrounds its beauties, obscures its luster, and prevents its usefulness.

The outer world is to us the quarry from whence we draw our material for the erection of the moral edifice. The aspirant who seeks to be admitted into a place in the temple figuratively represents the rough ashler, unimproved and uninstructed in those necessary qualifications which properly adapt him for usefulness; that, as the perfect ashler, truly adjusted and apportioned, he may be fitted for occupancy, permanency, and stability in the structure.

The mortal part is the perishable nature; it is the rubbish which surrounds the gem, the immortal part, and of which it must be divested and purified to be prepared for the temple of eternity. Our science is allegorical. We impart our instructions by symbols; we inculcate the necessity of erecting a moral temple by figurative illustrations.

By the moral application of the twenty-four inch gauge, we illustrate to the mind of the pupil the importance and value of time, the necessity of a proper distribution and useful appropriation thereof, that he may thereby enrich himself with treasures imperishable. By the common gavel we illustrate the purification of the affections; to divest them of sensual desires; qualify and direct them to pure and proper purposes; to teach the enjoyments of life, not the abuse of them.

The proper exercise of the virtues portrayed by these instruments prepares us for the better performance of the duties enjoined by the others. By a proper adjustment of our time, we become systematized to a more extensive and enlarged sphere of useful occupation; by the proper direction of our affections, we become more pure and elevated in mind and sentiment, better qualified for the discharge of the duties of life; we walk more consistent to the plumb-line of rectitude; appreciate true equality agreeable to worth and merit; make our acts conform and square to the principles of truth and justice, and more firmly cement the bonds of brotherly love with the trowel of sincere friendship; erect a temple consecrated and dedicated to honor and virtue; wear our badge with respectful dignity; honor God; live in obedience to his laws, and render ourselves more useful to our fellow-beings. These will be the results flowing from a proper application and practice of the moral precepts illustrated by the emblems at the head of this subject.

LECTURE IV.

HUMILITY, FIDELITY AND INNOCENCE.

He hath shown the, O man, what is good, and what doth the Lord require of thee, but to do justly, and to love mercy, and to walk humbly with thy God? —Micah VI: 8.

Arise, O Lord; O God, lift up thy hand, forget not the humble.—Ps. x: 12.

By humility and the fear of the Lord are riches, and honor, and life.—Prov. XXII: 4.

Now this was the manner in former time in Israel concerning redeeming and concerning changing, for to confirm all things; a man plucked off his shoe, and gave it to his neighbour: and this was a testimony in Israel.—Ruth IV: 7.

THE Shoe, although it covers the lowest extremity of the human body, occupies an important place in our rituals, and, in its significance, is fraught with the most useful instructions.

From the last quotation, we learn that it was formerly the custom in Israel, in order to confirm a contract entered into or stipulated for, that the party offering the proposition plucked off his shoe and gave it as a guarantee for the faithful performance and fulfillment of his obligation. It is from the practice of this custom that the shoe is found to possess and occupy a place in our rituals. No duty that we are called upon to perform should be more punctually observed and adhered to than the faithful fulfillment of our engagements. It establishes the character for probity and veracity; and the truthful man will always be regarded for his integrity. Its object, also, is to impress other matters upon the mind of the initiate equally useful and instructive in their intent.

There are numerous passages in the Sacred Scriptures in which particular reference is made to the shoe, all under peculiar circumstances or for some special purpose, for in all God's dealings with man his manifestations are made in similitudes or figures.

"And he said, Draw not nigh hither: put off thy shoes from off thy feet; for the place whereon thou standest is holy ground."—Ex. iii: 5.

Here was a direct command to Moses, when he was called by the angel of the LORD in the presence of his Creator, symbolized under the figure of a burning bush, to witness one of the most wonderful and remarkable circumstances human eyes were ever permitted to behold. And why the command to take off his shoes? Because he stood on holy ground, in the immediate presence of his God, the great I AM, and it was only in humility and meekness that he could be permitted to be in the immediate presence of the Divine Being. It is to the Royal Arch Mason that this symbol presents itself with the most august and intense feelings of reverence. "And the captain of the Lord's host said unto Joshua, Loose thy shoe from off thy foot, for the place whereon thou standest is holy: and Joshua did so."—Joshua v: 15,

Here the angel of the Lord appeared unto Joshua, under the similitude of the captain of the Lord's hosts, and he was commanded to put off his shoe from off his foot, because he stood on holy ground, in the presence of the Lord's angel. In this instance, as in the former, humility and meekness are powerfully illustrated; and the Mason who fully understands the moral application of the emblem at the bead of this subject, can not but realize the force of its instruction.

Humility and meekness are essential qualifications to a Mason. They are the first principles taught him upon the threshold of the arcana of our mystic temple. Every step he progresses, they are present to his mind. Man should ever be humble and meek. He has nothing to boast of. To-day he may be in the tide of prosperity and affluence; to-morrow, surrounded by misfortune and adversity. The fickle goddess of fortune is unstable in her favors; what she lavishly bestows upon us to-day, she may recall on the morrow. Hence, man should not pride himself upon worldly considerations; and he who is not lifted up by ostentations show, will be better enabled to sustain the adversities of life with becoming resignation. For our common mother earth receives us all on the level when we return to her embrace. She knows no distinctions and recognizes no inequalities in her children.

True and genuine humility and meekness do not require of us that we should feel ourselves debased, or that we should assume that sombre and melancholy aspect which is repulsive in its nature, and unbecoming us as intelligent beings; but it consists in that happy and contented disposition and frame of mind, through which we are enabled to bear up, against the events and vicissitudes peculiar to human life, with dignified deportment and courage—that pure Christian philosophy which fortifies and strengthens us to meet the varied incidents we are daily called to encounter, with becoming and obedient resignation—that undoubting and unwavering confidence and faith in God's promises, that he will never forsake the good and virtuous; for he who hath numbered the sands of the sea-shore, hath marked the sparrow's fall and numbered the hairs of the head, will never be unmindful of his faithful ones; and this is man's encouraging hope.

What a happy and cheerful state of being it must produce, when man can so control and constitute his mind as to regard all things for the best. The finite mind does not know and can not foresee what the day may bring forth; and most wisely for man is it ordained to be so, for if he could foresee the coming events of life, accompanied with their varied scenes and trials, he would be the most unfortunate, unhappy, and deplorable of beings. God alone knows all things, and, in his infinite wisdom, deals with man according to his just merits. He will be just to man, if man will be just to himself; and man, when just and true to himself, will be just and true to his fellow-man, and thus far he honors God.

What greater evidence can we desire of the necessity for cultivating a spirit of becoming humility and meekness than was manifested by the immaculate Son of God, on the occasion when he descended to wash the disciples' feet?— HE, as their Lord and Master, condescending to perform this most menial office, thereby to teach them of the true character in which they were to go abroad on their mission of charity and good works; that it was not by force and power, nor with a haughty and supercilious deportment, that they were to perform their labors, and through which convince an erring world; that it was God, and God alone, who claimed their first and highest considerations. And this principle is taught to the initiate, that his chief dependence is in obedience and conformity to his divine law.

It was the custom of the high priest, previous to entering the temple, to take off his shoes. This he did, although it was not a requirement of the Mosaic law, yet it was regarded as an act of becoming humility and veneration.

The custom of taking off the shoes before entering the temples or dwellings of persons of distinguished rank, has always been observed, and prevails to the present time among many of the Oriental nations. The Mohammedans follow most strictly the observance of this ceremony, and regard it as the greatest act of sacrilege to enter their temples with their feet covered.

In the primitive periods of the world the feet were protected by sandals, which consisted mainly of the sole, secured with thongs, laced to the foot and ancle, and they were more or less ornamental, according to the rank and station of the wearer. It was the custom of the Greek and Roman ladies to wear sandals or slippers; and, with those of distinguished rank, these were more or less richly ornamented with gold and silver, and precious jewels.

This emblem, however, holds and occupies a different position in our rituals. It conveys neither pride, ostentations display or show; but, like every other emblem in our Temple, it has its uses and purposes to serve, and its moral lessons to inculcate; and as such, it occupies its place, and is not less useful and instructive in the lessons it is intended to inculcate; and as a satisfactory reason is assigned for every form and ceremony peculiar to our Order, so is one assigned for its use and drawn from the great light in Masonry—the light of divine truth.

Humility is humbleness of mind—a sense of our own unworthiness; a submission to the divine will of God; freedom from arrogance, pride and ostentations vanity, whereby the sensibilities become blunted, harsh and selfish in their natures, and often make us indifferent to the welfare and interests of others.

Meekness constitutes mildness of temper, gentleness of disposition, amiableness of deportment, forbearance with moderation under wrongs, and charitableness toward the failings of others. These are the virtues portrayed by a humble and meek spirit; they are harmonious in fellowship, and are masonically symbolized under the emblem of the shoe. They are ornaments to beautify and adorn the character of man, and, as such, are virtues enjoined upon Masons to cultivate, and devoid of which he can not fully conform to the duties and requirements of the others.

THE RIGHT HAND OF FELLOWSHIP.

> Friendship is the cement of two minds,
> As of one man the soul and body is;
> Of which one can not sever but the other
> Suffers a needful separation—*Chapman.*

THE right hand has always been deemed an emblem of fidelity and a token of friendship, and as such it holds a conspicuous place in the rituals of our Order. Its symbolical signification betokens the virtue of that pure friendship which should distinguish Masons in their intercourse in life.

The Romans worshiped a goddess under the name of FIDES, or Fidelity, figuratively represented by two right hands joined, or sometimes by two human figures holding each other by the right hand. Temples were erected in honor of this goddess, and her attending priests were robed in white flowing garments, emblematic of sincerity and purity. They were conducted to her temples in chariots gorgeously decorated, and attended on such occasions with great pomp and show. No sacrifices were offered at her shrine requiring the slaying of animals or shedding of blood. Garlands fragrant with delightful odors were strewed upon her altars as the incense offered to this deity; and promises made or oaths confirmed by the symbol of this goddess were regarded as more sacred and binding than any others.

It was a custom that prevailed both among the Greeks and Romans, that all agreements, contracts and promises made or given, were regarded by the parties, when taking each other by the right hand, as a confirmation of their intention to adhere to them, and as the sealing token of their sincerity; and the violation of such pledges were regarded as the highest breach of fidelity, and it was rarely that any consideration ever restored the violater of his plighted faith to the confidence and enjoyment of his former favor. Such was the sacredness with which promises were regarded, when confirmed by the joining of the right hands.

The custom of confirming promises and contracts by joining the right hands also prevailed among the Jews and other nations. The Persians held this custom in the highest esteem, and regarded the joining of the right hands as conveying the most inviolable obligations of fidelity, and a guarantee of the most ample security of protection that could possibly be offered. This token, when extended, was a sure guarantee for safety under all circumstances for which it was pledged.

The right hand has always been used in the confirmation of oaths, mostly in an elevated attitude; but, since the introduction of Christianity, it is also used by placing it upon the Holy Scriptures. Among the Jews, also, an oath of fidelity was taken by placing the right hand under the thigh of the person administering it— as in the case of Abraham and his servant, that he should not select a wife for his son Isaac from a daughter of the Canaanites; also in that of Joseph, when he swore his brethren to carry his bones with them when they left Egypt for the land of promise. The right hand is regarded as the most efficient member of the body. It is significant of power, and a symbol of the inner emotions of man. It is raised in acts of devotion and prayer as well as in confirming of oaths.

The Scriptures abound in passages, figuratively, illustrative of the right hand.

And Abram said to the king of Sodom, I have lifted up my hand unto the Lord, the Most High God, the possessor of heaven and earth, that I will not take from a thread even to a shoe-latchet, and that I will not take any thing that is thine, lest thou shouldst say, I have made Abram rich.—Gen. xiv: 22, 23.

Here we have the manner in which Abram confirmed his oath unto the Lord, on his return from the rescue of Lot.

I have set the Lord always before me, because he is at my right hand, and I shall not be moved.—Ps. xvi: 8.

Thy hand shall find out all thine enemies; thy right hand shall find out those that hate thee.—Ps. xx: 8.

And I said this is mine infirmity; but I will remember the years of the right hand of the Most High.—Ps. lxxvii: 10.

Thou hast also given me the shield of thy salvation, and thy right hand hath holden me up.—Ps. xviii: 32.

These exclamations of the Psalmist seem to convey the idea that the right hand is the medium through which flow the thoughts, desires, and designs springing from the affections.

It is those alone possessed of true and genuine friendship that can truly appreciate the feeling of satisfaction from reciprocated tokens of fidelity. Animated by this noble principle, pure and sincere friendship will cause the affections to glow with ardent zeal and attachment. It opens the tender springs of affection with increased love and confidence of fidelity, cherishes a warm regard of interest in the welfare of others, and strengthens the bond of union and fellowship in man. It is the symbol which conveys expression of the affections, inward emotions of the mind, and acts as the medium of communication of our purposes and desires.

> Friendship is an abstract of love's noblest flame,
> 'T is love refin'd and purged of all its dross,
> The next to angels' love, if not the same,
> As strong in passion is, though not so gross;
> It antedates a glad eternity,
> And is a heaven in epitome.—*Cath. Phillips.*

Masons should pay a due regard of veneration to this symbol. Fidelity is one of the highest and noblest attributes that can adorn the character of man. The Mason endued with this principle will be just and upright, faithful to his engagements; he will live in the respect and confidence of his fellow-man; his example will be praiseworthy and God-like; he will live in the enjoyment of having acted well his part, and his memory will be cherished with grateful remembrance for his noble virtues.

No principle that can actuate man is more honorable than true and genuine friendship; no virtue can add greater dignity or luster to his character—none is more winning in its influence, social and genial in its nature, desirable in companionship, stronger in influence, lasting in memory, durable in gratitude, commanding in respect and esteem, than sincere friendship, based upon the virtue of truth; and no virtue can claim a higher or stronger consideration of Masons. He who possesses this virtue in honest and sincere purity will never be a dissembler or deceiver, but sincerity and truthfulness will be the motive-spring of his actions. Honor and integrity will ever be distinguished by sincere friendship.

No act can be regarded as more perfidious and unhappy in its influence, or more painful in its sting, than the betrayal of confidence reposed in friendship. It is the severing of ties sacred to the tender sensibilities of the affections that unite man to his fellow-man, and too often begets bitter hatred, and only leaves unrelenting enmity in its trail.

FRIENDSHIP.

Friendship, the noblest sentiment of the heart,
An offspring of love in kind affections grown,
Radiant with joy the countenance doth glow,
When true friend with friend in sweet communion meet.

Friendship, a heavenly plant, sprung from love divine,
A token of sincerity, when pure and holy in design;
With brothers faithful, a bond in union form'd,
When heart to heart, hand in hand, in love are join'd.

Friendship sincere, pure, holy and unalloy'd,
Gives joy and pleasure, true happiness and love,
When in genial streams of tender kindness flow,
Through true hearts in sympathetic union form'd.

Friendship the bond of union by which we stand,
Strongly cemented in brotherhood as one,
Guided by love and good will as Masons are,
Who by the plumb-line walk, just, upright, and true.

Friendship pure, sincere, from base deception free,
Is the brightest gem that can the heart adorn,
An ornament that true dignity imparts,
Gives confidence, worth, and nobleness to man.

Frindship—a symbol of love and harmony—
A token of affections pure and sincere—
A bond of union in sympathetic love,
Where man dwells with fellow-man in brotherhood.

Friendship is ever dear, consoling to man,
Soothing his moments of desponding grief;
Relieves the overburdened heart with sorrow pressed;
Gives joy and hope, stimulating courage true.

Friendship, criterion of a noble heart,
Genial in sympathetic kindness to man,
Is the standard of a Mason just and true
Guided by the precepts in our Order taught.

Friendship, constant, steadfast in affections pure,
With brotherly love and charity imbued,
Is the brightest ornament that can adorn
A brother who by the Golden Rule doth walk.

What is friendship? Love sincere; a plant divine;
A union of hearts firmly in kindness joined—
To deception or hypocrisy unknown
When brother in heart with brother is sincere.

THE LAMB, THE EMBLEM OF INNOCENCE.

The *Lamb* has, in all ages, been deemed an emblem of innocence; he, there fore, who wears the lamb-skin as a badge of Masonry, is thereby continually reminded of that purity of life and conduct which is essentially necessary to his gaining admission into the Celestial lodge above, where the Supreme Architect of the Universe presides—*Craftsman.*

THIS harmless and inoffensive animal has in all ages been deemed an emblem of innocence; hence its appropriate reference, in our rituals, under that symbol.

Frequent reference is made to it in the Sacred Scriptures. In the Pentateuch it is mentioned as the chief animal led to the altar of sacrifice as an offering for atonement. The holy prophets of old prefigured the coming Son of God under the similitude of the Lamb. When God commanded Abraham to take his son Isaac and offer him upon Mount Moriah as a sacrifice, it was under the similitude of the Lamb, typical of a coming event. And when the child, in the simplicity of innocence, said, My father, where is the Lamb? Abraham answered, "My son, God will provide himself a Lamb for a burnt-offering."—Gen. xxii: 8.

What must have been the keen anguish and tender emotions of parental sensibility that agitated and throbbed within the breast of the faithful patriarch when called upon to offer up his son Isaac, his child of promise, as a burnt-offering and sacrifice! What a moment of severe trial! Unaided by Divine Power, human nature could not have withstood the ordeal; and what strength of faith it must have required for a willing compliance with what apparently would seem so unnatural a command;

but it was this means God took to test the faith of Abraham, and he was faithful and obedient to the Divine call—unwavering in his fidelity to God.

"My son, God will provide himself a Lamb." Yes, Abraham's faith was firm—God did provide a Lamb; the patriarch's faith was tested, the child of promise speared, and, in due time, through that lineage, the Lamb of Life was made manifest in the flesh.

Isaiah, in prefiguring the peaceful reign of the coming Messiah, says: "The wolf also shall dwell with the Lamb." By this we see that the ferocious nature of this animal shall become so meek and submissive, and so partake of the harmless and inoffensive nature of the Lamb, as to become a tenant of the same fold; and it is typically illustrative to us of the necessity of subduing the passions of human nature, if we desire to enter and become tenants in the fold of the Lamb of Life.

"He was oppressed, and he was afflicted, yet he opened not his mouth; he is brought as a Lamb to the slaughter."—Isaiah liii: 7.

Here the prophet portrays the anguish and suffering to be endured by the Son of God, and the submissive meekness in which he would bear up under the trials he would be called to endure. The prophetic vision of Isaiah foresaw these coming events; and it was the power of God, the Father on high, that sustained the Lamb of Life under these trials; and without this sustaining aid, human nature could not have endured.

The Son of God represents his own spotless nature under the figure of a lamb; and when we regard the harmless and inoffensive nature of this animal, we can not resist the impression it must necessarily produce on the minds of those who seek to enter the fold of the Shepherd of their salvation. It typifies the inoffensive life and character of the Son of God, the great High Priest of our salvation, whose life was given as an atonement for our offenses, and through whose redeeming grace alone we are to be led, like lambs, to the fold of heavenly Love; and this is the decree of God.

But, to carry the subject no further than man's present state, what a beautiful moral lesson may he not draw therefrom for his present state of happiness and well-being, and the good of society in general; and what man would be if he walked by the Golden Rule as laid down in the precepts of this Divine personage. He would be refined and elevated in thought and sentiment, noble and dignified in nature.

To do justly, love mercy, exercise charity, and walk humbly before God, are the just requirements exacted thereby, and enjoined upon man to perform. It embraces all that is taught in our esoteric school, and surely we can offer no apology or excuse why we should not truly conform to its virtuous requirements, so essential to our peace, our happiness, and our social enjoyments in this life; for we all seek to attain these objects, and we enjoy them in proportion as we practice them, and through our influence are instrumental in extending them to our fellow-beings.

They are the true principles laid down for man's guidance in life, and, as such, are inculcated in our institution, and beautifully illustrated by our various symbols, and are in union and harmony with the laws of heaven; and as we cultivate them and make progress therein, so will our happiness proportionately be advanced, our influence for good more generally diffused, and our offices of benevolence more freely exercised; the bonds of brotherly love more firmly cemented in each other's welfare, the virtue of charity abide more liberally in our affections, of generous sentiment toward others; the attentive ear more cheerfully listens to wise counsels from the instructive tongue, and the confiding brother feel the greater security of confidence in the repository of a faithful breast. It will be as the corn of nourishment, imparting vigorous strength to the brotherhood —the wine of refreshment, gladdening the heart with joyful happiness—and the oil of joy, soothing the cares and trials of life. These will be the happy and beneficial results flowing from an adherence to the precepts of a just, virtuous, and upright life, such as Masons are taught to lead, and will lead, if they are consistent in their profession.

LECTURE V.

THE HIGHEST HILLS AND LOWEST VALES.

EAST AND WEST.

EVEN them will I bring to my holy mountain, and make them joyful in my house of prayer: their burnt-offerings and their sacrifices shall be acceptable upon mine altar; for my house shall be called a house of prayer for all people.—Isaiah LVI: 7.

Upon a lofty and high mountain hast thou set thy bed; even thither wentest thou up to offer sacrifice.—Isaiah LVII: 7.

FROM the foregoing quotations it will be seen that the highest hills or mountains were held in sacred veneration; and this is the highest authority we can possibly have of the sacredness for those elevated places. And in the last days the Lord will establish his house on the top of the mountain, and it shall be exalted above the hills, and all nations shall flow unto it. This is figurative of that elevation of God's supremacy, and of that worship he claims of us, as our first and highest consideration, as due to him. Even Moses desired to gladden his vision, and earnestly plead with the Lord that he might permit him to behold the mountains of Judea and Libanus.

The highest hills, or lowest vales, are said to have been the places where our ancient brethren formerly held their meetings. The situation of either was most appropriate, for thereby they were enabled to transact their affairs, free from intrusion, unobserved by the gaze of the profane, and their pious veneration more religiously observed. These localities also afforded ample opportunity to give them timely warning of the approach of cowans, either ascending or descending.

There are also other good and ample reasons to be assigned why the highest hills or lowest vales should have been selected as most befitting for the assembling of the Craft. These places having at all times, from the most primitive periods of the world, been held sacred to worship, both by Pagans as well as the faithful patriarchs of old, hence sacrifices were mostly performed on the highest hills, as they were deemed most suitable and appropriate for an acceptable offering.

Our ancient brethren, possessing a knowledge of the true God, and taught ever to admire the great works of nature, sought the highest hills or lowest vales as most suitable to enjoy the glorious works of creation and pay due reverence to their great Author as the chief Architect of the Universe.

> Spirit! whose life-sustaining presence fills
> Air, ocean, central depths, by man untried;
> Thou for thy worshipers hast sanctified
> All places, all times; the silence of the hills

> Breathe veneration; founts and coral rills
> Of thee are murmuring; to its inmost glade
> The living forest with thy whisper thrills,
> And there is holiness in every shade.—*Hemans.*

Our ancient brethren, being both operative and speculative Masons, it was proper, after their allotted hours of labor had closed, to assemble for brotherly communion, moral and intellectual culture and instruction. We being but speculative Masons, the various instruments used by them in their operative capacity are now symbolically used, figuratively, to more fully impress upon the mind the moral lessons they are intended to inculcate in the great duties we owe to each other in life, to erect our moral temple, and, as God's rational creatures, socially live in the more full enjoyment of the blessings he has bestowed upon us.

The great luminary in Masonry, ever to be kept in view, has already been shown to furnish us the most ample evidence of the veneration in which the highest hills and lowest vales have ever been held, and we need not go beyond God's Holy Word, as authority to confirm that fact.

"Take now thy son, thine only son Isaac, whom thou love, and get thee into the land of Moriah; and offer him there for a burnt-offering upon one of the mountains which I will tell thee of."—Gen. xxii: 2.

Here was a command given by the Lord to Abraham to test his faith: Take now thy son Isaac, whom thou lovest, the idol of thy heart, the child of promise, and offer him upon one of the mountains which I will tell thee of, and offer him for a sacrifice. It was upon this same Mount Moriah that the pious David subsequently erected an altar as an atonement for offense, to appease the avenging angel, and the Lord was pleased to manifest his approval of the act by fire from heaven upon the altar of burnt-offering. And at a still later period Mount Moriah was consecrated for and made sacred as the dwelling-place of the divine Shekinah, in the MOST HOLY OF HOLIES of the Temple erected by KING SOLOMON, and which he dedicated with such solemn ceremony to the MOST HIGH GOD, and where the Divine Being was again pleased to renew his favor and sanction the imposing ceremony in a flame of celestial fire descending from heaven, and consuming the burnt-offering and sacrifice, "And the glory of the Lord filled the house." Such should be the purity of sacrifice offered upon our altars and ascend from off our hearts if we desire them to be an acceptable offering to God. The former is but typical of the latter. Our affections are the ark—the sanctuary wherein purity and divine light should dwell.

"And there I will meet with thee, and I will commune with thee from above the Mercy-seat, from between the two cherubims which are upon the ark of the testimony, of all things which I will give thee in commandment unto the children of Israel."—Ex. xxv: 22.

So will God condescend to commune with us if the heavenly Shekinah—the divine light—shines within our hearts—as the repository of his love.

"And the Lord came down upon Mount Sinai, on the top of the mount; and the Lord called Moses up to the top of the mount, and Moses went up."—Ex. xix: 20.

It was on this occasion that Moses received the Decalogue; and here the Lord manifested his presence under the most tremendous thunders and lightnings, so that the mount shook to its very base, and the penalty was death for man or beast to approach the mount at that awful period.

Moses was not permitted to enter the Promised Land, but the Lord, to gratify his earnest desire, called him to the top of Mount Pisgah from whence he had a view of the whole land, through its whole extent; and he died, and the Lord buried his body in the valley opposite Bethpeor, in the land of Moab.

The ancient Persians had neither temples nor altars. They chose the highest hills as most appropriate for their sacrifices, and always selected a clean spot for that purpose. They worshiped the sun, the stars, and fire, not because they were the real objects of worship, but they were regarded as visible images and symbols of the Supreme Being, whom they believed to be the Creator and Sovereign Ruler of the Universe.

The Romans paid religious honors to several orders of deities. To those of the higher caste they erected altars on high or elevated positions, as being most acceptable in their worship to those deities of a celestial nature; to those of the lower orders they erected altars in depressed or excavated localities, as being more appropriate in the observance of the rites and ceremonies of the terrestrial or infernal deities.

Our highly-esteemed brother, the late Rev. Dr. Oliver, one of the most able Masonic writers of the age, says, in his Landmarks of Freemasonry, that it was the custom of the Fraternity in Scotland, as related by Scottish tradition, for the Masons of the ancient lodges of Kilwinning and other localities to assemble, in fair weather, on St. John's Day, early in the morning, on the tops of the hills, and form themselves into order, and from thence march to the place where they were to hold their festivities.

Previous to the building of the Temple, the tabernacle and the altar of sacrifice were at Gibeon, a city belonging to the tribe of Judah. It was about five miles north of Jerusalem, and situated upon a high hill.

"And the king went to Gibeon to sacrifice there; for that was the great high place; and a thousand burnt-offerings did Solomon offer upon that altar."—1 Kings iii: 4.

Here it was also, at the time of this offering by Solomon, that the Lord appeared unto him in a dream, and God said, "Ask what I shall give thee;" and the Lord was pleased with his request, as he asked neither for riches or honor for himself, nor the life of his enemy, but for wisdom and understanding, that he might walk according to his ways; that he might be able to discern between good and evil, and judge his people in righteousness; and the Lord granted him peace and prosperity, wisdom and understanding, such as we should seek, and which he will grant to us if we ask it at his hand.

The highest hills and lowest vales. These emblems are susceptible of illustrating man's nature; elevated, when he walks in the paths of virtue, integrity, and uprightness, guided by truth and justice. The lowest vales are illustrative of that spirit of meekness and humility in which he should walk before God. And it is only in this character he can truly do so; and when man feels his own dependence and humbleness, then his oblations and sacrifices, offered upon an altar high and holy to the Lord, will be an acceptable offering— ascending as incense to the mountain of joy. Such are the symbolical representations illustrated, and Masonically intended to convey, by the highest hills and lowest vales.

The highest hills and lowest vales, therefore, herein afford us a most happy illustration of man's nature and therein symbolize his character. When imbued with the principles and virtues which give tone, moral worth, and dignity to his character, he may be compared, in similitude, to those elevated places; for it is in possessing virtuous principles, and acting in conformity with their requirements, that man most truly assumes that elevated dignity and nobleness which may be symbolized by the highest hills, as true worth gives eminence and gains esteem; and while they afford this illustration, the lowest vales equally impress him with his humble and dependent state; for man governed by those virtues, which adorn his character with god-like beauty, will ever feel his own dependence, his humility, and meekness, for they are in harmony with the virtues which elevate and exalt his nature.

Man, although he may not be refined in intellectual culture, yet he may be elevated in sentiment, and governed by honorable motives; be free from vanity or superciliousness. Gentle and affable in his deportment, he will regard his fellow-man, not altogether for his worldly position or goods, but for his merited worth.

And as he cultivates the moral virtues, he will, to a greater or less extent, cultivate the intellectual growth and improvement of the mind.

THE MASON CREED.

It matters not, whether on the highest hill,
Lowest vale, level plain, or desert bleak,
Ocean's bosom, or mountain's top, Masons meet—
The language universal prevails to all.

Whether north or south, east or west, far or near,
From the center to the circumference around,
By the Mystic Signal, bond of union given,
Recognized and known as one in brotherhood.

A Mason's hail, by a Mason recognized,
In fellowship brings brother with brother near,
Gives mutual confidence, with man in man,
Who, otherwise far estrang'd, apart might be.

It matters not, what the tongue or language be—
What the nation, what the clime, or what the caste—
King or subject, prince or peasant, rich or poor,
Mason finds a friend wherever Masons be.

Such the bond of union, such the brotherhood,
Such the true fellowship in which Masons meet,
And, in fraternal concord united stand,
Firmly by the Mystic tie to be observ'd.

Bond of union, congenial in sentiment,
That from the kindred heart spontaneous flows,
Form'd indissoluble in affection's tie,
Is the cement by which we united are.

SITUATION OF LODGES.

Thus saith the Lord God The gate of the inner court that looks toward the east shall be shut the six working days; but on the Sabbath it shall be opened, and in the day of the new moon it shall be opened.—Ezek. XLVI: 1.

Now when the prince shall prepare a voluntary burnt-offering, or peace-offering, voluntary unto the Lord, one shall then open him the gate that looketh toward the east, and he shall prepare his burnt offering and his peace-offerings, as he did on the Sabbath day.—Ezek. XLVI 12.

And he brought me into the inner court of the Lord's house, and, behold, at the door of the temple of the Lord, between the porch and the altar, ware about five and twenty men, with their backs toward the temple of the Lord, and their faces toward the east; and they worshiped the sun toward the east.—Ezek. VIII: 16.

And his feet shall stand in that day upon the Mount of Olives, which in before Jerusalem on the east, and the Mount of Olives shall cleave in the midst thereof, toward the east, and toward the west.—Zech. XIV: 4.

THERE is not a subject or ceremony connected with our institution to which we may not find numerous scriptural passages appropriate and parallel; and we need desire no stronger evidence to establish the fact that it is based upon the foundation of God's Holy Word than is produced by this testimony. This also most clearly demonstrates its antiquity, as handed down through generations and ages, and it will continue to survive while time endures, as the principles inculcated therein are emanations from Deity, derived from his Divine law. It may be traced to almost every nation and people inhabiting the globe, and its language is understood wherever its standard is found. Its resources are inexhaustible—its principles elevating in their nature, and adapted to almost every stage of human life wherever human intelligence exists. No human institution ever devised is so extensive and liberal in its sphere. It was conceived in consummate wisdom, founded in endurable strength of truth, and is ornamented with all the virtues that can adorn and give beauty to the moral character of man. Its requirements are a just, virtuous, and upright life, a belief in an eternal God, and a dependence upon his supporting and sustaining hand.

Our lodges are said to be situated due east and west, and between the north and south, to denote the universality of our institution, and that Masons are found in all parts of the habitable world.

The tabernacle erected by Moses in the wilderness of Sinai was situated east and west; and for a full and minute description thereof, see Ex. xxv, and the following chapters.

The temple erected on Mount Moriah, and of which the tabernacle was the type, was also situated due east and west; and this, in both instances, was by Divine command; hence our lodges are, or should be, so situated, as they figuratively represent both tabernacle and temple.

The east is one of the four cardinal points of the compass —that particular part of the hemisphere in which the sun is seen to rise. It was a custom that prevailed with the Hebrews to express the east, west, north, and south by words signifying before, behind, right, and left, according to the situation of a man with his face turned toward the east. By the east they described the various countries surrounding Palestine—such as Arabia Deserta, Moab and Ammon, Assyria, Mesopotamia,

Babylon, and Chaldea; hence, in the primitive periods of the world, it held a supremacy in the mind of man.

The Star of Bethlehem, which shone in splendor above all other stars, appeared in the east, and by it the Magi were guided to the place of nativity of the Messiah. God located paradise in the east, in which he first placed man, and the entrance thereto was from the east; and when man, for disobedience, was expelled therefrom to be a wanderer upon the earth, he placed a cherub there with a flaming sword to guard the entrance.

The east, as the source whence light emanates and travels to the west, is significant in its meaning to Masons; and hence it symbolically illustrates to us the proper situation of our lodges. And this custom can not be disregarded or innovated without a violation of one of the fundamental principles of our Order.

The east, whence light emanates, conveys exaltation of mind, and typifies man's elevated nature. And as the rising sun, appearing in the east, ascends, and shines forth in splendor and beauty, so man, endowed with virtues of purity and holiness, like the luminary of day, sheds peace and happiness in the paths of life. The belief in the earthly paradise is the living principle influencing man; and when he walks uprightly, as designed by his Creator, so long he enjoys the pleasures typical of the celestial paradise; but when he departs from the paths of virtue and partakes of the forbidden fruit, he then sins against his Creator, and expels the Divine influence from the heart, the fountain of his mortal life; hence he becomes estranged from God, lost to his ways, is a wanderer in the paths of sin and vice, and reaps the bitter consequences thereof, and retards his progress to eternal life.

It was also the custom that prevailed in the primitive periods of the world by Pagan nations when they erected temples or places for sacrifice and worship, to select an elevated position, and place them east and west. The sun was worshiped by many of the oriental nations as a symbol of the Deity; hence, in their devotions, they always stood, knelt, or prostrated themselves with their faces toward the east, as being most acceptable to the object of their adorations. And as the great luminary of day that gilds the early dawn with refulgent rays of light, beams forth from the east, and descends with all his parting rays of glory in the west, so is it prefigurative of Masonic light and knowledge, which emanates from the east, travels to the west, and diffuses its good influences both north and south; and while the great prototype gives light, warmth, and animation to the material world, so does our institution, comprehending a universal brotherhood, inculcate the principles of love and charity, and diffuse its salutary influence for the happiness of mankind.

Our ancient brethren assembling on the highest hills or lowest vales figuratively illustrates our lodges as representations of the outward world, extending from east to west, between the north and south—from earth to the starry-decked heaven—and their bounds illimitable; hence it may, with just propriety, be said that they represent the outer world. Their supports are wisdom, strength, and beauty, and their living principles are faith, hope, and charity: faith in God, as revealed and made manifest to man; hope in immortality, as revealed through that faith; and charity to all mankind. So broad and comprehensive is our platform, that it extends to every point of the compass— radiating from one grand center, like the light of Divine Truth, the great light of our superstructure, around which the lesser lights radiate. What can be more beautiful— more sublime in conception or comprehensive in extent—than the universality of our institution?—a brotherhood hailing from every part and section of the habitable world, the great field of our operations, and wherein a portion of our labors may be employed to the service of our fellow-beings, conduce to their happiness, in connection with our own.

The Mason endowed with wisdom from on high, strengthened in the bonds of fraternal love, ornamented with the grace and beauty of holiness, living in the faith and promises of his God, hopes to enjoy the reward awaiting the just and perfect, that when faith shall have been lost in sight, hope ended in fruition, he may be admitted by the Theological Ladder, ascending from earth to heaven, and become a participant of that enduring charity enjoyed in the celestial realms of an endless felicity—where no east, no west, no north, no south, are known, but all absorbed in one great center—one uncircumscribed, universal domain— and, as the perfect Ashler, be fitted and garnished for the Eternal Temple dedicated to endless joys of bliss, whose Grand Master is the builder of worlds innumerable, and who will reward us according as we have labored in his service; for we all labor in this world, and our labors will be productive of good or evil.

EAST AND WEST.

First in the east the light effulgent rose;
Westward it journey'd, in its shining course,
Its rays refulgent spread both north and south,
Like charity, unbounded in its sphere.

First in the east God plac'd his creature man—
In paradise, the garden of his home,
Where sweet converse man with his Maker held,
Till, disobedient, he from favor fell.

At the east gate a sentry faithful stood—
A heavenly cherubim with flaming sword—
Pointing both right and left, on every hand,
To guard the same, that none should enter there.

In the east the Star of Bethlehem appeared—
A light with brilliant radiance shone,
To guide the wise men of orient land,
And lead to Messiah's nativity.

First in the east the morn of day beams forth;
The glorious sun, in rising beauty,
Illumes the heavens with his gilded rays,
Journeying onward in his westward course.

First in the east the Master stands supreme,
The Craft to call, their labors to pursue,
And the pillar of wisdom represents,
With those of strength and beauty—his supports.

LECTURE VI.

WISDOM, STRENGTH, AND BEAUTY.

Our institution is said to be supported by *Wisdom, Strength, and Beauty,* because it is necessary that there should be wisdom to contrive, strength to support, and beauty to adorn all great and important undertakings.—*Craftsman.*

So teach us to number our days, that we may apply our hearts unto wisdom.— Ps. xc: 12.

Wisdom is the principal thing; therefore get wisdom: and with all thy getting get understanding—Prov. IV: 7.

With him is wisdom and strength, he hath counsel and understanding— Job XII: 13.

The glory of Lebanon shall come unto thee, the fir-tree, the pine-tree, and the box together, to beautify the place of my sanctuary; and I will make the place of my feet glorious—Isaiah LX: 13.

> Wisdom and Spirit of the universe,
> Thou Lord that art the eternity of thought;
> And giv'st to forms and images a breath,
> And everlasting motion not in vain—*Wordsworth.*

WISDOM, STRENGTH, AND BEAUTY. These are said to be the supports of our institution. They are the pillars established upon the foundation of eternal truth, and upon which our superstructure is erected. Hence, it is with just propriety they are said to be its supports. They are also said to represent the three principal officers of the Lodge—the Worshipful Master, Senior and Junior Wardens. The Worshipful Master, by the Ionic column, which represents the pillar of Wisdom; the Senior Warden, by the Doric column, which represents the pillar of Strength; and the Junior Warden, by the Corinthian column, because it represents the pillar of Beauty. And they are triangularly placed—East, West, and South. They are the primitive orders, and, as such, are held in veneration by Masons, as being original in their invention.

The Worshipful Master, as the pillar of wisdom, should be possessed of that skillful knowledge and wisdom, essentially necessary to the well-being and proper government of the lodge, and without which its affairs could not be properly transacted, and confusion would soon exist amongst the Craft. Hence, judicious care should always be observed in the selection of the most expert, possessing ability and merit for this important position, as the welfare and prosperity of the lodge, in a great measure, depends thereon.

The Senior Warden, as the pillar of strength, should be strong in the affections of the Craft, for that is necessary to secure their respectful attention and give a proper direction to their labors; he should possess a proper and becoming dignity, and thus be qualified to render that aid to the Master, necessary in the administrations of his lodge. It is his duty to see that each receives his just equivalent for his labor, and that no disaffection exists, but that harmony prevails. And, as he is called to the discharge of the duties of the Master in his absence, he should be equally as well informed in Masonic usages and customs.

The Junior Warden, as the pillar of beauty, like the resplendent luminary of day, whose genial rays are refulgently shed upon all nature's works, and at meridian height, reminds him of the hours of repose from labor, and to refreshment, so should he be governed with equal regularity in the interest and welfare of the Craft. Promptness and efficiency should be the distinguishing characteristics of this officer, and he should be equally qualified for the position of his seniors in office.

Such ought to be the officers of a lodge, if desired to be governed with wisdom, supported by the united strength of the brotherhood, animated by the laudable ambition as to who can best work and best agree, and this will impart true ornament and beauty to our Mystic Temple and insure harmony and good fellowship among the Craft.

The wisdom of a Solomon, received from on high, the strength and support of a Hiram, cemented in the bonds of a fraternal union and friendship, and guided by the unrivaled skill and genius of an architect, whose designs were clothed in ornaments of beauty, produced a structure, the admiration and wonder of the beholder, unparalleled in the history of the world for its magnificence and splendor— a type of the celestial temple in the eternal city of the New Jerusalem, whose builder is the Grand Architect of heaven and earth, and to whose call we must sooner or later respond.

> Wisdom sits alone,
> Topmost in heaven; she is its light, its God.
> And in the heart of man she sits on high.
> Though groveling minds forget her oftentimes,
> Seeing but this world's idols. The pure mind sees,
> Sees her forever; and in youth we come,
> Filled with her sainted ravishments, and kneel,
> Worshiping God through her sweet altar-fires,
> And then is knowledge "good."—*Willis.*

Wisdom is that grand attribute in the nature of Deity by which he knows, orders, and controls all things for the promotion of his glory, and the happiness and good of his creatures. Strength is that omnipotent power by which the Almighty laid the foundations of the universe, to endure through endless ages when time shall cease to be. Beauty is that loveliness emanating from on high, ever adorning the universe with cheering pleasures for man's happiness, and which he enjoys and beholds on every side in the great landscape of nature's works. Whether in the early dawn, meridian, eve, or in the midnight shades, on every hand he beholds works calling forth admiration, gratitude, and adoration to the great I AM. All the works of infinite creation are founded in wisdom, strength, and beauty, and move in perfect order and harmony.

"And I have filled him with the Spirit of God in wisdom, and in understanding, and in knowledge, and in all manner of workmanship."—Ex. xxxi: 3.

"And God gave Solomon wisdom and understanding exceeding much, and largeness of heart, even as the sand that is upon the sea-shore."—1 Kings iv: 29.

"Give me now wisdom and knowledge that I may go out and come in before this people: for who can judge of thy people that is so great?"—2 Chron. i: 10.

"The fear of the Lord is the beginning of wisdom: a good understanding have all they that do his commandments: his praise endureth forever."—Ps. cxi: 10.

"My mouth shall speak of wisdom; and the meditations of my heart shall be of understanding."—Ps. xlix: 3.

"No mention shall be made of coral, or of pearls: for the price of wisdom is above rubies."—Job xxviii: 18.

"The sluggard is wiser in his own conceit than seven men that can render a reason."—Prov. xxvi: 16.

"O Lord! how manifold are thy works! in wisdom hast thou made them all; the earth is full of thy riches."—Ps. civ: 24.

STRENGTH.

> "T is by thy strength the mountains stand,
>   God of eternal power;
> The seas grow calm at thy command,
>   And tempests cease to roar."

Strength is that quality or power of the body by which it moves itself along. It is the agent or means through which it moves other bodies. It is also that quality by which we sustain and resist force, and this is what is denominated physical strength.

Strength, as intended to be understood and applied in our Masonic illustrations, is mental. It pertains to the vigorous energy and power of the mind. It is the cultivation and improvement of the intellectual faculties, through which man's more elevated qualities become developed, and his usefulness more generally diffused. By intellectual culture, his argumentative faculties and powers of reasoning become more fully developed, and which enables him with the greater force successfully to carry conviction to the mind by the strength and power of his logic. His knowledge and judgment, when well matured, are founded in strength. Such is the application by which we symbolize the pillar of strength, one of the supports of our institution. And surely nothing can add more to the stability of our structure than the diffusion of useful knowledge, and the intelligence of its votaries, for the more elevated and refined the mind, the nearer we approximate to the standard of a true and genuine Mason.

Intellectual improvement and cultivation of the mind are pursuits enjoined upon Masons, and he who complies with these requirements, and applies his knowledge for the promotion and happiness of his fellow beings, stands as a pillar of strength in our temple, based upon the foundations of truth. He is a pillar, ornamented with the graces, which give true dignity and strength to his moral character, enrich his mind with a fund of information as a treasure of useful knowledge.

"It is God that girdeth me with strength, and make my way perfect."—Ps. xviii: 32.

"Bat the salvation of the righteous is of the Lord; he is their strength in the time of trouble."—Ps. xxxvii: 39.

"I will go in the strength of the Lord God; I will make mention of thy righteousness, even of thine only."—Ps. lxxi: 18.

"The king shall joy in thy strength, O Lord; and

in thy salvation how greatly shall he rejoice."—Ps. xxi: 1.

"Behold, God is mighty, and despise not any; he is mighty in strength and wisdom."—Job xxxvi: 5.

BEAUTY.

>What is beauty? Not the show
>Of shapely lines and features? No;
>These are but flowers,
>That have their dates and hours
>To breathe their momentary sweet, then go.
>"T is the stainless soul within
>That outshines the fairest skin—*Sir A. Hunt.*

>Some souls lose all things but the love of beauty,
>And by that love they are redeemable,
>For in love and beauty they acknowledge good,
>And good is God.—*Bailey's Festus.*

By the expression of the term beauty, we understand that which is pleasing to our senses. Beauty produces joy and gladness, whether we behold it in the works of nature or otherwise. Whatsoever is pleasant and agreeable to our senses, presents itself in the form of beauty, whether to the affections, imagination, or thoughts.

When God made his covenant with Noah, that he would no more destroy the world in a deluge, he confirmed that covenant by the appearance of the bow in the heavens, arrayed in heavenly colors of pristine beauty. What can possibly present itself to the imagination more lovely or more beautiful than this token of God's love? And what a delightful symbol does it present to us of that beautiful harmony which exists among brethren governed by the ties of brotherly love—

mutual confidence and sympathetic affection—blended together, like the colors of the bow, or interwoven, like the net-work and ornaments upon the chapiters surmounting the pillars in front of the Temple, encircled with the wreaths of the lily—an emblem of purity.

The term beauty, as comprehended in its Masonic sense, is faith, hope, charity, brotherly love, relief, and truth; and it embraces the cardinal virtues of temperance, fortitude, prudence, and justice. These are the ornaments that give grace and loveliness to the temple and surround it with a halo of beauty; they are its jewels, its gems, purified and glowing in brilliant luster.

Hence the pillar of Beauty stands in the south, like the glorious sun at its meridian height, which is the ornament that beautifies and illumes the day. So the moon, as she sheds her gentle and mellow rays of light, imparts her cheerfulness to the night; and the twinkling stars, in the blue-arched vault, shine forth, as a galaxy of beauty that adorns the heavens and inspires the mind with feelings of profound reverence and affection for God, the center of our affections, and the glory and beauty of the universe; so a Mason should stand in our temple as a pillar of Beauty, imbued with the virtues which give ornament and beauty to his moral edifice, for they are the endowments bestowed upon him by his Creator—the apportionments of his temporal estate that produce him true happiness.

"And thou shalt make holy garments for Aaron, thy brother, for glory and for beauty."—Ex. xxviii: 2.

"Give unto the Lord the glory due unto his name,

bring an offering, and come before him: worship the Lord in the beauty of holiness."—1 Chron. xvi: 29.

"O worship the Lord in the beauty of holiness; fear before him all the earth."—Ps. xc: 9.

"Let the beauty of the Lord our God be upon us, and establish thou the work of our hands upon us: yea, the work of our hands, establish thou it."—Ps. xc: 17.

"Thine eyes shall see the King in his beauty; they shall behold the Lord that is very far off."—Isaiah xxxiii: 17.

The preceding scriptural quotations have been selected as suggestively appropriate to the pillars of Wisdom. Strength, and Beauty, and as illustrative of the elevating and moral tendency of our institution, and an observance of them is necessary as a just support to man's moral edifice; and they fully establish, to the satisfaction of the inquiring mind, that true wisdom emanating from Deity, with strength commensurate, as we seek and apply ourselves to profit thereby, to beautify and adorn our characters, as we walk in wisdom's ways, are the only true and safe supports to man's happiness.

The good and virtuous Mason, endowed with wisdom, is ever prudent and circumspect in his acts; strengthened in the affections of a kind and benevolent heart, is ever generous to the wants of others; ornamented with the graces of charity, is ever willing to look with tender sympathies upon the frailties of his erring brother, and will be ever ready to extend to him a supporting hand in need. Imbued with the virtues of brotherly love, relief and truth, faith, hope, and charity, he walks forth arrayed in the panoply of beauty, enrobed in heavenly virtues, as the supports that adorn, beautify, and sustain the moral Temple of a good and upright Mason.

WISDOM, STRENGTH, AND BEAUTY.

Conceived in wisdom infinite, laid in strength
Omnipotent, in beauty's celestial robes
Arrayed, a glorious fabric arose—the Architect
DIVINE. A universe created was,
Perfect in all its works, as designed to be,
And all things therein contained. Six days the work
Accomplished—the great Architect surveyed,
And said 't was good—the seventh, consecrated
And hallowed to holy rest. Angels on high
Their harps attuned, and, in symphonious concert,
Sung anthems of heavenly praise; the sun,
Stars, and beauteous queen that reigns at night—
The mountains, hills, and valleys—harmonious,
In acclamation joined in universal
Praise; the blue-arched vault of heaven, eternal—
Dome on high-re-reverberating with celestial joy,
Alleluia, reëchoing to that praise—
Glory, glory to the Architect Supreme;
To Jehovah God, Eternal, Infinite—
The Great I Am—praise and honor ever be,
Such as is due to the Majesty on high,
Who alone justly can adoration claim
From man, creation of his great work,
As an homage of obedience to Him.

The whirlwind's rapid flight, lightning's vivid flash,
And pealing thunder's roar; the ocean billow's

Surge heave wild, with frantic rage, lash their rockbound
Shore, furiously recoiling back again,
And, with gathered strength, the combat fierce renew;
Thou! Omnipotence, Most High, but say the word,
When obedience submissive promptly yields:
"Be still, thou troubled elements; cease thy strife—
Thy discordant, inharmonious jarring
Cease. Promptly the mandate from on high obey,
Obedient to my will submissive be,
And each to his peaceful quietude return.
'T is my command to thee given—thine to obey,
For thou the offspring of my creation are:
Thou the creature be—I the Creator am;
Obedience to the Will eternal yield;
My bidding—as becomes thee and thine to do"—
And all is hushed in the still and silent calm.

    Man thou didst create, in thine own image formed—
Just and upright, last and best of all thy works—
And in a tenement of clay gave us life—
Immortal life. Free-will thou according to him,
And in thy garden, paradise, didst place,
Lord and Master of all on earth here below,
Except the tree of knowledge. Thou didst forbid
To touch or partake thereof—death, the penalty
Prescribed for disobedience of the law
Thou hast now my just commands received;
Go forth—the inheritance bestowed enjoy,
And all else here shall submissive be to thee,
For thou, as my superior work, monarch

Thereof shalt be—so ordained, decreed by me.
Thus was the mandate given—thus the penalty
Prescribed—for man when placed in paradise—
Eden—God's garden—to be his happy home.

    Wily, seductive, artful in influence,
The evil tempter came—man transgressed and fell.
All nature stood aghast, convulsed; angels wept,
Mournfully sorrowing his untimely fall.
Conscious of transgression—disobedience
To the injunction from God Divine received—
And dreading his just wrath therefore to come,
With remorse of guilt, he seeks the darkened shade,
And with his consort, companion-mate, him given,
Seek to hide their shame from the light of heaven.

    But, hark! a footstep, in the cool of evening,
Approaches; a voice divine is heard:
"Adam, where art thou? What hast thou done, to hide
    thyself
From the presence of thy God, thy steadfast friend?
Him with whom thou dost commune and converse hold,
And who thy good and thy happiness desires,
And placed thee here in paradise therefore?
Hast thon, disobedient to my command,
Partaken of the forbidden fruit, whereby
Thou thine inheritance here hast forfeited?
Else, why shouldst thou avoid and shun my presence?
Come forth." They, with grief and shame, in humble
    mien,

Approach, and in his dread presence trembling stand,
Their condemnation, just sentence, to receive.

The fiat went forth: "From henceforth thou shalt till
The earth; from the sweat of thy brow thy bread
Shalt earn. Henceforth, wanderers upon the earth
Shalt be; cares and sorrows shall attend thy way;
Labor, pain, anguish, and trials shall afflict
Thee and thine untold posterity to come.
Death, the penalty for disobedience!
Mortal death to thee, and thy race is doomed.

"Cursed shall be thy enemy, thy deadly
Foe; thou shalt bruise his head, whilst he shall bruise thy
Heel. Enmity and strife shall between thee be,
And with thy unborn posterity, till death—
Destroyed shall be—swallowed up in victory.
Thus the doom upon thyself and thine hast brought,
For disobedience to my law divine."
The doom pronounced, hand in hand, mournfully
Dejected, they leave their once heavenly state—
Paradise—their happy, joyful, peaceful home.
No more in presence with their God, their heavenly
Father, sweet communion hold; banished from his
Presence, outcast, forlorn, wanderers they are,
To and fro, upon the wide world, to them unknown.

Propitious heaven and mercy intervened;
Grace, love divine, in fallen man's behalf
Interceded. Restoration promised—

Redemption from the power and dominion
Of sin and death—he disenthralled shall be.
Such the plan Almighty God designed for man;
For through the chosen seed, in course of time,
A second Adam came, by whom, through faith,
Through hope, and universal charity,
Man will be restored again. So decreed;
Then sin and death will be destroyed—swallowed up
In victory; the heavenly hosts shout with joy,
Make the ethereal welkin ring with joyful
Praise, in glory and honor to God on high,
Infinite, Eternal, Majesty Supreme;
Then, wisdom infinite, strength omnipotent,
Beauty in celestial robes arrayed, Time
Will be no more, eternity intervened—
All centered in one unbounded universe,
Uncircumscribed, endless, eternal domain.
Then God of Love, God Divine, God Supreme,
Omnipotent, Omnipresent, Omniscient,
Will be all in all.

LECTURE VII.

FAITH, HOPE, AND CHARITY.

AND he dreamed, and behold, a ladder was set upon the earth, and the top of it reached to heaven; and behold, the angels of God ascending and descending on it—Gen. XXVIII: 12.

> Faith lights us through the dark to Deity; Whilst without light, we witness that she shows
> More God than in his works our eyes can see, Though none but by those works the Godhead knows.
> Sir W. Davenport.

> Faith builds a bridge across the gulf of death,
> To break the shock blind nature can not shun,
> And land thought smoothly on the farther shore.
> *Young's Night Thoughts.*

FAITH, HOPE, AND CHARITY. In our Masonic illustrations, these virtues are said to be the three principal rounds in Jacob's Ladder. Their figurative signification, as set forth and illustrated in our rituals, is to have faith in God, hope in immortality, and charity to all mankind:—Faith, as established upon the undoubted truth of the divine word; hope, of unwavering confidence in the realization of the promises set forth therein; and pure charity, as essentially necessary to secure the bestowments promised through faith and hope.

What is faith? It is that belief we have in the credit we give to the promises made, whether directly or indirectly, expressed or implied, on or by the authority of the person making it. And as a large share of our knowledge is derived from the statements of others, we give credit thereto according as our confidence is established in the veracity of our informer, or the source of the intelligence received; and the more reliable the evidence, the stronger is our faith.

"And he dreamed, and behold, a ladder was set upon the earth, and the top of it reached to heaven; and behold, the angels of God ascending and descending on it."—Gen. xxviii: 12.

Here was a vision manifested to Jacob, in which God renewed to him the promises he had made to Abraham, that through his lineage the nations of the earth should be blessed. It was the promise of an event that was to transpire at a remote period, and which, through faith, was believed and proclaimed by prophets and holy men of old. What gave strength and force to the faith in these promises? It was the source from whence they emanated—an unfaltering evidence.

You would place but feeble reliance upon a statement made by one of an easy conscience for truth and veracity, and, the more wonderful and mysterious the narrative, the more doubtful and credulous would be your faith. Hence, a well-established faith is based upon undoubted authority.

"And behold, the Lord stood above it, and said, I am the Lord God of Abraham thy father, and the God of Isaac."—Gen. xxviii: 13.

This was the authority and evidence of heaven, and surely no higher could have been desired to have secured the most ample faith in the fulfillment of the promises made to the patriarchs of old.

St. Paul says: "Now faith is the substance of things hoped for, the evidence of things not seen."—Heb. xi: 1.

Perhaps no more beautiful or replete illustration of the power of this virtue is to be found in the sacred Scriptures than that given by Paul in his Epistle to the Hebrews, embraced in chapter xi: 1-31. After having stated what constitutes faith, narrated the numerous instances of its power, he sums up the chapter by asking the question, "And what shall I say more? for the time would fail me to tell of Gideon, and of Barak, and of Samson, and of Jephthae; of David also, and of Samuel, and of the prophets;" and closes with what they endured and what they accomplished through faith.

Faith in the promises of God! No man hath at any time seen God, yet he has been pleased to manifest and reveal himself in various ways for man's special benefit, through the instrumentality of the patriarch and prophets of old, and through the more immediate source of the light of revelation; and we have daily manifestations of his goodness to man, and these are the evidences of our faith in him and in his promises.

A firm and abiding faith in the promises of God, as made manifest to man, will secure him the most ample enjoyment of his favors. It will fortify him with true courage to bear up against the trials of life. It will be his strength and support in the desponding hour of need. It will afford him comfort and consolation, under all circumstances of adversity, and lead him in the paths of contentment and happiness, for the adversities of life are the tests of a man's faith. And nowhere in our esoteric department may we observe this virtue more fully illustrated than in the beautiful emblem of the Ground Floor of our Mystic Temple. It inspires the mind with a true conception of man's own insignificance, and of his dependence upon God, as the chief source of his reliance.

The mariner upon the broad ocean's billows guides his vessel by the points of his compass, and his faith to reach his place of destination consists in the confidence he has in its reliability; and if he possessed any doubts as to its reliability, he would be reluctant in hazarding upon uncertain adventures. Before the discovery of this instrument, he was guided in his course by the aid of the heavenly bodies alone.

The husbandman, when he prepares his ground in the spring-time for seed, has his faith in refreshing showers, and the genial rays of heat and warmth emanating from the sun, which warms the earth and gives vitality to the unseen germ, and through faith he looks forward in anticipation of realizing a coming harvest.

No man has ever seen, felt, heard, tasted, or smelled a soul. It is not tangible to the human faculties, although clothed in a human form. It is too pure and divine in its nature to be made manifest to any of the powers that actuate the mortal parts of man. But no man of sane mind will deny its existence. Every impulse, action, or sentiment of the mind, which places him above the common brute creation, carries the evidence and conviction of its existence, and the more pure and elevated the mind, the more powerful is the evidence, and the stronger is man's faith. And to more fully confirm and establish man's faith, God has revealed to him, through the record of Divine truth, his ultimate purpose and Divine will, and has given it to him for his compass and unerring rule of faith.

HOPE.

> Hope, with uplifted foot, set free from earth,
> Pants for the place of her etherial birth,
> On steady wings sails through the immense abyss,
> Plucks amaranthine joys from bowers of bliss,
> And crowns the soul, while yet a mourner here,
> With wreaths like those triumphant spirits wear.—*Cowper*.

What is hope? It is that anticipation we have of realizing and enjoying some object we are in pursuit of. It is that enlivening principle within the mind which affords greater or less joy as we approximate the object of our desires. No passion seems to be more natural or stronger within man than hope. With what strong feelings and emotions of pleasure do we look forward to the realization of a reunion with those dear to us in life after long separation! What tender sympathies of affection awaken within the mind for departed ones, dear to us in life! With what longing and joyful hope do we look to the realization of a happy reunion in a better and higher sphere! Have you ever lost a cherished friend, an affectionate companion with whom you have journeyed in the trials and turmoils of this life; a child, as the tender offspring of affection, ripening to the years of maturity, that you have not, in your moments of quiet and retirement, dwelt upon, and with anxious hope looked forward to a happy meeting and tender embrace? If you have not, you have no hope, and it is a dark and gloomy reflection, a bewildered road you journey.

Surrounded by the cares and trials incident to the uneven, varied, and checkered span of human life, man, devoid of hope, would be a dreary, heavy, and spiritless being. Whatever his condition or circumstances—high or low, rich or poor, toiling with daily labor for the simple sustenance to sustain life, or in the enjoyment of the comforts and luxuries of ease—his hope is ever watchful, looking forward in bright anticipations of greater joys.

The good man's hope leads him to look forward, through undoubting faith, to the enjoyments of a happy eternity, founded on the promises of his God, through the righteous offices of a Mediator—man's light, his life, his crowning joy of happier spheres.

"That they might set their hope in God, and not forget the works of God, but keep his commandments."— Ps. xxviii: 7.

"The hope of the righteous shall be gladness, but the expectations of the wicked shall perish."—Prov. x: 28.

"Blessed is the man that trust in the Lord, and whose hope the Lord is."—Jer. xvii: 7.

"And now, Lord, what wait I for? my hope is in thee."—Ps. xxxix: 7.

"For thou art my hope, O Lord: thou art my trust from my youth."—Ps. lxxi: 5.

"And hope make not ashamed, because the love of God is shed abroad in our hearts."—Rom. v: 5.

"For we are saved by hope. But hope that is seen, is not hope: for what a man see, why doth he yet hope for?"—Rom. viii: 24.

"But let us who are of the day, be sober, putting on the breastplate of faith and love; and for a helmet, the hope of salvation."—1 Thess. v: 8.

"Which hope we have as an anchor of the soul, both sure and steadfast, and which enter into that within the vail."—Heb. vi: 19.

CHARITY.

Fairest and foremost of the train, that wait
On man's most dignified and happy state,
Whether we name thee charity, or love,
Chief grace below, and all in all above.—*Cowper*.

True charity, a plant divinely nursed,
Fed by the love from which it rose at first;
Thrives against hope, and in the rudest scene,
Storms but enliven its unfading green;
Exuberant is the shadow it supplies,
Its fruit on earth, its growth above the skies.—*Cowper*

In faith and hope the world will disagree,
But all mankind's concern is charity;
All must be false that thwart this one great end;
And all of God, that bless mankind, or mend.—*Pope*.

If we have asked the question, what is faith, or what is hope, with what stronger feelings of emotional interest may we not ask, what is charity? Charity is as unbounded and extensive in its sphere as the universe. Its philanthropic principles know no limits. It is that heaven-born principle, that ennobling virtue, that highest attribute of Deity, which lives beyond this sphere, through endless ages of eternity. When faith shall have been lost in sight, hope ended in fruition, charity will bloom and fructify in vigorous growth. It is love to God, with all our heart, soul, and mind; love to our neighbor as ourselves. True charity is an active principle. It is a fountain within the heart, whence all the benign virtues of candor, forbearance, and generosity flow, as so many native streams, meandering and diffusing themselves, through varied channels, in love and good-will to all. It inspires within us a humane and forgiving disposition. It forms gentleness of temper, with affability of manners, and a liberality of sentiment broad and catholic in principle. It is the soul of social life—the sun, whose rays of love enliven and cheer the abodes of men—a luminary, ever radiant with benignant love and good, refreshing as the gentle dews of heaven.

Pure charity is a plant of Divine growth, celestial in its nature, exuberant in benevolence and love, fragrant with pleasures delightful to contemplate—the choicest plant man can cultivate in the garden of his affection. It is the incense that flows from the sanctuary of the heart, the fountain of life, and infuses its heavenly influence through the various channels connected therewith, and returns with invigorated and renewed strength, ever refreshing to the soul.

St. Paul, in his Epistle to the Corinthians, chapter 13, has given us one of the most sublime, beautiful, and touching illustrations of this divine principle that could possibly be conceived of by mortal man, and sums up the whole with the superiority of this most liberal and truly benevolent of all the heavenly virtues as paramount to all others. So particular is his description in enumerating them, that its import may be fully understood. And what greater evidence need we desire than that given by Paul, as to the power of this virtue; having himself, at one time, been a most violent and intolerant persecutor, and having in turn experienced an equal degree of persecution, he certainly was, through the school of experience—which is said to be the best for discipline—well qualified to judge of its powers and influence, and, therefore, could so well and beautifully describe and illustrate this heavenly virtue.

"And now abide faith, hope, and charity, these three; but the greatest of these is charity."—1 Cor. xiii: 13.

"And to godliness, brotherly kindness; and to brotherly kindness, charity."—2 Pet. i: 7.

"I know thy works, and charity, and service, and faith, and thy patience, and thy works; and the last to be more than the first."—Rev. ii: 19.

From the preceding scriptural quotations you will perceive that we have been drawing quite liberally again, from the inexhaustible treasury of Divine truth, passages applicable to the virtues of faith, hope, and charity. We can not resist the inclination to do so, and have no desire to do it if we could, for the connection is so intimate, the field so extensive, the garden so profusely interspersed with fragrant flowers, that we delight to cull them and strew them in the pathway, in the hope that it may lead others into the same delightful pursuits. It is the oasis in the barren desert, where the weary sojourner may rest and enjoy the refreshing repose, as the reward of the trials and turmoils he endured in the desert.

Faith, hope, and charity—a noble trio in the bonds of fraternal union, affectionately interwoven with the celestial cords of Divine love, are inseperable in association; for where we have faith, we look forward with hope, and through which we anticipate the enjoyment of love and charity.

The true and consistent Mason will ever endeavor to cultivate and live in the practice of this virtue. Endowed therewith, he will be slow to anger and easy to forgive his erring brother; ever ready to give him advice, admonition, or reproof, in gentleness, and with brotherly kindness. He will never lend an ear to the slanders or reproaches of a brother, but will ever vindicate him against unjust assaults, and give him timely notice of attending dangers; he will ever remember and put forth his supplications in his behalf, and regard the interest and welfare of a brother in connection with his own. Selfishness will find no resting-place in the breast of a brother, from whose heart flow the gentle streams of charity.

To live in the bonds of fraternal love is inculcated in our institution, and is one of the chief principles upon which it is founded, and every Mason who lives in obedience to its precepts will be kind and gentle in heart, affable in deportment, humane in disposition, tolerant to the opinions of others, free from vindictive or unjust resentment, always looking upon the frailties of his brother with the most charitable construction. Man by nature is fallen, and prone to err; hence, be not unjustly severe and unforgiving to the errings of your brother, as you know not what may attend you in life, but exercise that noble principle of charity, love, and mercy; endeavor by gentle means to restore him, that, as the perfect ashler, he may be fitted for his place in the temple, and you will enjoy the happy reflection of having acted well your part in the performance of one of the sublimest duties enjoined upon you, as a Mason.

The ancients used to depict the virtue of charity in the character of a goddess, represented as seated in a chair of ivory, holding a wand in her right hand, and wearing a golden tiara upon her head, set with precious stones. Her vesture was of various colors, representing chastity and universal benevolence. Like the light of heaven, her throne was unpolluted and unspotted by passion or prejudice. The gems of her fillet were intended to represent the inestimable blessings flowing variously from her hand of bounty. Such was the veneration paid to this virtue, and thus symbolized in the figure of a goddess to more fully illustrate and inculcate its divine and heavenly principles.

Charity is a perennial plant; it is the evergreen of the soul. The chilling blasts of adversity do not destroy or interrupt its growth; its vitality is as vigorous and active in its influence under adverse circumstances as well as in the most cheering moments of joy. It is the germ of our supplications—the sunbeam of our affections, ever glowing in ardent love. It constitutes the living principles of our faith and the inspiring element of our hope. Have Faith in God, Hope in immortality, and Charity will glow with ardent zeal within your hearts.

FAITH, HOPE, AND CHARITY.

What is Faith? A belief in God unseen,
To human eye invisible—not seen
But through revelation and nature's works;
Man believes, sees God therein, and has faith.

What is Hope? Joy and pleasure not possessed—
Anticipated happiness to come—
The goal, with desire longing to possess,
Seen through the eye of faith, afar, unreached.

What is Charity? Love supreme to God.
Man's first, great, and chief duty is to do
To his neighbor as himself, next is due.
And this is charity, "pure and undefiled."

Faith, Hope, and Charity, sweet sisters three,
Of celestial birth, sprung from love Divine,
Hand in hand, with heavenly mission joined,
In man's behalf they journey on their course.

LECTURE VIII.

BOOK OF THE LAW.

EVERY well-governed lodge is *furnished* with the *Holy Bible, Square,* and *Compasses.* The Holy Bible is dedicated to God, the Square to the Master, and the Compasses to the Craft.—*Craftsman.*

Take this book of the law, and pat it is the side of the ark of the covenant of the Lord your God, that it may be there for a witness against thee.— Deut. XXXI: 26.

This book of the law shall not depart out of thy mouth; but thou shalt meditate therein day and night; that thou may observe to do according to all that is written therein; for then thou shalt make thy way prosper, and then thou shalt have good success.—Josh. I: 8.

And Hilkiah the high priest said unto Shaphan the scribe, I have found the book of the law in the house of the Lord; and Hilkiah gave the book unto Shaphan, and he read it.—2 Kings XXII. 8.

So they rend in the book in the law of God distinctly, and gave the sense, and caused them to understand the reading.—Neh. VIII: 8.

BOOK divine, holy law, to man is given—
His guide, his light, his faith, his hope, his joy;
A precious boon from God Supreme on high—
The polar star, that guides the way to heaven.

The light Divine, unerring rule and guide,
The rock securely based we stand upon;
As the foundation whereupon we build
Our faith, our hope, our happiness to come.

The light divine, undoubting guide of faith,
In the center, upon our altar lies;
Illumes the journey through the life we pass,
Gives faith and hope, cheering our onward way.

Light Divine, hope inspiring gives to man,
His thoughts from earth to heaven it elevates.
Leads him the joys and bliss to contemplate,
Attendant on a just and upright course.

The Holy Bible, as we have already observed, lies constantly upon the altar of Masonry; upon it rests the square and compasses—and they are, masonically, inseparable, and are technically said to constitute the furniture of the lodge.

To remove the sacred volume, with its accompanying symbols, from the lodge, would be an innovation of our landmarks which could not possibly be permitted without undermining the foundation of our structure. It would soon cause it to totter, fall into interminable ruin and destruction—buried in the grave of chaotic darkness. Such would be the deplorable condition and unhappy results attending the removal of the greatest of our luminaries.

In our rituals, we say that every well-governed lodge is furnished with the Holy Bible, Square, and Compasses. The Holy Bible is dedicated to God, the Square to the

Master, and the Compasses to the Craft. The Holy Bible, as God's inestimable gift to man, is the rule and guide of his faith and practice. It is the channel of communication between God and man, and through it he has been pleased to more fully reveal himself and his divine nature and purposes than through any other agency; hence he is the most proper person to whom it should be dedicated.

The Holy Bible is the great light in our moral temple, which gives us vitality and strength, and prepares us, as living stones, for an immortal inheritance in the spiritual temple. What would be the state of man without this revelation of the Great I AM? He would soon sink into savage and degraded barbarism. Man, by nature, is harsh, rude, and overbearing—tyrannical in the exercise of power; hence he needs the soothing influence of Divine favor to curb and bring into subjection the rougher passions of his uncultivated nature.

From this great light we also learn the moral application of the lesser lights, and draw from it the beautiful lessons of morality which are figuratively illustrated by our various symbols.

As Masons, we meet upon the Level—no wealth, rank, title, or nobility gives preference, but, as God's noblemen, we are, masonically, on the level. It is true worth and merit alone which give rank and distinction; and as we are consistent in our profession, and apply ourselves according to our talents, with industry, in the pursuit of our occupation, so will be our reward, for him to whom much hath been given, from him much will be required.

We act by the Plumb. Uprightness, as the rule of our conduct, is the true principle by which Masons should be governed and act toward one another and the world at large. It is in a faithful conformity with the precept of this principle that a Mason walks consistent with the rules of rectitude, and thereby honors his Creator.

By the application of the Compasses he learns so to circumscribe and control his passions and desires as to keep them within due bounds of moderation and proper restraint, conducing to his own welfare.

We part upon the Square—the square of truth and justice. This is one of the natural results consequent upon a strict adherence to the practice of the precepts as taught in the moral application of the Level, Plumb, and Compasses, with the aid of the Holy Bible as our great light and the chief rule for our government.

The Holy Bible, as the great light in our Mystic Temple, sends forth the rays of Divine truth, from its center to the circumference, like the brilliant luminary of the day, which diffuses its genial warmth far and wide, giving light and animation from its center to its utmost bounds. These are but figurative illustrations of what a Mason should be who walks according to his light and knowledge, and whose good influence and example shed rays of light and virtue within his sphere. In this illustration, he may very appropriately apply the Compasses, to ascertain if he meets its just requirements; if not, he may then bring into requisition the use of the Gavel and other implements necessarily required to properly adjust him, that he may be transformed from the rude to the perfect ashler, so that the jewels of his affections may display their beauties and usefulness.

The Holy Bible is always held in the highest veneration by the good and true Mason. He regards it as the fountain from whence are drawn the many excellent precepts he has so often heard in the lodge, and enjoyed with such refreshing pleasure; and he who lightly esteems and disregards the sacred volume, can not but fail in the performance of the great duties it enjoins upon him, and may be regarded as a brother groping in darkness, whose vision has not yet been illuminated by the true light—a stumbling-block, a rough ashler, unprepared for the builder's use.

The Holy Bible is the rock upon which we have laid our foundation—the corner-stone of our structure; and, as already observed, divest it of this, and our beautiful fabric could not survive the separation. And when that event transpires, we may mourn in sorrow. Every ennobling virtue that dignifies and adorns the character of man would give way to some baser passion. Where peace and happiness reigned, misery and sorrow would intervene; where pure and sincere piety flourished, infidelity and atheism would reign supreme.

The Holy Bible is the Masonic store-house; it is the mine from whence we draw our moral instruction—the garner that furnishes us with heavenly food—the fount from whence we quench our spiritual thirst. It is amply sufficient in its resources to meet the wants of all. Your drafts upon it may be liberal; it will honor them if properly made. Such are the merits it possesses, that it is never-failing in its supplies. It promises an ample reward for virtuous deeds and labors faithfully performed, while at the same time it warns you against a violation of its precepts, and the bitter consequences resulting therefrom. As a sure and steadfast friend, you need not be troubled with doubts or misgivings; it is reliable—it will never deceive you; it is God's Holy Word—it can not possibly deceive. You are secure on that score. Make it the man of your counsel; it will prove to be your steadfast friend and counselor in life. You may consult it under all and every circumstance; it is adapted to every sphere and condition in life, without exception. When you are desponding, from care and sorrow, consult it, and it will open a door of relief. If you are overburdened with cares, anxieties, and perplexities, seek its aid and counsel, and it will point out the way of release and ease; if you are over-solicitous about your worldly gains, ask its counsel and advice, and it will tell you of riches imperishable, and to which your present are but as dross. Then, as your beacon-light, let it illuminate your pathway, lead you where you will know no cares and sorrows to be relieved—no burdens of anxieties and perplexities that need release; no solicitude about your over-accumulated worldly gains, for it will provide you a better treasure, and lead you to the enjoyment of endless felicity in the haven of peaceful rest.

Such are its ample provisions, and with such it invites your earnest attention; surely you will not, or you ought not, to be indifferent to its solicitations. If the various symbols presented for your consideration claim so highly your admiration, why should not, then, this symbol of your faith lay a higher claim, not only for your admiration, but for your exalted and pious veneration, and, as Masons, that it may be truly and consistently the rule and guide of your faith and practice through life? That your deportment toward each other may be affectionate, your emulations be such as to who can best work and best agree, and the approval rest upon its own merits, without envy or discord. That love and harmony may prevail throughout the Mystic Temple, the bonds of brotherly love and relief be more strongly cemented in the principles of Divine truth— that faith, hope, and charity may be more fully exemplified— faith, that, in your integrity, your uprightness and fidelity, you may confidently look forward with joyful hope in anticipation of that unbounded charity that brings goodwill and peace to all; and, as a reward for your labors, you will be fitted and prepared for a happy transit from your earthly to your spiritual temple. Such, my brethren are the reflections based on the illustrations and teachings of our symbol of faith.

The book of the law holds a more intimate connection with the institution of Masonry than many of its votaries conceive of, and this fact is more fully elucidated in the higher degrees. The three primitive degrees in Masonry are symbolic in their instruction, and they inculcate the great duties man owes to his God and to his fellow-man; they portray the various virtues of morality enjoined upon him to cultivate and practice in his intercourse with his fellow-beings, and impress upon his mind the necessity of intellectual culture and improvement for his more full enjoyment of happiness in the social relations of life, as God created man for social enjoyment and happiness; and they sum up with a most beautiful and impressive allegory, wherein he is admonished of his corporeal mortality and the immortality of the indwelling Spirit of eternal life.

It is in the higher degrees, which are historical in their nature, that we learn the full import and relation Masonry holds with the book of the law. Solomon possessed great wisdom and knowledge, for God had promised and bestowed it upon him, and doubtless he foresaw, through the prophetic range of vision, that the children of Israel, as they were surrounded by idolatrous nations, would depart from the worship of God, and fall into sinful and idolatrous ways, and through which a knowledge of the true God might become lost to them; hence, in order to prevent so dire a calamity, he made provision for its safety.

When the Temple was destroyed by the armies of Nebuchadnezzar, and the holy vessels and sacred treasures, together with the children of Israel, were carried away into Babylonish captivity, every means and effort was made to destroy and obliterate the worship and knowledge of the true God, for Nebuchadnezzar had erected a huge brazen image, before which he required the Israelites to bow down and worship, under the penalty of death. But the evil designs of their conqueror were frustrated, and in due time the children of Israel were, by the Divine will, through the instrumentality of Cyrus, permitted to return to the land of their fathers and rebuild their city and Temple, and the book of the law was found preserved. Such was the will and providence of God, and the evil designs of man could not frustrate it.

THE BOOK OF THE LAW.

On Sinai's mount, before Jehovah God,
In a cloud of glory veiled, amid lightning
And thunder's roar that shook the mountain's base,
Moses, leader of Israel's favored flock,
In the cleft rock, in awful silence stood.
Forty days and forty nights' converse sweet
With Israel's God this faithful servant held,
And from the hand, unseen to human eye,
Invisible, unobserv'd, veiled in the cloud,
The Sacred Law Divine for man received—
The Law of God, supreme on high—to be his
Rule, his guide in life, whereby to walk, as man
Should do, obedient to the Law Divine.

The thronging multitude await, impatient
His return. Murmurs and discontent arise,
Clamorous disaffection throughout the camp
Prevail—disobedience in Israel's hosts.
Corrupting evil on their affections seized;
False gods they sought, menial, vain, idolatrous.
Ingrates to God, the true and living one, were
The favored, chosen flock, Jehovah's special
Care—by him from Egyptian servile bondage
Freed—forth to go—the promised land inheritance
To them bequeathed, and by them to be enjoyed
As his peculiar, favored, cherished flock.

Meantime, Aaron the golden calf had made—
An image from golden trinkets formed—
High on an altar raised: "These be thy gods,
O! Israel; reverence and homage show"—
When lo! behold, forth came the multitude
And prostrate before the idol image fall,
And to their false gods adoration pay;
Not adoration to God Supreme, Most High,
Pure and Holy, observed—just and due to him—
But to vain idolatry, the handicraft,
The work of frail, mortal man, they vainly
Bowed, to their own humility and shame;
While shouts of acclamation rend the air—
Not shouts to God—Eternal, Infinite God
On high—but to unhallowed idolatry.
Such the acclamation, reverberating
Far and near, from the hosts around the image
Formed, that reached the ear of Moses on the mount.
Hark! 'tis not the voice of those with victory crowned,
Nor the cry for mercy by those overcome,
But shouts of merriment, heard far and near,
From those who to the false image homage pay.

The Law Divine, from God on high received,
Charged with the mission faithfully to perform,
Slowly the mount descending, the precious boon
He bears, with countenance reflecting glory
In effulgent brightness, with luster shone—
Unseen, unknown to him, who in the presence
Of his God had stood—veiled in the cloud with him,
The Great Jehovah, Eternal Holy One.

From afar he beholds the chosen flock—
Observes, views them as around the image formed—
The multitude of Israel, seed of Abram,
Congregated for unhallowed purposes,
Amazed, astonished, he descries vile, servile
Idolatry within the camp, by Israel's
Hosts, the chosen ones, God's reserved special care.
With anguish keen and deep—painful to behold—
Base infidelity to God he observed;
Witnessed their sinful, degraded sacrifice
Offered to an idol image raised on high;
Angered for their willful disobedience,
Their departure from God's holy will and law,
With deep remorse of shame for them, he dashed
Aside the holy Law from God Divine received—
The Law upon the tablets inscribed by HIM.

Seized with sudden anguish and dread remorse
At their own perfidious and inconstant course,
Conscious of disobedience and of sin—
Guilt to be atoned—they, with trembling fear,
Dread his approach, fearful of his just wrath
And indignation for their transgressive course,
For they had sinned a great and grievous sin,
And purged must be thereof—the offense atone
By them committed against God the Most High,
Ere the camp could proceed again on its way.

"Who's on the Lord's side? Let him come forth
Arrayed, the just cause to vindicate,
That atonement for the mischief done be made.
Let every man put on his sword—from gate

To gate, the camp throughout, brother, neighbor,
Man and companion slay, that this foul sin
Be blotted out and justly atoned therefore;
The camp from polluted sin be purified,
The offense against him the Most High appeased,
That his people purged and cleansed their from might be
Ere the camp proceed again upon its way."
Such the mandate from Moses, servant of God,
Leader of Israel's hosts, given the faithful ones,
To be enforced—be strictly adhered thereto—
Until reparation, atonement in full
Be justly made, God's just cause to vindicate.
And faithfully the command observed was,
Strictly in prompt obedience to his will;
And of idolaters in Israel's camp
That day, three thousand fell—the offense atoned.

    Peradventure, God's just wrath to appease,
His mercy and forgiveness to obtain,
Moses interceded in their behalf,
Sought forgiveness for their offenses past
In purification, and atonements made,
Such as was justly due, pardon to obtain—
Sacrifices and purifications made
For their perfidious errors and wanderings,
Their idolatrous, evil, and sinful course.
God, ever propitious, ever merciful,
Forgave, and the Law Divine again restored.

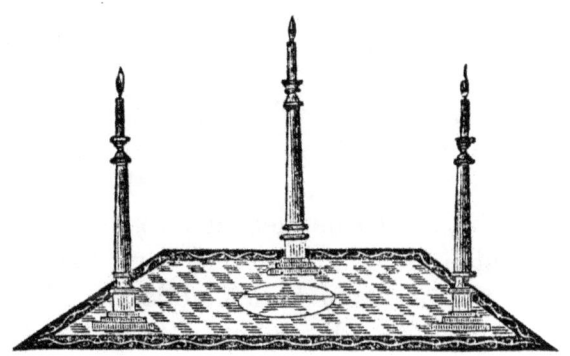

LECTURE IX.

THE ORNAMENTS AND LIGHTS OF A LODGE.

The ornaments of a Lodge are the *mosaic pavement, indented tessel,* and the *blazing star.* The *mosaic pavement* is a representation of the ground-floor of King Solomon's temple; the *indented tessel,* of that beautiful tesselated border or skirting which surrounded it; and the *blazing star* in the center is to remind us of the omnipresence of the Almighty, overshadowing us with his Divine love and dispensing his blessings among us.

The *mosaic pavement* is emblematical of human life, checkered with good and evil; the *beautiful border* which surrounds it, of those manifold blessings and comforts that surround us, and which we hope to enjoy, by a faithful reliance on Divine Providence, which is hieroglyphically represented by the blazing star in the center—*Craftsman.*

THE MOSAIC PAVEMENT, INDENTED TESSEL, AND THE BLAZING STAR. Of such are said to consist the ornaments of a Lodge, and which, in their symbolic illustrations, are fraught with the most useful lessons of instruction, well calculated to impress the mind with the uncertain and varied events incident to human life, and of the instability of man's earthly pursuits. They are also to teach us that man's final destiny is a higher sphere; and yet as he lives in obedience to the precepts of the Divine and moral law, blessings and enjoyments attend him through life, intermingled with its cares and solicitudes.

The great Author of our being destined man for happiness, but when he transgressed the Divine law, he forfeited the inheritance bequeathed to him, and through that transgression he fell from his high estate, and the bitter consequence of disobedience subjected him to the ills and afflictions incident to his fallen nature, and the penalty of death.

The Ground-Floor.—The Mosaic Pavement consists of small stones of various colors, beautifully interwoven and closely laid together. The ground-floor of the temple is said to have been constructed in this manner. It was also a custom that prevailed among the ancients, to lay the ground-floors of their temples and other important edifices with checkered and variegated work, doubtlessly intended to convey some useful instruction as well as for its ornamental beauty.

What can more appropriately or more powerfully impress the mind with man's true state, his dependent condition, of the various scenes of life through which he passes, than this emblem, in the important lessons it is intended to teach? To-day, we are in prosperity; to-morrow, cast down in adversity. Elated with joy and happiness, or in the depths of sorrow and grief; vigorous in health, or languishing on the conch of sickness and pain; administering aid and relief to others, or ourselves the recipients of kind and benevolent offices; in the giddy height of fame and honor, or down in degraded anguish and humility. Such are the precarious events of the uncertainties attending the transitory journey of human life, and are forcibly symbolized by this checkered ornament.

What a befitting emblem for contemplation, for the consideration of the INITIATE upon his first introduction to the ground-floor of our Mystic Temple! But when he casts his eyes around, and surveys that, beautiful tessellated border with which it is surrounded, what feelings of joy should it not inspire within his breast, that, amidst all his cares, anxieties, and solicitudes, his pathway is strewn and interspersed with flowers, fragrant with happiness and pleasures; that every bitter cup has its corresponding and refreshing draft of sweetness, every sorrow its joy, and every grief its soothing balm.

The Tessellated Border.—This ornament is wisely designed, in its illustration, to teach us that man, amidst all the trials and anxieties he is called to experience in life, is sustained by the reviving joys of hope, that hope which animates him with the prospect of happier and more cheerful days. Hope is the invigorating stimulant of the soul. It is that encouraging beam of light which guides man through the gloomy labyrinths of the uneven paths he treads, to illumine and cheer his desponding way. Devoid of hope, life would be a dreary blank—a weary burden to sustain—and man would sink and perish in despair.

The Blazing Star.—This cheerful and brilliant ornament, the center of affections, is the ACME of man's joy and hope. Through this ornament, he looks forward with an inspiring faith to GOD, and hopes through the fruition of that faith to enjoy that bliss which lies beyond the scenes of this life. By it he also learns that the practice of brotherly love, relief, and truth; combined with the virtues of Faith, Hope, and Charity; established within his affections, nurtured with the love of God, and stimulated with the anticipated joy of heaven, will strengthen him with fortitude to endure the trials of life, and secure him an interest, when his earthly labors shall have ceased, into that Celestial Lodge, whose ambrosial founts are draughts of refreshing and life-giving joys.

What reflections for the contemplative mind does this beautiful emblem with its various and checkered ground-floor, its beautifully-ornamented and tessellated border, and its blazing star in the center, present! It impresses the mind with our own insufficient and dependent state. It inspires it with joyful hope in the realization of happier days. It opens and expands the affections with kind and tender sympathies to the unfortunate, and of love and charity to all. It makes man feel and realize his dependence upon the all-sustaining hand of God. It is to him as a refreshing spring of joy, the manna that invigorates him with strength to bear up against the ills of adversity, the talisman that directs his footsteps to that light which leads to the haven of peaceful rest.

Such, my brother, are the illustrations and lessons drawn from this symbol, and intended to be inculcated and impressed upon your mind, for we can not be too often or too forcibly reminded of the constant changes attending man through life. He knows not the events of the coming hour, and thus it is wisely provided for him to be so, for could man foresee the various uncertainties that accompany him in his worldly journey, whether intermingled with joy and pleasure, or alloyed with care and sorrow, he would be the most unhappy of beings. His present state is, therefore, one of probation, and as he learns to encounter and meet its adversities with becoming resignation, so their counterparts afford him the greater pleasure in the enjoyments thereof, and the more willing acquiescence to endure its trials.

If the ways of man were smooth and even through life, unattended by any of its cares and solicitudes, he would be but illy fitted to exercise the humane virtues of benevolence and charity. Haughty, supercilious, and selfish in his nature, his charities would be bestowed in that character, and would not emanate from sympathetic affections, keen and sensitive to the wants of others. He would be illiberal and contracted in sentiment, and proscriptive to the opinions of others. Selfishness would influence him and be the governing motive of his heart.

A Mason can not contemplate this beautiful emblem without being deeply impressed with the important lessons it is intended to convey, and of the necessity of being so fortified and strengthened by its just consideration, as to be at all times prepared to meet the adversities he is daily called to encounter; for such are its purposes, and such the illustrations it is intended to inculcate.

This emblem embraces within its scope and portrays

the lessons of the various implements symbolized for your moral instruction, and impressively illustrates the several virtues you are taught to inculcate and exemplify in life.

The Square, Level, and Plumb, to square your action by truth and virtue, in all your dealings with your fellowman, ever remembering that in God's presence all are on the level of equality, and that no distinctions are recognized by him, except as merited by an observance and conformity to his will. And by the plumb-line, as the index which points from earth to heaven, to elevate the mind from groveling cares, to contemplations of bliss; always remembering the application of the compasses, that by keeping your passions, sensual and mental, circumscribed within due bounds of moderation, you can not materially err, or be far astray.

Brotherly Love, Relief, and Truth, that you should be courteous and respectful toward a brother, affable in your deportment; and this will secure you his respect. Kind and solicitous for his welfare, ever ready with a generous hand of charity to extend toward him that aid and relief his circumstances may require; governed by candor and truthfulness in all your actions toward him, whatever his frailties or errors may have been, whether through misfortune or by imprudence, ever remembering that be is a brother, and that the germ should not be destroyed, but restored if possible; and this will constitute true and heavenly charity.

Faith, Hope, and Charity. The checkered ground-floor illustrates the necessity of having faith; faith in God's promises, as revealed in his Divine Word. The beautiful border leads you to look forward with a hope which, through that faith, you may be called to the enjoyments of the blessings promised, and in which you will participate according as you have fulfilled your obligations, and surely, the reward will be amply sufficient for all the labors you are required to perform.

Temperance, Fortitude, Prudence, and Justice. Not merely that restraint of intemperance to which the carnal passions of man are more or less subjected, and to which, through the weakness of his nature, he yields, but that temperate moderation which should be observed and govern his actions toward his fellow-man. He is always endued with that fortitude which will enable him to meet the various encounters of life with true moral courage, firmness, and consistency. Prudent in action and expression, carefully guarded and governed on all occasions, avoiding any intentional injury or wrong to others, and with justice to be fair and honorable, prompt to all his engagements, and truthful in word and sincere in motive; and thus he sums up the virtues, beautifully symbolized and illustrated by the checkered ground-floor, surrounded by the beautifully tessellated border, and from whose center radiates the brilliant star, his hope, and his blissful joy.

Man's trials, cares, and anxieties in life are often more or less the result of his own imprudent acts than otherwise, for every departure from a correct line of rectitude, or deviation from the principles of truth and justice, has its corresponding equivalent to meet—its trial or affliction to endure. It is an inevitable law of nature, which can not be avoided or escaped, for the debt contracted must be canceled. Hence, man needs a monitor as a talisman, to impress him with the necessity of constant vigilance against the infirmities of his nature, and to keep him in the paths of virtue. If he would so learn to control and form his mind, as to be governed by the principles of rectitude, truth, and justice in all things, moderation and forbearance toward others, he would then be fortified with the virtue of prudence, through the exercise of which he would be enabled to overcome many of the seeming difficulties he is called to encounter; often inflicted as the trials of his faith, for God's ways are not as the ways of man, for he deals with us for our good.

Correct and virtuous principles are taught us as Masons. They are inculcated in our esoteric schools, and every Mason is in duty bound, as a good member of society, to observe them; and when he fails to do so, he fails in the faithful performance and discharge of his most sacred duty. He tarnishes the badge he has promised to preserve unsullied, is inconsistent in his professions, and does not reflect honor to the Fraternity. He walks as a benighted brother, and is an erring stumbling-block in the ways of virtue; an inclined column devoid of beauty or ornament, not in conformity with the principles of rectitude, as required by the plumb-line; an undressed ashler, unfit for the builder's use, and to which the moral application of the Gavel may be profitably employed, to fit it for its proper use in the temple.

Hence, how important it is then for us, as Masons, to be circumspect in our deportment through life, to observe with profit the instructions presented and illustrated, for our moral edification, by our various symbols; to apply them in their moral bearing, and act in conformity to their requirements, and thereby fit ourselves, as living ornaments, to adorn and beautify the temple—the moral temple of man—to walk in rectitude and harmony with our profession, to live in the bonds of brotherly love and good fellowship, enjoy true happiness, be living ornaments, reflecting honor and dignity to our noble Order.

In our ritual, we say that the three principal rounds of Jacob's ladder are denominated Faith, Hope, and Charity; and they are illustrated as having faith in God, hope in immortality, and charity to all mankind. If these virtues are symbolized by this emblem, may we not with equal propriety say that the beautiful Ornaments of the lodge are susceptible of the same illustrations? What can impress the mind with a stronger or more forcible necessity of faith, than the diversities represented in the ground-floor of the temple? If it is intended to symbolize the varied and checkered events peculiar to human life, it must also symbolize the necessity of having faith; for whilst we tread upon this emblem. we are reminded of the trials and conflicts man endures in his probationary state of dependence, and that he should feel the necessity of having faith in that Being, upon whom he is called to place his chief reliance for support and aid.

For we need aid, we need counsel and advice, and to whom can we go, or look to with greater confidence, or with a stronger assurance of hope, than the Creator of our being, our chief reliance; for his promises are, "Seek, and ye shall find; ask, and ye shall receive; knock, and it shall be opened unto you." These are the inviting assurances he has extended to us, but we must come with our petition in faith; hence the altar, as an emblem of devotion, is to remind us of Him from whom we are to seek aid and counsel, and who will withhold nothing from us for our good.

How beautifully does this accord with the principles of our institution, in respect to the outer world, with those desiring fellowship and admission into our sanctuary: they seek information through a lawful channel; make their desires known to one of the Fraternity, ask, and all that is necessary is communicated; and if found worthy, they knock, and the door of Masonry is opened unto them. And here they are taught to acknowledge their dependence on that God whose Divine aid and favor is ever to be sought and implored in all good and laudable undertakings.

And as the mind is directed to look forward and behold the beautiful Tessellated Border which surrounds the ground-floor, as symbolical of the manifold blessings and comforts with which we are surrounded in life, so does it inspire and enliven us with the cheering prospects of that hope man has in a firm and well-grounded faith—that hope which inspires within him an invigorating energy and perseverance to battle the adversities of life, ride triumphantly over its tempestuous billows until safely moored in the peaceful harbor of security.

The Blazing Star, symbolized as the Eye of Omniscience

ever wakeful to man's happiness and comfort, is to remind him that his reliance and dependence should always be placed in Divine Providence, as the chief object to whom he is indebted for his being and every comfort and blessing he enjoys. How forcibly does this emblem impress itself upon the mind, with God's love, his goodness, and his superabounding care for our welfare! And how beautifully does it symbolize that heavenly principle of love and charity, which should ever be extended toward our fellow-beings—that charity which is liberal in sentiment and in harmony with God's love toward his creatures.

How beautiful is this ornament of the ground-floor surrounded by the Tessellated Border, illumined from its center by the Blazing Star, emblem of Divine love! It is in heavenly harmony and in unison with the virtues illustrated by the Theological Ladder, the three principal rounds of which are Faith, Hope, and Charity; three tenets of our order, inculcating the virtues of Brotherly Love, Relief, and Truth; three supports to our institution—Wisdom, Strength, and Beauty; three lights in our mystic temple—East, West, and South, all supported by the great light of Divine Truth; three Jewels, which teach us Truth, Justice, Equality and rectitude of deportment in life; three Jewels also, which illustrate man's rude and imperfect nature, his more refined and advanced stage of improvement, and his final adaptation as a living stone for God's temple on high; three Grand Masters, as the superintendents of the Craft at the building of the temple.

The number three is a triad sacred to Freemasonry.

It constitutes the three symbolic degrees, and upon which the several rites or higher system are based; it beautifully illustrates the three principal stages of human life—youth, manhood, and old age; it inculcates man's mortality, his resurrection, and immortality.

HUMILITY.

The checkered Ground-floor whereupon we meet
Humility and meekness inculcate;
Impresses man with his dependent state,
And reliance on God's supporting hand.

The Tessellated Border it surrounds,
Within us cheering hope inspiring forms;
Animated with courage, let us pursue
The onward course, that leads to peaceful joy.

The Blazing Star, within its center placed,
Shines brightly forth in rays of glowing light,
Illumes our way with joyful hope through life,
And confirms our faith in God's promise made.

Pride not thyself upon thy worldly state,
Thou know not what the day may yet bring forth;
Honor and riches are but worldly gain,
That false pride in the heart of man beget.

With meekness, in the paths of wisdom's ways,
Humility better becometh man;
As pride lifts up the heart to vanity,
With vain imaginations and conceit.

True humility is true dignity,
When with meekness and modesty combined;
An ornament that adorns the paths of man,
With true pride, honor, worth, and mein to him.

Humility and meekness virtues are
That give merit and character to man,
Beautify and adorn his walks in life,
With God—like attitude, as they will do.

THE LIGHTS OF A LODGE.

And god said, let there be light, and there was light—Gen. I: 3.

And the Lord went before them by day, in a pillar of cloud, to lead them the way; and by night in a pillar of fire, to give them light; to go by day and night—Ex. XIII: 21.

He will bring me forth to the light, and I shall behold his righteousness.— Mich VII: 9.

Bat the path of the just is as the shining light, that shine more and more unto the perfect day.—Prov. IV: 18.

God is light, and in him is no darkness at all.—1 John I: 5.

Thy word is as a lamp unto my feet, and a light unto my path—Ps. CXVII: 105.

THE three burning tapers represented in the Lodge—placed east, west, and south—are masonically called the three lesser lights, and they have an emblematical representation. There is none in the north. There were three entrances to the Temple—east, west, and south; also to the tabernacle, which was the type of the Temple. There were also three principal rounds in Jacob's ladder, denominated Faith, Hope, and Charity, illustrative of these virtues; and there are three principal officers of a lodge, represented by the pillars of Wisdom, Strength, and Beauty.

We have previously referred to the three great lights in Masonry—the Holy Bible, Square, and Compasses—and these are surrounded by the three lesser lights. The Holy Bible, as the greater light, like the luminary of day, is the center surrounded by the lesser lights; from it radiate the effulgent rays of Divine truth—that truth which will guide us in the paths of virtue, and lead us in the way to eternal life.

The Square is a figure of four equal sides, parallel; it is also a mathematical instrument, forming a right—angle. In the hands of the operative it is the instrument by which he adjusts his work, and by its application he ascertains its fitness and adaptation for its intended place in the building. The moral application of this instrument is intended to impress upon our minds the necessity of conforming to correct principles, and of being governed in our actions by truth and justice, as two shining lights that beautify and adorn our moral characters.

The Compasses is the instrument for circumscribing circles. In the hands of the operative, its application enables him to ascertain and find his circle and such figures as pertain thereto. In the moral application of this instrument, we are reminded of the necessity of keeping the passions so circumscribed as to be within the bounds of moderations, as prescribed by the virtues of temperance, fortitude, prudence, and justice. The principles inculcated by the cardinal virtues are to be fully observed if we desire to live in obedience to the precepts of the three great lights—the greatest of which is the Divine light of truth.

Thus we illustrate the three great lights of our temple: the Holy Bible, through faith, enlightens our minds as to God's will, and teaches us to walk obedient thereto; the Square, that we should conform to correct principles, equal and just to all, and thus we form true parallels; the Compasses, from the center to the circumference, confine our passions and desires, and admonish us to keep them within the limits of moderation and rational consistency.

Of all the wonderful productions of God's works in the creation of the universe, the most desirable and cheering to man is light—it prefigures knowledge; and the light of knowledge is the source through which we know God.

"In the beginning God created the heaven and the earth. And the earth was without form, and void; and darkness was upon the face of the deep, and the Spirit of God moved upon the face of the waters. And God said, let there be light, and there was light."—Gen. i: 1, 2, 3.

> Hail, holy light! offspring of heaven—first-born—
> Or of the eternal, co-eternal beam—
> May I express thee unblamed? since God is light;
> And never but in unapproachable light
> Dwelt from eternity—dwelt then in thee—
> Bright effulgence of bright essence incarnate.—*Paradise Lost.*

Light is prefigurative of life. On the fourth day of God's work, he created the sun, moon, and stars—the sun to rule the day, and the moon to govern the night—emblematically illustrative of that regularity with which the Master should rule and govern the lodge over which he presides; hence they are symbolized as emblems of regularity. The sun, as the greater of the lesser lights, whose effulgent rays of warmth impart life to the vegetable creation, was, in the wisdom of the Great Architect of the Universe, designed to rule the day, and the moon, whose mild rays emanate from this luminary, to govern the night. It is with regularity and concert of harmony that the Supreme Master of the Universe governs his works; and as he is our great prototype, so should we endeavor to imitate his example.

God is the effulgent essence of Divine light. To seek light is, or ought to be, the great object of our desire. When Moses received the Divine instruction in reference to the tabernacle, light was an essential prerequisite. The golden candlestick, with its seven burners, is particularly described. The quality of the oil consumed thereby is also specified to be pure oil olive, beaten for the lamps; and it was made a statute of the tabernacle that they burn continually. In the Temple, also, was the golden candlestick, with five burners on the right hand, and five burners on the left hand.

Lights have been used in religious ceremonies in all periods of the world. When the children of Israel departed from Egyptian bondage, the Lord placed before them a pillar of cloud, which went before them by day, and at night as a pillar of fire, that they might journey by night as well as by day; hence, the book of Divine light being our guide, our altars are illuminated by the three burning tapers.

"Moreover, the light of the moon shall be as the light of the sun, and the light of the sun shall be sevenfold, as the light of seven days, in the day that the Lord binds up the breaches of his people and heals the stroke of their wound."—Isaiah xxx: 26.

"The sun shall be no more thy light by day; neither for brightness shall the moon give light unto thee: but the Lord shall be unto thee an everlasting light, and thy God thy glory."—Isaiah lx: 19.

"Then shall thy light break forth as the morning, and thine health shall spring forth speedily, and thy righteousness shall go forth before thee; the glory of the Lord shall be thy reward."—Isaiah lviii: 8.

"As the appearance of the bow that is in the cloud in the day of rain, so was the appearance of the brightness round about. This was the appearance of the likeness of the glory of the Lord. And when I saw it, I fell upon my face, and I heard a voice of one that spoke."—Ezek. i: 28.

"For with thee is the fountain of life; in thy light shall we see light."—Ps. xxxvi: 9.

"For thou wilt light my candle, the Lord my God will enlighten my darkness."—Ps. xviii: 28.

From the foregoing quotations you will perceive that the light of Divine truth abounds copiously in illustrations figurative of the symbol of light, and under which symbol the Son of God prefigured himself as the light of the world.

Whatever our pursuit in life may be, when laudable, light is a desirable consideration to the attainment of our object. To gain knowledge is to gain light. The effort is commendable; and he who seeks this attainment worthily, merits the honor of a true son of light, he reflects honor to his profession.

The man of an enlightened understanding will be governed by reason and judgment in all his acts. Liberal and enlarged in his views, he will accord to others a just and proper consideration of respect. He will be free from prejudice and bigotry, liberal and candid, reasonable and agreeable, frank and honorable in his intercourse; while he with the benighted mind, contented to grovel in ignorance and grope in darkness—satisfied to feed upon the husks—will be but as an empty vessel—an ornament devoid of intrinsic value—a vain bauble and show—a dull and heavy being—a light enshrouded in the mists of darkness—and but poorly qualified for the great duties of life.

As light is prefigurative of life, so is darkness that of death, which is the absence of light. Darkness is one of the plagues inflicted upon the Egyptians, for the obstinacy of Pharaoh in persistently refusing to allow the children of Israel to depart for the Promised Land according to God's command. It lasted for three days, and is said to have been a most terrible darkness—so much so, that not one of the Egyptians stirred out of his place for three days, during its continuance. And yet, during this dark period to the Egyptians, the children of Israel enjoyed the light, which remained visible to them.

The light of the Shekinah was visible in the Most Holy of Holies of the Temple. It was the Divine light of Heaven—the visible manifestation of God's holy presence—the Divine oracle which the high priest was permitted to consult, for the interest of God's favored people. But when they departed from his ways and forsook his laws, and their minds became degraded to darkness and idolatry, then the divine light departed, and they paid the penalty for their transgression.

Ignorance and darkness are incompatible with God's holy law—they are at variance with the virtues that elevate and dignify man—uncongenial in association with an enlightened understanding and knowledge—incapable of virtuous and meritorious worth. They are the counterparts of what should constitute a Mason, in the proper sense of that term, for light is essentially necessary to the well-being and prosperity of our science. The light of a pure mind makes it the receptacle of divine and moral truths.

The Mason who properly comprehends the great object of our institution will be industrious in the pursuit of knowledge. He will strive to gain that light and general information portrayed in its teachings, and live in accordance to its precepts, and thus give honor to the Fraternity; he will be a shining light in the galaxy of the brotherhood, a pillar of wisdom, strength, and beauty, and a worthy ornament in the temple.

Light is the illumination of the mind; it is the possession of knowledge that gives power and strength to the intellect; and he who seeks the attainment thereof may truly be said to walk in the paths of light.

Light is divine and moral in its nature, and be who seeks the Divine light, elevates the mind in the pursuit of that knowledge which is spiritual in its nature, and through which we derive our knowledge, and form our ideas of Deity; and as we are, to a greater or less extent, imitative beings, so we form our own characters according to our conceptions of the Divine Being. Moral light consists in the knowledge of those laws God has given us as the rule and guide of our actions in life—conformity to which is required of us, as the duties we owe to each other, to observe, for our moral comfort and happiness.

A Mason who applies himself in the pursuit of useful knowledge, and lives in obedience thereto, may be said to be a light in the temple, and reflects the virtues inculcated therein. As the eye is the light of the body, so he stands as a worthy son of light, reflecting the beauties that adorn the moral temple.

God is the source of light. He created man in his own image, and infused within him light and life; hence they are the living principles inherent in his nature—and he prescribed laws for his guidance, both divine and moral; and as man conforms in obedience to those laws, so far he reflects the light of his Creator; and as he departs there from, so the light within him becomes proportionately obscured; and thus far he is not in accordance with God's will, and his responsibility will be proportioned according to the light and knowledge he possesses; for Divine justice demands this, and we can not set it aside. These principles are taught us in the several departments of our esoteric institutions; hence light is one of the essential prerequisites in our mysteries—it prefigures life, is symbolic thereof.

LECTURE X.

THE JEWELS OF A LODGE.

The *rough ashler* is a stone as taken from the quarry in its rude and natural state.

The *perfect ashler* is a stone made ready by the hands of the workmen, to be adjusted by the working tools of the Fellow-Craft.

The *trestle-board* is for the master workman to draw his designs upon.

By the rough ashler we are reminded of our rude and imperfect state by nature; by the perfect ashler, of that state of perfection at which we hope to arrive by a virtuous education, our own endeavors, and the blessing of God; and by the trestle-board we are also reminded that, as the operative workman erects his temporal building agreeably to the rules and designs laid down by the Master on his trestle-board, so should we, both operative and speculative, endeavor to erect our spiritual building agreeably to the rules and designs laid down by the Supreme Architect of the Universe, in the great book of revelation, which is our spiritual, moral, and Masonic trestle-board. - *Craftsman.*

THE jewels of a lodge are said to be six in number: they are the Square, Level, and Plumb; the Rough Ashler, Perfect Ashler, and the Trestle-Board.

The Square, Level and Plumb are the first in enumeration, and, as such, are the jewels worn by the three principal officers of the lodge, designating their rank and stations.

In the second degree they are presented as the working tools of a Fellow-Craft; and it is here where their moral signification is more fully illustrated, although, in every stage of advancement we make, wherever they are referred to, the moral principles inculcated and symbolized through them are more or less elaborated as they are intimately interwoven throughout our system in beautiful harmony.

The Square is the jewel pertaining to the Worshipful Master, and its application in that connection is intended to impress his mind with the responsibilities of the station he occupies; and keep constantly in his view the fact that great Masonic knowledge is essentially necessary to the well-being, regularity, and proper government of his lodge, whereby he preserves that peace and harmony which should always exist among the Craft, that their work may be true and square, fully according with the principles inculcated by the moral illustrations as drawn from this jewel.

The Master of a lodge, as the pillar of Wisdom, should be well informed in Masonic Law—the usages and customs by which the Fraternity is governed; and unless he is so, he falls far short of the proper requisitions necessary for its well-being. Much depends upon his skill for its harmony and prosperity; hence he should fully realize the responsibilities of the exalted position he is called by his lodge to occupy. His deportment should be characterized by courtesy, condescension, and affability; he should be prompt and decisive in the discharge of his duties, watchful over the interests and welfare of his lodge; he should reprove and admonish with moderation, as a faithful guardian, the irregularities of those over whom he presides, as a duty strictly incumbent upon him. His example should be one of candor and frankness, not swayed by petty caprice, but consistent and firm, conforming in duty to the moral principles illustrated by the jewel he wears, the badge of his distinction, and thus he will not only honor his station, but will secure the respectful consideration and esteem of the brotherhood.

The Level, as the jewel pertaining to the Senior Warden, inculcates equality, and a frequent recurrence thereto is to remind him of the duties pertaining to his office. It is his duty to give proper aid and support to the Worshipful Master; and that can only be done by preserving unanimity and harmony among the workmen. See that no contention exists—that true merit is only attained through the maxim as to who can best work and best agree. This alone should be the proper stimulant and motive to action—the only consideration to just and merited preferment. Such principles and such actions will always be attended with good and beneficial results to the lodge, and strengthen the affections of the brotherhood in the performance of their labors.

The Senior Warden, as the second officer of the lodge, should not only qualify himself for the discharge of the duties thereof, but should be equally well informed in

Masonic usages, to enable him to give proper aid and support to the Master. As the pillar of Strength, much depends upon his ability to do so, for in the absence of the Master, the responsibilities of his position devolves upon him, and he should, therefore, prepare himself to assume its requirements and discharge its duties.

The Plumb, as an emblem of rectitude, pertains to the Junior Warden. It is to direct his mind to the necessity of promptness and faithfulness in the discharge of his duties. As the glorious luminary of day moves regular in his diurnal course, and reminds him of meridian height, so ought he to be ever watchful and prompt to the interests of the Craft, that their hours of labor and refreshment be duly observed, that neither overwrought hours nor indolence be permitted to interrupt and disturb the peace and harmony of the Craft. Ever directed by the counsel and wisdom of the Worshipful Master, supported by the strength of the Senior Warden, and guided by the meridian beauty of the day, he sustains the dignity of his station with regularity and order, and reflects the beauty that ornaments the south.

The Junior Warden, as the third officer of the lodge, represents the pillar of Beauty. Regularity and promptness in the discharge of his duties should be his governing considerations, as these qualities impart beauty to his position, and qualify him for the performance of the higher stations should he be called to the discharge of them.

Hence it will be observed how necessary it is for a

lodge to be judicious in the selection of its officers, as its prosperity. peace, and harmony, depends greatly thereon, Neither should officers be retained too long in service, because it does not give the lodge an opportunity to test the abilities of its members; nor does it preserve that vigorous state of activity which infuses life and spirit among the brotherhood. Good address should also be considered as necessary to the officers of a lodge; they thereby secure respectful attention, and are enabled to acquit themselves with becoming dignity and decorum. The example has a salutary influence upon the members.

The Rough Ashler.—As a stone taken from the quarries in its natural state is unfit for the builder's use, and must first undergo the process of adjustment by the application of the tools used by the operative, who brings it into proper shape and form for the use and purpose to which it may be applied by the master-builder, so it is with man in his natural state; he is rude and imperfect, confined by no restraints, and governed by no laws except force and necessity, and herein he morally represents the Rough Ashler.

He must first undergo the necessary process of that education and discipline through which the better qualities of his nature become developed, suitably prepared and fitted, before he can be adapted to the occupancy of that sphere of usefulness to the position he may be called to assume, and which illustrates him as the Perfect Ashler.

Man, uncultivated and unimproved in mind, is rude and harsh in his nature, fierce and turbulent in disposition.

Consideration and reason are not the principles that govern his actions; force and power predominate within him. His own innate instincts are the ruling passions that influence and prompt him to action; and as he is enabled to wield and exercise his power, he generally becomes more or less intolerant in demeanor and tyrannical in his bearing, regarding others as subservient to the advancement of his own selfish purposes.

The untutored savage delights to inflict torture and pain; he binds his victim and consumes him by slow process at the stake, relishing the scene and agony of his victim with a gusto of elated pleasure and a composure of mind, feeling conscious in the justification of what he deems a just retribution for some injury received. It is the feeling of passionate instinct, the desire for revenge, which governs his unrestrained passions and unimproved condition. Such are the influences that control the uneducated and uncultivated mind, and the rude character of man is here in similitude to the Rough Ashler.

The Perfect Ashler.—Having, by the application of the operative, been divested of its inequalities, and undergone the necessary adjustment and preparation for use—tested by the Square, and found just and true in all its parts—is securely laid in its proper place by the builder. Leveled and plumbed upon its base, it gives strength and support to the edifice. So man, through the influence of education and intellectual improvement of the mind, becomes refined, and divested of his ruder qualities, cultivates the higher and nobler principles of his nature, and thereby prepares and fits himself as a useful member for society. Endowed with virtuous principles, he walks in the integrity of his heart, just and upright; ever kind and benevolent, conscious in the rectitude of his deportment, he enjoys the pleasing satisfaction flowing there-from—is an ornament to society, and honors his God.

Such are the contrasts resulting from education and a refined state of mind. It is the improved condition of society which produces friendly intercourse and relations of good-fellowship, conducive to our real happiness, comfort, and pleasure. It divests us of the repulsive harshness of our unimproved natures, and begets within us those amenities and courtesies which are reciprocal in a well-regulated state of society, and extends our influence for its well-being.

As the Perfect Ashler, we are thereby fitted for useful purposes, prepared to occupy and adorn our position in community, and thereby give strength and support to society, and extend our sphere of operation for each other's welfare; and thus we illustrate our improved condition by the Perfect Ashler.

The Trestle-Board.—Upon this the Master Architect prepares and draws his designs for the Craft to pursue their labors. Here he displays the power of his skill and ingenuity in the various designs conceived in his imagination, either for utility or ornament.

But when we look around on every side, take a survey of the great landscape of nature, observe it in all its harmony and beauty, we behold with astonishing wonder the grand designs drawn upon the Divine Trestle-Board of the Supreme Architect of the Universe;

we behold and view the stupendous fabric clothed in ornaments of celestial beauty and glory with feelings of mingled awe and admiration, and fully realize our own insignificance, our want of knowledge, and limited capacity to comprehend the vast machinery of the universe.

The finite mind becomes lost and bewildered in the giddy maze of incomprehensible wonder and astonishment. Worlds innumerable surround us on every side; all move within their spheres with the most perfect harmony, regularity, and order. The various seasons going and returning at their appointed time, producing the varied elements of their nature, and supplying man with his necessary wants; the whole animated creation filling their day and destiny, and passing away; hills, valleys, plains, and mountains, oceans, rivers, lakes and rivulets—all surrounding nature—is vocal in his praise—worlds innumerable all attest the wisdom, strength, and beauty, and the infinity of their great Author, the Master Architect of the Universe.

Such is the great Trestle-Board of nature, and given for man's study and contemplation—a field beyond the scope and comprehension of the finite mind—infinite throughout eternity.

Well might the Psalmist of Israel exclaim, "I will praise thee; for I am fearfully and wonderfully made: marvelous are thy works; and that my soul knoweth right well."—Ps. cix: 14.

What can be more worthy, or lay a higher claim to our consideration—what more elevating in mind, thought, and sentiment—what more sublime and heavenly in contemplation—what more elevating and exalting to our better natures—what more deeply impress us with our own insufficiency and dependence, and lead us to a more exalted degree of reverence—what more strongly inspires the mind with sincere love and devotion, and produces a warmer glow of pious reverence for the Deity than the study of the great works of nature, productions of unfathomable wisdom?

Such themes and such contemplations inspire the mind with pure and lofty sentiments of love to God, and surely no object can lay a higher claim to our affections. For love to God is love to our fellow-man, and this we are taught in every precept of the Great Book of light, our guide and faith of practice in life. Man has his moments of inspiration, and they gush forth in eloquence of thought and simplicity of mind, such as language can not convey. They are the emanations flowing from a soul inspired with the grandeur produced by the Great Architect of the boundless creation—the outpouring of an overcharged fountain, gushing forth in streams of heavenly joy that fills the mind with gratitude and adoration—the spring of the affections that flow with inspiring reverence and love to God.

He views the heavings of the ocean's billows, whose restless agitation, if caused to cease, would produce a pestilence of contagion and disease, loathsome malaria. He hears the pealing thunders and their reverberating echoes; beholds the lightning's flash, and feels the rushing tornado's force, and although they cause him terror and dismay, yet they are the purifying elements of our atmosphere, designed by infinite wisdom for our good. He views planets of immense magnitude, and at remote distance, all moving in perfect harmony and order, and he becomes absorbed in thought, and is lost in bewildering astonishment, and he instinctively asks, are they not inhabited? He realizes his own incompetency to comprehend the mysterious works of Deity—the incomprehensible Jehovah God, infinity of mind who alone knows all, and disposes according to his supreme and infinite judgment.

To the reflecting mind, these themes are heavenly in contemplation—they cause man to meditate and consider his own welfare; they elevate his intellectual nature, and imbue his mind with serious thoughts of the future; they impress him with the futility of worldly greatness and honors, teach him to regard them as of a secondary consideration, proper in their place, but not his reliance at the tribunal of eternal justice.

They produce exalted reverence for their great Author, and enlarge man's affections toward his fellow-man. How befittingly, indeed, were the highest hills selected for the assembling of our ancient brethren! How appropriate for their hours of devotion and meditation—their service to God—whom they were taught to adore and worship as their Great Grand Master! The highest hills give a most beautiful figure illustrative of exalted excellence, and the lowest vales of a pure spirit of humility and meekness, walking in the paths of virtue and chastity.

The pious David had his moments of inspiration, producing some of his most sublime thoughts and conceptions, yet he was not permitted to build the house of the Lord, because he had been engaged in wars. He also departed from the paths of rectitude, for which he paid the penalty; but the Almighty never forsook him, and when he repented of the errors he had committed, the repentance was acknowledged, and he was restored to favor.

To study the great Trestle-Board of nature, is the sublimited field for a Mason's leisure moments. It qualifies him for the better enjoyments of the bestowments of life, and prepares him for a higher and more exalted sphere.

Hence our Trestle-Board, upon which we draw our designs, is figuratively intended to illustrate and draw our mind to the great Trestle-Board of Divine light and truth—the unerring guide of our faith. It is herein we draw the designs for our moral and spiritual edifice, and if we work agreeable to the plans laid down therein we shall erect an edifice worthy of our profession, and a temple of enduring inheritance.

A laudable ambition is praiseworthy and commendable; it gives eminence to man, and establishes his character for usefulness. A Mason has no apology to offer for indolence, but, on the contrary, has every inducement presented to draw forth his energies in the pursuit of some useful object. He is taught to be actively engaged in life—not only in the amount of physical labor he may perform, but also in the culture and improvement of the mind, and in the performance of good works. This principle is most beautifully illustrated to him in the moral application of the twenty-four-inch Gauge, where he is taught to apportion his time for labor, refreshment, and repose, and service to God, and the relief of the distressed and needy, These requirements, when fully exemplified, comprehend the chief duties of a Mason, and are applicable to the Trestle-Board.

Jewels are beautiful ornaments, desirable to possess, but they only show forth their sparkling attractions, when divested of their external covering. So it is with man; he only shows forth the beauty and excellence of character when divested of the rubbish of vice with which his nature is enthralled. Properly trained and educated in mind and thought, imbued with sentiments of honor and true nobility, governed by the principles of truth and justice, consistent to the virtues of morality, he then may be said to be a jewel whose luster shines forth in his virtues.

THE JEWELS OF A LODGE.

Act by the SQUARE as thy rule,
If thou desirest just to be.
For justice to all is due,
And just men are ever true.

Brothers, on the LEVEL meet
If you desire to be true,
In love on the Jewel part,
As brothers in friendship do.

Walk by the PLUMB as your guide,
And thou wilt not be far astray;
Uprightness by man observed
Will its just reward secure.

The Square, the Level, and the Plumb,
Jewels illustrative are,
Of virtues man to govern
And in wisdom's ways to guide.

Love thy brother as thyself,
Is God's just and righteous law;
For if thou thy brother hate,
Then thou dost break the Law.

In the quarries an Ashler lay,
Rough and unfinished as it was;
Yet strong and firm an Ashler good,
As from the quarries hewn could be.

The Ashler dressed was good and true,
When finished and prepared it was,
By Gavel, Level, Square, and Plumb,
For architect and builder's use.

The Master Architect, upon
The Trestle-Board he plans and draws,
Designs and ornaments to be
For beauty or utility.

As the rough Ashler, so is man
In his uncultivated state,
Vindictive, fierce, and turbulent,
By nature so when unrefined.

As the Perfect Ashler, so man
By education form'd becomes,
The ruder passions learns to curb,
Be friend to man, as man should be.

The Trestle-Board of light Divine,
Unerring rule of guidance true;
Man's just designs when drawn therefrom,
Are virtue's paths to happiness.

Seek then to walk in virtue's ways,
The Golden rule with man observe;
Love God as you are taught to do,
And love Divine will follow you.

For God, the Architect Supreme,
Rules in Heav'n above, on high;
On earth beneath o'er all his works,
And obedience to him is due.

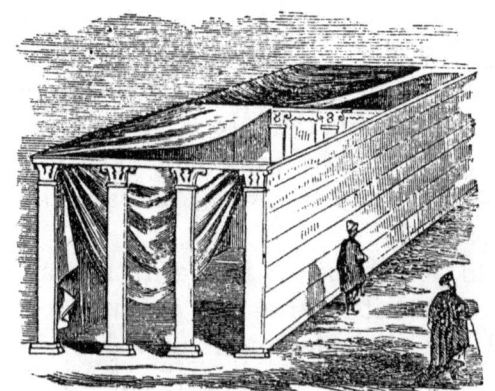

LECTURE XI.

DEDICATION.

LODGES were anciently dedicated to King Solomon, as it is said he was the first Most Excellent Grand Master; but Masons professing Christianity dedicate theirs to St. John the Baptist and St. John the Evangelist, who were two eminent Christian patrons of Masonry; and since their time, there is represented, in every well-governed lodge, a certain *point within a circle*—the *point* representing an individual brother; the *circle,* the boundary line of his conduct, beyond which he is never to suffer his prejudices or passions to betray him. This *circle* is embordered by two perpendicular parallel lines, representing St. John the Baptist and St. John the Evangelist, and upon the top rests the Holy Scriptures. In going round this circle, we necessarily touch upon these two lines, as well as upon the Holy Scriptures; and while a Mason keeps himself circumscribed within their precepts, it is impossible that be should materially err.—*Craftsman.*

THUS we monitorially illustrate who our lodges were anciently dedicated to, and to whom they are at present dedicated; and we also illustrate the two eminent patrons of our Order by two perpendicular parallel lines bordering on a circle, and upon the top of which rests the Holy Bible;

and in the center of the circle is a point which is intended to represent an individual brother, whose mind should be constantly directed to the light of Divine truth and to the virtues exemplified in the lives of those two eminent personages represented by the parallels; and the circle as a symbol of eternity, and the Book of Faith as his compass and guide of safety.

"And behold, I will build a house in the name of the Lord my God, to dedicate it to him, and to burn before him sweet incense, and for the continual shew-bread, and for the burnt-offerings mornings and evenings."—2 Chron. ii: 4.

"So was ended all the work King Solomon made for the house of the Lord, and Solomon brought in the things which his father David had dedicated."—1 Kings vii: 57.

Our halls are dedicated to Masonry, Virtue, and Universal Benevolence; our lodges to St. John the Baptist and St. John the Evangelist.

In one of our preceding lectures we have already referred to lodges—how they were situated, and the reason therefor. When Masonic halls, for want of suitable locality, can not be so constructed as to be placed due east and west, they are, for Masonic purposes, in accordance with our requirements, internally so arranged, the east being regarded as the source of light; hence, when we enter the lodge, the attention is directed toward that point, as from thence emanates the light and knowledge we seek to obtain.

Our lodges, as well as our halls, are dedicated. At

the building of the first temple, lodges were dedicated to King Solomon, as he was our first Grand Master; and this custom still continues in all Jewish countries.

In England, lodges are dedicated to "God and his service," and the two perpendicular parallel lines represent Moses and Solomon. The similitude certainly is in consonance with the antiquity of the institution; and we can not conceive of a more appropriate person than Deity, to whom Masonic lodges should be dedicated, as our first and supreme service and duty belongs to him, The first consideration to which the mind of the initiate is directed is God; hence there is a beautiful analogy and consistency in making God the person to whom our lodges should be dedicated. In this country, and also in other localities, Masonic lodges are dedicated to the Sts. John—St. John the Baptist and St. John the Evangelist—and they are represented by the two perpendicular parallel lines referred to, as representing Moses and Solomon in the English lodges.

Whether the two Sts. John were Masons or not, there is probably no authentic information or reliable authority about it. There is, however, a Masonic tradition that St. John the Evangelist had been initiated into the Fraternity at an early period of life. The Essenecs were a sect distinguished for their virtues and piety. Many of them led lives of celibacy, while others entered into a matrimonial state, as a Divine ordinance, to propagate the human species. They had forms and ceremonies of admission into their order. In their state of probation, they were clothed in white garments, to denote their purity and innocence. Their schools were esoteric, and their instructions communicated by symbols; hence there was a strong similarity between them and Freemasons. They also wrought at various handicrafts, and held their goods in common—paid a strict regard to charity and to the wants of the necessitous. They also had means of recognition; hence some authors claim that they were the descendants of the Freemasons of the Temple. The lives of these two eminent men were therefore in accordance with the principles professed and practiced by this sect.

During the turmoils and the disturbances produced by the wars in which the Jewish nation had been engaged by the Romans, the Fraternity suffered severely thereby, and fell into decline. Its character and mission being of a peaceful nature—to ameliorate man's condition—these disturbances were incompatible with its divine mission, and it became much neglected, in consequence of which it was found necessary, for a restoration thereof, that some eminent and worthy brother should be called to assume the Grand Mastership of the Fraternity. Accordingly, a deputation of Masons waited on the Evangelist to solicit his acceptance of that office. Although at that time being far advanced in years, and also occupying the position of Bishop of Ephesus, yet he responded to the call, and assumed the position, and the Fraternity soon rose to its former state of usefulness, under his administration—recovered from its languishing state, and became healthy and vigorous in its labors.

While Jewish lodges are dedicated to King Solomon, and the English lodges dedicated to "God and his service," ours are dedicated to the Saints John, because they were pious and good men, eminent patterns and pure exemplars of Masonic virtues, Illustrious examples of the virtues Masons are taught to revere and enjoined to receive and practice, and while time lasts, the memories of these two eminent personages will be cherished and revered by all good and true Masons.

Dedications of temples and public edifices, have prevailed from the earliest periods of the world, by Pagan, as well as by Christian nations. No event, however, has transpired since the foundations of the world were laid, that equaled the magnificent splendor, sublime and exalted piety, that was manifested and witnessed at the dedication of the first temple by King Solomon; and perhaps the world will never witness such another imposing ceremony until the dedication of the celestial temple in the New Jerusalem; beyond the confined limits of time.

The Temple having been erected by Divine instruction, first communicated to David, and afterward renewed to King Solomon, was, under the same favorable auspices, carried on to completion.

Under the guidance and wisdom of Solomon, aided by the friendship and facilities of a powerful sovereign, the skill and ingenuity of an unrivaled architect, and the most favorable circumstances of peace and prosperity having attended him in his labors during its erection, the structure, when completed, was the admiration and wonder of the world.

Whilst a period of two hundred and twenty years was consumed in the erection of the famous temple of

Diana of Ephesus, the splendid edifice on Mount Moriah was constructed and finished in the short space of seven years and six months. The former was erected and dedicated to idolatry and false worship, while the latter was erected and dedicated to the ever-living and true God. Having the influence of the Divine favor during its erection, the work went forward with regularity and unanimity. By the wise regulations of King Solomon, the most perfect harmony prevailed among the several bands of workmen, and no discordant element was permitted to enter and interrupt their labors.

At the time appointed for the dedication of the Temple, King Solomon assembled all those bands of workmen and masters who had served him faithfully during its erection, together with the Chief Priests and Elders of the people, for the purpose of dedicating it to the Most High God. The prayer offered by Solomon on this occasion, for its humility, eloquence, and piety, is unparalleled. The Divine favor of the Great I Am, approved and sanctioned the occasion by a manifestation of his presence in a flame of Divine light, descending from Heaven, and which consumed the "burnt-offering and the sacrifice, and the glory of the Lord filled the house;" and with devout and humble reverence, the whole assembled congregation prostrated themselves with their faces to the ground, and worshiped and praised the Lord, saying: "For he is good; for his mercy endureth forever."

But this magnificent structure, modeled and planned under divine instruction, erected under the guidance of the most profound wisdom with which man could be endowed, its foundation laid in strength to endure through ages to come, ornamented with the most exquisite skill of architectural richness and beauty, and dedicated with sublime and magnificent grandeur to the Most High God with solemn and impressive ceremonies and costly sacrifices, such as were never witnessed by human eyes; honored with the glory of the Divine presence, and its inward sanctuary, the Most Holy of Holies, wherein rested the Ark of the Covenant, overshadowed by the outstretched wings of the cherubim, became the dwelling-place of the Shekinah, and from whence the invisible Deity was pleased to commune with man, yet it scarce survived the short period of the third of a century ere its glory and purity of holiness departed, its exalted prestige dimmed, the invisible Shekinah, as the light of Heaven and means of communion with man, departed and ascended on high— false worship and idolatry had intervened, God's chosen people became estranged from him and wandered in the ways of idolatry, and the effulgent glory and beauty of the Temple became obscured and enshrouded in darkness.

The Temple, with all its splendor and magnificence, hallowed by the most sacred associations, was a type of the moral temple of man, formed just and perfect with the indwelling Spirit of life, as the Shekinah, from whence emanates the Divine light to guide and direct him in the paths of virtue and holiness; and whilst he walks thereby, so long is the moral temple preserved in its pristine beauty and luster; but when desecrated by vile and sinful lusts, prostituted to impure and unholy desires, the glorious light becomes dimmed, the spiritual orbs are obscured, and man walks in the Valley of Death enshrouded in darkness, and his communion with God is ended.

This magnificent structure, in this connection, presents itself to the mind, as one of the most beautiful allegories of which the imagination can conceive. It is susceptible of being most beautifully and instructively symbolized, and it figuratively illustrates to us what man should be, and what he was designed to be by his Creator. Man, as a moral temple, is endowed with all the virtues of goodness; and were he to live in obedience to those virtues, and be guided by the Divine light—the heavenly Shekinah would dwell within him, and be his constant and reliable counselor. But when he desecrates the temple, and pollutes it with vice and corruptions, it is then not a fit abode for purity and holiness, for God can not dwell in an unsanctified and an impure place. Hence, the Temple of Moriah is presented to you as a symbol, and, like all the symbols presented, is for your edification, your profit, and your good. It is offered for your consideration, as a beautiful model of what you ought to be, to be truly and properly dedicated to the Most High; and such should be your honest and sincere desire.

Dedicate your lives to God and his service, and thereby they will be dedicated to the performance of works which will beget love and good-will to your fellow-beings—will imbue the mind with benevolence, charity, and liberality toward others. It will show forth the nobler qualities of your better nature, afford you true pleasure and happiness in the contemplation of an upright life dedicated to the performance of virtuous actions, which, as a sweet incense, will ascend from off the altar of your hearts to the throne of heavenly love and mercy.

He who seeks to gain admission to our Fraternity, seeks to gain light and acquire knowledge, the acquisition of which is to enlarge his sphere of operation, and thereby extend his abilities for usefulness. His admission requires obedience to our rules and regulations and a cheerful conformity to all our requirements. The obligations of a just and upright life are enjoined upon him to be observed; the cultivation and practice of the virtues of morality, imbued with the principles of faith, hope, and charity, practically exemplifying the tenets of brotherly love, relief, and truth, and living in conformity with the cardinal virtues of temperance, fortitude, prudence, and justice, are duties enjoined upon him to be observed, and as the precepts to be the rule and guide of his actions; and the book of the law is ever open to him, that he may not, through want of knowledge, err; hence we perceive how extensive is the field of our labors—every good principle and every virtue calculated to advance man's happiness is within the circumscribed bounds of our duty.

In the north-east he lays the corner-stone of his Masonic edifice, and receives the necessary instruction to erect a moral temple endowed with all the virtues of excellence, consecrated to the labor of good works, and dedicated to the service of the Grand Architect and Supreme Master of the Universe.

These ceremonies are pregnant with solemnity, and can not fail, when properly observed, to make their impression upon the reflecting and truly sincere mind. And a Mason consecrates and dedicates his service to God and to the general good of his fellow-beings; and a departure from it desecrates the temple, and pollutes it to idolatrous sin.

THE DEDICATION.

On Moriah's mount, sacred to memory dear,
And hallowed with associations divine,
Abraham, the faithful patriarch of old,
Servant of the living God, obedient
To his command divine, the child of promise
Led. An altar raised for holy sacrifice—
The offering to be the child—promised one—
Through whom salvation was to come for man.

Obedient to the call, God's will obeyed:
Dark and mysterious as the mandate was,
Dreadful as was the deed to be performed, yet,
Unfaltering, unwavering, undoubting
In God's promises, sustained by faith in him,
He led the child, offspring of affections
Dear, forth to the mount—the sacred mount—where,
By command divine, he there the altar raised,
And placed thereon the promised one, Lamb of Life,
Upon the altar pile, a sacrifice to be—
An offering—holy one—to God on high.

With trembling hand, ere the fatal blow was struck,
He call'd, in humble pray'r to God, the Father

Of Mercies from on high, for sustaining strength
In that dreadful, trying moment of needful
Aid. The suppliant's prayer was heard, faith tested—
Undoubting faith—such as was required of him,
Whom God had set apart, and through him ordained
That his name—His Holy Name—should be preserved,
And through whose lineage man would be restored.
Such was the Divine decree, the heavenly will,
Manifested to the faithful patriarch
Of old—Abraham, father of Israel.

In obedience to God's will—his command—
Swiftly from on high, an angel descending,
Came, a messenger of heavenly relief,
To save the child—to save the life—promised one—
Through whom redemption was decreed for man.
Hark! a rustling sound nearly is heard, an arm,
Invisible—unseen—stays the fatal blow;
When, lo! within a thicket near—an offering
To be the sacrifice entangled was.
Such was the relief, mysterious to him,
Timely aid swiftly on wings ethereal came—
The child restored from seeming death to life;
Abraham's faith confirmed, consecrated, and
Dedicated to the Eternal God on high.

   Sacred the mount—hallowed the place—Solomon,
Israel's king, in after times the Temple raised—
The Temple to God on high. Hiram, Tyrian's
King, steadfast friend, faithful ally—the Master
Architect, to Solomon sent—the trio,
Solomon of Israel, Hiram of Tyre,

And Hiram the architect of great renown,
The Craft in unanimity of concord
Formed, no discordant, disturbing elements
To intervene, interrupt their fellowship,
And thereby to impede the glorious work,
Or mar the harmony of the brotherhood.
Such was the wisdom, and such the strength combined,
That united effort in due time produced
A fabric, the pride and glory of Israel's hosts.

    The plan designed by God on high, to David
First was given, thence to Solomon renewed,
A prince of peace, whose happy, prosperous reign,
Had not interrupted been by cruel wars.
Preparation for the work was amply made,
The foundation firmly laid—the building reared;
Seven years and six months—the work completed—
When finished the admiration and wonder;
The gorgeous structure to the beholder was,
Its magnificence and splendor beyond compare.

    The faithful Craft, Elders, Chiefs of Israel,
By Solomon's command in congregation
Assembled were, to dedicate the same,
For holy service to God on high be given.
The jubilee auspicious celebrated
Was, by Israel's hosts in acclaims of joy,
Sanctioned the occasion was—manifested
By a gleaming ray from Heaven descending—
Celestial—etherial flame—light divine—
The sacrifice consumed, and incense pure,
Filled the house with joy and glory to the Lord.

And the vast congregation that assembled
Was, the imposing spectacle to observe,
In pious reverence and veneration
Deep, with sincere humility humbly bowed
In acknowledgment of the favors—divine;
And with audible voice of exclamation
Praised the Lord Most High, saying, "For he is good,
For his mercy endure forever." Thus
Was God's supremacy—his goodness acknowledged,
And thus was consecrated—dedicated
To the Most High—the Temple on Moriah's Mount.

   Who walks in wisdom's ways, just and upright;
Guided by the unerring rule of faith;
Observant of the just and righteous law,
Walks in fellowship and harmony with God—
As man should do to honor and glorify
His holy name. Man—a living temple is—
Moral edifice—reflecting refulgent
Rays of light that virtue's paths illuminate
When in due obedience and observance
To the law, both moral and divine he is.
And thus in conformity to rectitude
Justly he stands erect before God and man,
A moral temple, dedicated to good
And noble works, such as becomes him to do.

   Light Divine—unerring guide that leads to life;
Man's faith, his hope, his joy, his peace on earth;
His shield, his staff, consoling and sustaining
Aid, whilst in weary pilgrimage he walks
The paths of life. His higher hope, brighter joy

That guides the way beyond this mundane sphere,
To realms celestial, of eternal, never-Ending
bliss. Who walks thereby upright in faith,
A living temple is, endowed with wisdom
Pure, sustained by strength Divine, and beautified
With holiness, whereby thus he consecrates
And dedicates his life and services to God
Supreme, most high—as justly due to Him.
Life is but a transitory, fleeting show,
Surrounded with its cares and solicitudes;
Of no permanent stability is man's
Abode on earth—his works confined to the brief
Space of time, and, with its duration, must pass
Away; his earthly labors cease—absorbed to be
In eternity. Exhumed from the quarries
Of mortality, adjudged according to
Its works, the vital—the living part must be
For immortality—inheritance
Bequeathed—prepared there its abode to be
Of happiness that awaits the "just made perfect"
In the celestial temple of endless joys
For works done and deeds of charity performed,
As the award for a virtuous and faithful
Life, devoted to the performance of labors
Useful, and dedicated to the service
Of God, the Architect Supreme, on High.

LECTURE XII.

THE TENETS.

BROTHERLY LOVE.

By the exercise of brotherly love we are taught to regard the whole human species as one family—the high and low, the rich and poor—who as created by one Almighty Parent, and inhabitants of the same planet, are to aid support, and protect each other. On this principle, Masonry unites men of every country, sect, and opinion, and conciliates true friendship among those who might otherwise have remained at a perpetual distance.—*Craftsman.*

THE practice of this virtue inculcates within us the principles of love and charity; it embraces that spirit of universal benevolence we should ever exercise toward all mankind, but more especially to those of our own household. Brotherly love is one of those ennobling and elevating traits of character which spring from the tender affections of the heart, and opens its sympathies to the appeals of others. The kind offices we perform by the exercise of this virtue not only soothe the cares and sorrows, mitigate the trials and burdens of others, but it affords us, in our moments of reflection, a happy and pleasant enjoyment in the contemplation of virtuous actions performed.

Masons are taught to practice this virtue with kind and affectionate obedience, and live in conformity to its requirements, not only in affording relief to the necessitous, but in that practical exemplification of those social relations in life which tend to make up the sum of human happiness; for God designed us as social and rational beings, and we can only enjoy this privilege by cultivating a spirit of brotherly love and living consistently with the principles laid down therein.

A confiding faith in the integrity of a brother—a cherished sympathy of regard and affection for each other's welfare—thereby more firmly cementing that union by which we are united in the bonds of brotherhood, is one of the most praiseworthy and commendable maxims inculcated in our esoteric schools; it is true charity—divine in its nature.

To counsel, advise, admonish, aid, and sustain a brother, commiserate his errors and frailties, and with kindness, give him encouraging hope for the better, is one of the great objects and aims of our institution; and as we claim these considerations from a brother, so we ought, with the same generous liberality, be ever ready to extend them to others. And this principle is inculcated in every stage of progress we make—from the incipient step to the highest grade of elevation.

"Thus speak the Lord of Hosts, saying, Execute true judgment, and show mercy and compassion every man to his brother."—Zach. vii: 9.

"So likewise shall my Heavenly Father do also unto

you, if ye from your heart forgive not every one his brother their trespasses."—Matt. xviii: 35.

"That no man go beyond and defraud his brother in any matter, because that the Lord is the avenger of all such."—1 Thess. iv: 6.

"Speak not evil one of another, brethren; he that speak evil of his brother, and judge his brother, speak evil of the law."—Jam. iv: 11.

"And this commandment have we from him, that he who love God, love his brother also."—1 John iv: 21.

"But, as touching brotherly love, ye need not that I write unto you; for ye yourselves are taught by God to love one another."—1 Thess. iv: 9.

You perceive, from the foregoing quotations, that we have again been drawing from the oracles of Divine truth. The passages are so appropriately applicable and illustrative of this virtue, that we desire your particular attention to them. And the oracles abound so copiously with material for our edification that the influence to do so is irresistible; and if they will lead you to the same source, we shall feel happy in the reflection that our labors have not been in vain. You have an equal privilege to draw from it, and of which, it is to be hoped you will avail yourselves. Fear not being satiated because your capacity of mind and desire will expand as you seek to store it with knowledge. The nutriment is healthy and invigorating; and surely it is better to partake of healthy nourishment than that which is nauseating.

The mind, like the body, needs food, and none is

more vigorous and beneficial to intellectual growth and strength than that drawn from the source of Divine truth. We are so formed and constituted by nature that we can not be indifferent to surrounding circumstances; we must either progress or retrograde; and surely, in our sane minds, we can not desire the latter course. If we seek true happiness in life, we must first apply to the true source, use the proper appliances, and then all things will be added. This will constitute true wisdom, give vigor to the mind, and ornament man's life with the beauty of holiness.

The principles of brotherly love require of us, as Masons, to avoid all controversies and contentions that have a tendency to disturb and interrupt the peaceful harmony that should exist among brethren. Difficulties and misunderstandings should be amicably adjusted between brethren, in order to avoid public notoriety and litigations, which ought not to be resorted to if avoidable. Brethren governed by the principles of love and good-will, as inculcated and enjoined upon them, will always first seek to reconcile their differences, with the aid and counsel of their brethren, ere resorting to other means; and by so doing, they give true strength and support to the institution, and more firmly cement the bonds of good-fellowship.

Brotherly love also enjoins upon us to be circumspect in our deportment toward each other, avoiding all uncharitable and unkind expressions and illiberality of thought; to be careful and tenacious of a brother's character, for that is a tender thing to deal with; keen and sensitive to unjust censure or reproach; hence, too great attention can not be paid to avoiding the formation of inconsiderate or hasty conclusions.

The brother who endeavors to govern and circumscribe his passions by the moral application of the Compasses will avoid unnecessary and improper controversies. He will not be governed by unjust and hasty censure, unkind or improper expression, but charitable and liberal in feeling, ever ready to make just and proper acknowledgments for errors or wrongs committed, and, with equal magnanimity, forgiving in disposition; for the who can honorably acknowledge and retrieve an error, can, with noble generosity, forgive one. Such actions will constitute true brotherly love, the symbol illustrative of pure affections.

No principle inculcated in our institution is perhaps more strictly observed and sacredly adhered to than that of brotherly love; none certainly exercises a greater influence over the mind and passions of man than this virtue. However greatly at variance Masons may be religiously or politically; however widely separated in sentiment upon matters of controversy, whether in hostile array and conflict upon the sanguinary battle-field, or turmoil of political excitement, the potent influence and power of this virtue, like an angel of mercy, intercedes with its Divine influence, and at once checks and softens the most bitter and rancorous hostility. Rarely is the instance that this virtue is disregarded, for so strongly is its influence imbued in the affections of a true Mason, that he bails the opportunity to exercise its benevolent power.

The late sanguinary conflict through which our beloved

country has passed could furnish volumes of evidence to establish this fact. Even the patriots and fathers of our country, in their days of revolutionary struggle and conflict, would lay aside their hostility, and, as Masons, meet upon the broad platform of brotherly love.

Upon the merits of this virtue we place our institution secondary to none. Its influence will accomplish what others fail to do. It is a bond of union that draws man to his fellow-man, however widely apart; gives mutual confidence and protection, whatever his caste or creed may be—a brother TRUE will ever recognize a brother's hail.

Spurned as unworthy of association would be him who would fail to recognize, or who would disregard a brother's appeal in the hour of adversity; and, although at variance in opposing fends and hostile conflicts, yet a brother never will, nor should, disregard this most sacred of all obligations, Hence, we perceive that the true bearing of this principle extends beyond the mere bestowments of small acts of relief, and that it enters into the more enlarged and extended operations of our duties—succoring aid, protection, restoration, and all the lawful appliances we may bring to bear for each other's safety, are inherent in the virtues of brotherly love, and should be faithfully observed.

When brothers meet—it matters not where, or when — far remote, or near—what clime or country they may hail from—however remotely asunder, or what may be their language or dialect—their recognition is acknowledged, a mutual reliance of safety is felt, and confidence in each other's integrity. Mutual friendship and interest for each other's welfare is the bond of union that exists. Such are the safeguards of confidence and protection guaranteed, and all true Masons recognize them in the bonds of brotherhood.

The potency of this principle exists in the fact that Masonry unequivocally excludes from its halls every thing that is at variance with the requirements of a universal brotherhood. Forms and ceremonies peculiar to religious or political creeds and sects are matters of private concern, and these must be respected when lawful in their pursuits.

BROTHERLY LOVE.

I would not a brother be, and not feel for a brother's woe,
What ever his failings, errors, or his misdoings may have been;
Human he is, and by nature weak, prone to sin degraded.
Such is man's fallen, unhappy state—and needs the pitying eye.

I would not have a heart indifferent to a brother's wants,
What ever his wanderings, weakness, or his follies may have been;
Who can foresee or tell what their own state yet in life may be?
Man's strength, unaided by light Divine, is but a feeble staff.

I would not turn a deaf ear to a brother's appeal in want,
But, like the good Samaritan of old, kindly give relief,
What ever his transgressions or his iniquities may have been—
A brother still, though an erring one, with hope to be reclaimed.

I would not close the hand—iron-grasped, insensible to feel—
Or steel the heart to pharisaical selfishness and show,
Or shut the gentle streams that from the affections kindly flow;
What ever a brother's wants may be, a brother still he'll find in me.

I would not lend an ear to slanders unjust of a brother's name,
But would vindicate, defend the same, where wrongfully traduced,
As brother to brother, in honor, is ever bound to do
When brother with brother is constant, faithful, sincere, and true.

I would not a slanderer be, and thereby tarnish a good name,
Which, above the price of rubies, pearls, or costly gems, should be.
These are but ornaments, glittering show, false pride to gratify—
No solid worth, substantial merit, or happiness produce.

RELIEF.

To relieve the distressed is a duty incumbent on all men, but particularly on Masons, who are linked together by an indissoluble chain of sincere affection. To soothe the unhappy, to sympathize with their misfortunes, to compassionate their miseries, and to restore peace to their troubled minds is the grand aim we have in view. On this basis we form our friendships and establish our connections.—*Craftsman.*

To be ever ready, with a generous heart and willing hand, to relieve the wants and sufferings of our fellow-beings, administer aid, give comfort and relief to the afflicted, restore peace to the troubled mind, and sympathize with the unfortunate in their desponding cares and sorrows, is that virtue which acts in sympathetic harmony and union with the tenets of brotherly love, and shares the enjoyments afforded it in the performance of its kind and benevolent offices. They are intimately associated in companionship, and you can not exercise the duties of one of these kind offices without fulfilling the obligations of the other: hence, brotherly love and relief go hand in hand, for where the principles of brotherly love prevail, relief is ever constant to exercise its privileges.

The duties of this virtue, the twin companion of brotherly love, are inculcated in our system of instruction, and enjoined upon Masons to discharge according to their abilities and circumstances.

To turn a deaf ear to the appeals of the suffering and afflicted is incompatible with the feelings of humanity; and although we may be able to do but little, yet when our kind offices are attended with a cheerful willingness and administered with a kind hand, they are ever grateful to the recipient. We may often find ourselves the dupes of cunning and artful deception; yet this should not deter us from the performance of acts of kindness, for it is better to give to the undeserving than that the truly good and worthy should be permitted to suffer or languish for the want of attention.

As we have already drawn quite liberally from the oracles of Divine truth, and as we desire to keep them constantly in view for your consideration, to show the identity thereof with the principles of our institution, we have selected two very appropriate parallels, illustrative and applicable to the subject under consideration:

"And if thy brother be waxen poor, and fallen in decay with thee, then thou shall relieve him; yea, though he be a stranger or a sojourner; that he may live with thee."—Lev. xxv: 35.

"Learn to do well, seek judgment, relieve the oppressed, judge the fatherless, plead for the widow."— Isaiah i: 17.

The principles of Masonry are philanthropic in their nature, humane and charitable in their purposes, ever dispensing its bounties and liberalities for the improvement and advancement of the human race in the scale of happiness; free from any selfish considerations. Its principles are love and good-will to all; its charities are widely and liberally bestowed, and are felt wherever Masonic organizations exist. Masonry is the friend and benefactor of man, and will ever extend the hand of relief when circumstances require.

This praiseworthy and truly benevolent virtue, relief,

enjoined upon us, as Masons, to observe, can not be too carefully considered or properly regarded. No one can tell or foresee the uncertainties of human life, for although we may to-day be engaged in administering to the wants and necessities of our fellow-beings, yet, ere the morrow, penury and want may overtake us, and we ourselves may become the recipients of kind and generous acts of bestowments from the hands of others. And yet if, in the order of a kind Providence, it should be our good fortune to escape the calamities with which we are beset on every side, we shall at least enjoy the happy satisfaction of having been instrumental in the alleviation of the necessitous, and in due time receive our just recompense, for every good act performed with pure motives receives its corresponding reward.

The duties of this benevolent virtue do not cease in the performance of its kind offices upon the demise of a brother; neither is it indifferent to the wants of those who may through imprudence have proved themselves undeserving of its favors. Masonry is too benevolent and philanthropic in its nature ever to be indifferent to the wants of suffering humanity.

The fatherless and widow are ever objects of care and solicitude to Masonic lodges. It is a duty incumbent upon lodges of Masons to keep a careful supervision over the interest and comfort of those who may have been deprived of their natural means of support, and render such aid and attention as the nature of their circumstances may require from them; and especially those of young and tender years, that they may grow up, prepared and fitted by some useful occupation, as good members of society. Idleness is not to be encouraged or tolerated under any circumstances, as it would be incompatible with our precepts, and would be injurious in its effects upon those whose welfare we seek to advance.

These are duties required of us to perform, especially to those of our own household; and a failure or neglect to do so falls far short of a Masonic duty and obligation—fails in the performance of one of the most benevolent objects that can flow from the affections, and falsifies the great aim and object of our institution.

We are but stewards in God's heritage, and he will require of us a just account of our stewardship, for he is our Great Grand Master, and to him we must make our final reckoning. Then how important and necessary for us to be careful in the exercise of our labors, that they be directed in the proper channels; that we may so have wrought our hours faithfully, that, as the finished and perfect ashlers, we may be prepared to occupy our places in the spiritual lodge on high, where our labors will be honor and praise to HIM who rules and governs all things; and our refreshment, the joy and happiness flowing their from.

As an illustration of the charitable tendency of our institution, we make the following selections: The Grand Lodge of England, in the year 1724, during the Grand Mastership of the Duke of Richmond, under a proposition of the Earl of Dalkeith, an institution was organized for the relief of distressed and decayed Masons. It was supported by quarterly collections, made on the lodges according to their ability, and the funds put into a joint stock, and placed into the hands of the treasurer at the quarterly communications of the Grand Lodge, and distributed according to the directions of the charitable committee.

In 1835, the Freemasons of London established an institution known as the "Asylum for Worthy, Aged, and Decayed Masons," and to which was subsequently added an "Asylum for the Widows and Orphans of Indigent Masons. There is also in London the "Royal Masonic Benevolent Institution" to provide for aged and decayed Masons.

In France there is a central house of relief (Maison Centrale de Secours), established by the Grand Orient in 1840. Its object is to receive destitute Masons, provide for their immediate relief, and obtain employment for them.

At Lyons there is a society, formed by Masonic lodges, for the benefit of poor children, designed to educate and instruct them in some useful occupation.

There is also at Berlin, in Prussia, an institution for the support of children and widows of Freemasons.

It is endowed by annual subscription of all the Prussian lodges.

In 1753, there was an institution established at Stockholm, in Sweden, as an asylum for orphans. It was sustained by the contributions of Swedish lodges.

There are also institutions in our own country formed for the same benevolent object.

We briefly enumerate these instances to show the tendency of our institution in its charitable and benevolent designs. Many more might be referred to if necessary to do so. In many instances liberal bequests have also been made from the private hands of the more wealthy members of the Fraternity. In foreign countries the nobility and persons of distinguished rank have been liberal patrons of our Fraternity, and of the truly benevolent institutions reared by its hands.

We feel fully warranted in making the assertion that the time is not far remote when every State in our glorious Union will establish and endow similar institutions for more fully carrying out the great objects of benevolence to the needy and afflicted: and every truly good and worthy brother will give cheerful acquiescence thereto in extending the glorious principles of brotherly love and relief.

RELIEF.

Hail to the auspicious day, when benevolence and charity,
Brotherly love and relief, shall cheer the way,
Soothe the cares and sorrows of affliction's pain,
Dry the widow's tear, and still the orphan's cry.

Such the noble precepts of our Order are;
To mitigate the grief of dependent man,
To give relief and succoring aid where due,
Is heavenly, angelic—is love divine.

Who would not labor in such a glorious cause?
The noblest work, the highest attribute—
God-like—to adorn the character of man,
And crown his life with pleasures of happiness.

Calloused must be the heart, unworthy of man,
That would shut the tender sympathies of love,
Close the affections—insensible to woe,
Indifferent to frail humanity's call.

Forbid it, heaven! that such among us be
To mar the beauty of our love and harmony;
No abiding place within our brotherhood
May such unworthy elements ever dwell.

Brotherly love and relief go hand in hand,
Joined in charity and sympathetic love;
In kind fellowship are ever constant found,
On their heavenly mission of love for man.

TRUTH.

TRUTH is a divine attribute, and the foundation of every virtue. To be good and true is the first lesson we are taught in Masonry. On this theme we contemplate, and, by its dictates, endeavor to regulate our conduct; hence, while influenced by this principle, hypocrisy and deceit are unknown among us, sincerity and plain-dealing distinguish us, and the heart and tongue join in promoting each other's welfare, and rejoicing at each other's prosperity.— *Craftsman.*

TRUTH is the foundation upon which all other virtues stand. GOD IS TRUTH. The Divine law he has given man for his guidance in life is truth; and as our maxims are drawn from there, and we have made it the rule and guide of our faith and practice in life, we are in duty bound to receive it as truth revealed from God.

Truth is in contradistinction to falsehood. It ennobles and dignifies our natures, while the latter degrades and debases them. It gives honor and elevation to our characters, while the latter reflects dishonor and degradation; it strengthens man in the confidence of his fellow-man, while the latter makes him an object of distrustful doubt; it commands love and respect, while the latter produces derision and contempt; it causes man to honor and glorify God, while the latter pollutes his soul and buries it in sin and vice. Such, my brethren, are some of the noble virtues inherent in truth, and are in contradistinction to falsehood and deception. Hence, truth should be the principle governing our actions.

To further illustrate this virtue, we can not resist the temptation of selecting a few appropriate passages as a chaplet to wreathe its noble brow, and we make the selection from its own source, Truth—God's revelation to man, the fountain from whence flows truth, emanating from Him. To personify truth, the mind elevates to Deity as the highest conception upon which it can center.

"Only fear the Lord, and serve him in truth with all your heart."—1 Sam. xii: 24.

"Now, therefore, fear the Lord, and serve him in sincerity and truth."—Josh xxiv: 14.

"I know it is so of a truth, but how should man be justified with God."—Job ix: 2.

"I beseech thee, O Lord, remember now how I have walked before thee in truth, and with a perfect heart have done that which was good in thy sight."—2 Kings xx: 3.

"Lead me in thy truth, and teach me; for thou art the God of my salvation."—Ps. xxv: 5.

"But for me, my prayer is unto thee, O Lord, in an acceptable time: O God, in the multitude of thy mercies, hear me in the truth of thy salvation."—Ps. lxix: 13.

"For thy kindness is before mine eyes, and I have walked in thy truth."—Ps. xxvi: 3.

"O send out the light and thy truth; let them lead me, let them bring me into thy holy hill."—Ps. xliii: 3.

"Of a truth it is that your God is a God of gods, and a Lord of kings, and a revealer of secrets."—Dan. ii: 27.

"But I tell you of a truth, there be some standing here which shall not taste of death till they see the kingdom of God."—Luke ix: 27.

"Rejoice not in iniquity, but rejoice in the truth." —1 Cor. 13 : 6.

Faith, hope, and charity, brotherly love and relief, the handmaids of truth, are all merged, in the great fundamental principles of this virtue. It is the wisdom, strength, and beauty—the foundation stone of our structure. It is the living rock upon which we stand; the ÆGIS of our hope; the great I AM; the talisman of our souls; our happiness on earth; our joy in heaven; the noblest attribute that can embellish the character of man. Then, my brother, let truth be the standard of your actions, and, as a brilliant gem, it will give dignity and honor to your position.

The character established upon the principles of this virtue will always command the respectful consideration and confidence of others, and he who adheres strictly thereto will be an example of true nobleness and worth, and live in the respect and esteem of his fellow man. Hence, Masons should pay a due regard to this excellent and sublime principle, and live in the daily practice it inculcates, for by so doing, they add dignity and give tone to their own characters, cultivate elevated sentiments, and live in obedience to one of our most exalted precepts; are worthy ornaments to the brotherhood, and shed a ray of lustre upon our time-honored institution.

The Mason who walks by the plumb-line of truth will not likely err, or fail in the performance of the other virtues, for so intimately are they interwoven and blended together that he who is fully imbued with this principle must, of necessity, partake of the others; otherwise, he can not be consistent to his profession, for truth, properly considered, adheres to every other virtue, and is the basis upon which they stand, and no one devoid of them can be truthful. Hence, to be truthful is to be virtuous and consistent in all things.

Profanity and intemperance are vices. By the former we blaspheme the name of our creator, and thereby violate the seventh commandment. By the latter we dethrone reason and prostrate the God-like form below the level of the brute. In both instances we falsify our characters for truth, for when we profane the name of God, with that very breath that should be to his praise, infused by Him within man when he became a LIVING SOUL, we prostrate ourselves to degraded sin, and surround the soul with pollution. Endowed with intellectual powers of discriminating, we depart from truth, and are false in our duty toward God. Intemperance stultifies the intellectual and reasoning faculties, and unfits man for the social relations of life, makes him a disgusting object—abhorrent to others as well as to himself when in his more rational moments.

If the sun should refuse to perform his diurnal journey, or the moon her mission at night, you would say they were false to their purpose. So every departure of man from a strict line of rectitude, a violation of any of the moral obligations he is required to perform, stamps his character with infidelity and falsehood, shows him to be an ingrate, and he falsifies the purposes and objects of his creation. The brute dieth and pass-eth away, but man, created and endowed with immortality, is destined for joy and happiness.

Truth is a maxim—divine, unchanging, undying, and everlasting, and although it may, through injustice, fraud, and corruption, be, for the time, crushed to the earth, yet it will, in time, rise triumphant, in its vigor and prevail. When time shall have passed away, and the scenes of this mundane sphere have ceased to exist, truth will then be triumphant in its majestic power. It will shine forth in its resplendent glory of wisdom, strength, and beauty. Almighty truth—Omnipotent, Divine. Let truth, then, be your motto, your rule, and guide of action. True to man—true to every principle of honor and virtue, and you will be true to yourself, true to God, and true to your creation, and noble in the estimation of your fellow man.

Is this not, then, an object desirable to be attained? Is it not worthy of your highest consideration? Is it not consistent with the dignity of a true and upright Mason?

Does it not inculcate every principle of virtue, illustrated and symbolized in the beautiful system of our science? Is it not in harmonious concert with brotherly love and charity? Does it not comprehend the cardinal virtues of temperance, fortitude, prudence, and justice? Is it not one of the first principles taught you in your incipient steps in Masonry, and in every stage of your progress has it not been your constant attendant, as the living oracle, whose wise counsels, if adhered to, will be the ornament to beautify your life, and make you a glorious illustration of an upright and consistent Mason—a true and worthy son of light?

BROTHERLY LOVE, BELIEF AND TRUTH.

What is brotherly love? A heavenly fount,
That from the heart, in gentle streams, doth flow,
Of affection's love in just kindness shown
For a brother's welfare in weal or woe.

What is relief? A kind attention shown,
Of interest in a brother's wants when known,
Whether in deeds of charity bestowed,
Or, in kind and gentle words are given.

What is truth? An attribute of Deity;
Honor, integrity, and probity;
A nobleness that dignity imparts,
Which man should imitate as just and true.

Brotherly love, relief, and truth—virtues
In bond of union, and in concert joined,
Hand in hand, in fraternal fellowship;
A trio of tenets in beauty stand.

LECTURE XIII.

THE CARDINAL VIRTUES.

OF TEMPERANCE.

TEMPERANCE is that due restraint upon our affections and passions, which renders the body tame and governable, and frees the mind from the allurements of vice. This virtue should be the constant practice of every MASON, as he is thereby taught to avoid excess, or contracting any licentious or vicious habit, the indulgence of which might lead him to disclose some of those valuable secrets he has promised to conceal and never reveal, and which would consequently subject him to the contempt and detestation of all good MASONS.—*Craftsman.*

> "Temperance in every place—abroad, at home—
> Thence will applause, and hence will profit come;
> And health from either he in time prepares
> For sickness, age, and their attending cares."—*Crabbe.*

TEMPERANCE, FORTITUDE, PRUDENCE, AND JUSTICE. These are the cardinal virtues, and of which, agreeable to our arrangement, Temperance stands first in the enumeration. The precepts inculcated by this virtue consists in that government we are required to observe and exercise over our appetites and passions, so as to use the things of this world with rational consistency, and not in the abuse of them. By the exercise of this virtue we are enabled more fully to meet and act in conformity to the requirements of the others.

The virtue man is said to be possessed of who moderates his sensual passions is Temperance. It is by the judicious exercise of this virtue that he learns to control his appetites and desires, and keep them restricted within the proper bounds of prudence. Governed by this virtue, he will not indulge in excessive gluttony, because the habit of so doing is injurious to health, at variance with comfort, corrupts the system, engenders disease, and enfeebles man, instead of imparting physical strength.

Neither will he be given to indulgence in the pernicious use of intoxicating stimulants, because an undue use thereof tends to degrade the dignity of his character as a man, formed in the image of his Creator, prostrates him from the plumb of rectitude, and, while under its baneful effects, reduces him to the grade of the brute.

The mental passions of man are restrained by the same laws; Temperance regulates his actions. Governed by this principle, he will not be given to unrestrained rashness of temper, because, in an unguarded moment of passionate and ungovernable anger, reason becomes dethroned, and enraged excitement often leads to violence and the commission of acts that, on sober reflection, cause painful regret, unhappiness, and remorse to the unfortunate victim of passion, and the evil consequences of which frequently follow him through life, attended with anguish and suffering, often unhappily terminating it in dishonor and shame.

He will not indulge in the debasing and unmanly vice and practice of profanity, because the habit of this vile practice derogates from his dignity as a man, commands neither obedience nor respect, and is offensive and stunning to the sensitive feelings of a refined nature. It is also a sin against God, whose pure and holy name he pollutes with a foul breath, that should be pure and vocal to his praise, and for which he is indebted to that God, whose holy name he has profanely used and taken in vain.

By the proper exercise of this virtue, as rational beings we enjoy our moments of social refreshment with respectful and becoming dignity, interspersed with an intermingling expression of sentiment, intellectual and instructive, and through which we secure the attainment of knowledge, which, to a greater or less extent, we derive from others. Through its salutary influence, in a consistent and evenly course of temperament, we experience the enjoyment of human happiness, avoid the evils of sin, and its concomitant elements.

The Mason who lives in the practice of this virtue will be carefully guarded in his deportment, avoid and shun the ways of sin, which tarnish his character, stain it with dishonor, and bring degradation in its trail. He will seek to walk in the paths of virtue, because they lead to peace and happiness, are the true channels to the well-being of society, and the associates of man's higher and better qualities. And, as this is the desire and aim of a true Mason, he will ever be moderate and consistent, exercise due prudence, and govern his actions with circumspection, as becomes a good and useful member of society; be an honor to the Fraternity, and a benefactor to his fellow-man.

What can be more becoming or suitably embellish the character of a Mason than that exemplary and consistent deportment of conduct which secures the respectful esteem of his fellow-associates than a faithful adherence to the principles required by the virtue of temperance? His example of elevating is worthy of imitation; and his influence salutary to society. Honored and respected for his virtues, he enjoys the bestowments and privileges of life with becoming satisfaction, and escapes the evil consequences resulting from irregularities produced by excessive indulgence of appetite, or the gratification of passionate desires and intemperate government of the mind.

Every well-disposed Mason will endeavor to regulate his course of action consistent to the principles of Temperance. He will strive in the school of discipline so to train his passions, and govern his desires with moderation in all things. The virtue of Temperance when duly observed purifies the affections, elevates the mind with noble thoughts and sentiments, and assimilates man in conformity to his Creator. The good example of its influence is beneficial, and is felt by others; and surely this is a desirable consideration and a commendable object to attain. God designed man for happiness, and he can only enjoy the boon by consistent obedience to his Supreme will. So says the Divine law; and this is our standard of authority.

Shun the ways of sin and iniquity, learn to walk in the paths of purity and uprightness, and you will be consistent to your profession; you will be better qualified to live in the bonds of brotherly love, extend the kind offices of benevolence and relief to the less fortunate, and charitable and liberal in sentiment; augment the intellectual storehouse with increased knowledge that imparts wisdom and strength, and ornament it with moral beauty, and, as a temple of virtuous excellence, you will become a noble exponent of our institution.

Temperance is the symbol of those virtues which stand in contradistinction to vice in all its various forms. It elevates and dignifies man in all the social relations of life, whilst the latter degrades and debases his moral nature, and transforms him from honor to shame and remorse, unfits him for the duties and purposes of life, estranges him from his fellow-man, and alienates him from God.

To live in obedience and conformity to the rules of Temperance begets within us calmness of disposition and evenness of temper, and moderation in the exercise of our passions. It endows us with true courage, and surrounds us with that fortitude which makes us act with firmness and consistency, to bear adversities with becoming resignation, and to be magnanimous and forgiving in disposition. It enables us to govern ourselves with prudence, act with becoming circumspection, and judge of things with proper consideration. It forms within us a just equilibrium, whereby we act with equanimity, governed by the principles of justice, in all things with our fellow-beings, as well as for our own interest and welfare.

TEMPERANCE.

He who learns his passions to restrain,
By the rule of Temperance guided,
Will not to gluttony be given,
Licentiousness, or lascivious lust.

No sordid passion, or desire
Unholy, groveling, low, impure—
Unworthy man's noble, high estate—
Will the moral temple desecrate.

To good, to pure, for such unhallowed use,
Man should strive to shun the evil course,
Walk upright in paths of virtue's ways—
Just, erect—as God designed he should.

Happiness and pleasures just and pure
Are the objects man should have in view;
True felicity follow in their train—
Treasures worthy of pursuit in life.

Temperance, when justly exercised,
The various virtues doth combine—
Ennobles and elevates the mind
In purity, sentiment, and thought;

Exalts man with true and noble worth,
Such as his great Creator designed—
God-like in form and attitude,
Just, upright, and true in all his ways.

FORTITUDE.

FORTITUDE is that noble and steady purpose of the mind, whereby we are enabled to undergo any pain, peril, or danger, when prudentially deemed expedient. This virtue is equally distant from rashness and cowardice, and like the former, should be deeply impressed upon the mind of every Mason, as a safeguard or security against any illegal attack that may be made, by force or otherwise, to extort from him any of those secrets with which he has been so solemnly entrusted; and which virtue was emblematically represented upon his first admission into the Lodge.—*Craftsman.*

BY the principles illustrative of the virtues of Fortitude, we are, whilst under the trials of surrounding difficulties, enabled always to act, agreeably to right reason, and stand firm in the maintenance of the position we occupy, when based upon justice and honor as the correct sentiments, to influence our motives, and the true principles to govern our actions.

> "T is easiest dealing with the firmest mind—
> More just when it resists, and when it yields,
> More kind.—*Crabbe.*

Fortitude is a virtue, or quality of the mind. It is considered in the same light as courage, though in a more strict sense, there is a difference. Courage resists danger, whilst Fortitude invests us with firmness to endure pain or adversity with rational courage consistent with our love of duty. Courage may be either a virtue or a vice, according to the situation in which we are placed that calls our powers into action; but Fortitude is always a virtue, however we may be placed, or under whatever circumstances we are required to act. It surrounds us with proper considerations, and is the basis of genuine courage.

> Fortitude is not the appetite
> Of formidable things; not inconstant,
> Rashness; but virtue fitting for a truth;
> Derived from knowledge of distinguishing
> Good, or bad causes.—*T. Nabb.*

By the exercise of this virtue we are neither rash, cowardly, hasty, nor precipitate, but are governed by calmness and consideration—well fortified and prepared to meet perils and dangers with a steadfast firmness, and await their approaching issue. Courage, based upon a sense of honor, is generally governed by the virtues inherent in the principles of Fortitude. A truly courageous man is not given to impetuous rashness, but acts with due circumspection, as his safety often depends thereon.

We often speak of desperate courage. A man may, under circumstances, be so placed as to require some impulsive and extraordinary effort where imminent danger exists—where life is periled. Here might be required a sudden effort, where decisive action was necessary. That would properly be said to constitute an act of desperate courage. A disregard and reckless contempt of danger may also be called courage. But there can be no such thing as desperate, or reckless, Fortitude, and we never speak of it in this sense. This virtue is rational, steadfast, and considerate—governed by reason and judgment, and based upon a sense of honor, and a conscientious regard to duty.

The Mason who is governed by Fortitude is neither reckless nor imprudent, but guarded and circumspect in his words and actions. He is not hasty or inconsiderate, but calm and collected; not violent and impetuous, but mild and moderate; not wavering or doubtful, but firm and steadfast; not inconstant or variable, but constant and reliable. Such are the various qualities that distinguish this virtue in contradistinction from their opposites, and whilst the former lead to safety and security, the latter are attended with dangers and difficulties.

With a sincere confidence and trust reposed in God, he who is endowed with the virtues of Fortitude, is, under all circumstances, enabled to stand firm and undismayed. Surrounded by dangers and difficulties, he bears up under them with firm and becoming resignation, prepared to meet the varied vicissitudes he may be called to encounter. Supported with strength that looks forward with hope, and sustained through faith, he is enabled to withstand the trials and changes that attend him on every hand; is firm under the most discouraging events. He is ever true and faithful, steadfast and consistent to duty, unwavering in his confidence in God's promises as his great source of reliance under all circumstances. Such are the precepts inculcated by this virtue, and enjoined upon us as Masons, to inculcate and exemplify.

The excellent precepts for the safe guidance of a Mason are possessed in the cardinal virtue of Fortitude, and the possession of which enables him to maintain that calm, considerate, and deliberate state of mind, and self-control, that under whatever adversities he may be placed, whatever trials or temptations called to endure, he finds himself firm and constant, unwavering and inflexible in good principles and truth. Guarded and fortified on every point against the assaults he may be called to encounter, whether from fanaticism, bigotry, or persecution, either in personal attacks or for the defense of others. He who possesses the qualities inher-in this virtue is thereby strongly fortified to meet and endure their corresponding trials.

> Brave spirits are a balm to themselves;
> There is a nobleness of mind that heals
> Wounds beyond salves.—*Cartwright*.

Fortitude is the symbol of true courage, based upon the moral law of justice and honor. It is inherent in the principles of truth, and can not stand upon any other foundation, and he who is devoid of this virtue can not be said to possess true fortitude.

The Mason who squares his actions by the square of truth and virtue, regulating them upon the level of merited equality, and circumscribes his passion by the moral application of the compasses, and is guided by the unerring rule of Divine light, may truly be said to possess Fortitude.

As a most happy illustration of this virtue, we may, with pride, cite the immortal Washington, the father of his country. A noble brother, distinguished for his many excellent qualities, and amongst which none were more conspicuous, or shone forth in greater splendor than that of Fortitude. By the exercise of this virtue, whilst under the most trying circumstances man could be called to endure, he was ever calm and considerate, cool and collected. Amidst surrounding difficulties and dangers, wherein was involved the fate of his beloved country, and under which ordinary minds would have sunk, he was firm, steadfast, and constant in the pursuit of his object. But in all this be did not rely upon his own individual resources; he looked to a higher source, to higher aid, for that wisdom and strength which alone could sustain him under trying ordeals. His confidence and trust reposed in the strong arm of the Almighty. He possessed that firm faith in the ruler of the universe which gave power to his efforts; and he sought him on the tented field, through supplication, and this was the crowning beauty of his character. He knew that God alone could guide and give victory to his cause. Here was an example of faith, an example of Fortitude, practically illustrated, well worthy of imitation.

As a man deeply imbued with a religious sentiment, well grounded in faith, he looked to God as his chief support and reliance for success. In all the relations of life, he cheerfully acknowledged and reciprocated the courtesies due to his fellow-man, irrespective of rank or position, and this constituted true and noble courage.

Few such as Washington the world has, or perhaps ever will, produce, and it would not be amiss, and certainly not out of place, but in good taste, if every lodge in the land were to have a Washington placed in a niche in the east, as a symbol, illustrative of the virtues of this great and good man, this illustrious brother.

True courage consists in honorable action, rectitude of purpose, and a fearless discharge of duty, and although we may not always gain the immediate applause of favor, yet we enjoy the consciousness of being faithful to our duty, steadfast to our principles, and in due time will receive our merited and just award.

True courage, based upon a conscientious conviction

of mind, constitutes man's real greatness. It imbues him with correct and honorable sentiments, and sustains him in a fearless discharge of duty. It does not fear to meet responsibilities where the cause of justice demands it; for to be strictly just and true to principle requires courage—moral courage—which alone enables us to resist and successfully withstand the alluring temptations surrounding man, and which cause him to swerve from the paths of integrity, at the peril and sacrifice of reputation. Hence, moral courage invests man with strength to resist temptations, and escape the consequences resulting from their corrupting and pernicious influences.

These are the principles of courage we inculcate and illustrate under the virtue of Fortitude, and they comprehend the moral duties and obligations of man; hence, Fortitude embraces every virtue calculated to surround him with true courage, whether it be in the resisting of wrong, or the restraint of sensual passions.

Courage is a constituent part of Fortitude; and while it embraces a spirit of bravery, the latter affords the additional merit of bearing with patient resignation pains and adversities with calmness. Courage impels us to daring and intrepidity, while Fortitude supports us with consistency, Courage may forsake us, and be overcome by cowardice, but Fortitude imbues us with firmness of purpose, and enables us to remain steadfast and patiently await the coming issue. It also inculcates a spirit of forbearance and magnanimity of forgiveness for injuries received. Such are the contrasts that distinguish between courage and Fortitude.

PRUDENCE.

PRUDENCE teaches us to regulate our lives and actions agreeable to the dictates of reason, and is that habit by which we wisely judge and prudentially determine on all things relative to our present as well as our future happiness. This virtue should be the particular characteristic of every Mason, not only while in the lodge, but also when abroad in the world. It should be particularly attended to, in all strange or mixed companies, never to let fall the least sign, token, or word, whereby the secrets of Masonry might be unlawfully obtained.—*Craftsman.*

PRUDENCE is the knowledge and choice of those things we must either reject or approve, according to the dictates of a matured consideration. It implies to consent and deliberate, judge and resolve, conduct and execute, wisely and well, in all matters relating to our interests in the affairs of life.

> Prudence, thou virtue of the mind, by which
> We do consent to all that's good or evil,
> Conducting to felicity, direct
> My thoughts and actions by the rules of reason,
> Teach me contempt of all inferior vanities—
> Pride in a marble portal gilded o'er,
> Assyrian carpets, chairs of ivory,
> The luxuries of a stupendous house,
> Garments perfumed, gems valued not for use,
> But needless ornaments; a sumptuous table,
> And all the baits of sense, a vulgar eye
> Sees not the danger which beneath them lie.—*Nabb.*

Of all the virtues, Prudence may properly be said to be the leading one. It is that virtue by which words and actions are suited according to the nature and circumstances of things duly considered; or, in other words, it is that rule of rightly reasoning upon such subjects as present themselves to the mind for consideration, and through which it arrives at just conclusions.

By the exercise of Prudence we are better qualified for judging what is just and proper both in the means and end desired to attain; and he who exercises Prudence, will not be found likely to violate any of the rules governing the principles of Temperance; for these, like those of Fortitude, are governed by, and are subject to the same laws.

Prudence and wisdom are synonymous, and bear a close relation to each other; yet they differ in degree. The former is the weaker, while the latter is the more consummate and matured habit. We often speak of individuals as being prudent and wise, but never speak of Deity in this sense, for Deity comprehends all the virtues summed up in infinite wisdom. All the minor virtues are combined in the attribute of his wisdom— infinite, unbounded, and unlimited in its resources— omnipotent, omnipresent, and omniscient.

Man, as a finite being, is endowed with the lesser faculties, and of which Prudence is the greater; for by the use of this faculty he reflects and reasons, matures and judges, and, with the combined wisdom drawn from there, he is able to gather and consummate his plans for execution.

The prudent man may be said to be wise. He acts by reason in all his doings. His actions are not based upon the impulse of the moment, but are governed by a calm and considerate mind. He views objects deliberately, and regards matters and things thoroughly in all their bearings. He reasons upon and considers their proximity, and relations, and their bearings toward each other, judges and concludes as to their fitness and adaptation, and by the exercise of these several faculties his mental powers are brought into play, and become fully matured; and in this he displays his prudence through a well-digested and matured consideration of mind.

Not one of the virtues can want Prudence. Devoid thereof to guide them, zeal would run into fanaticism, courage into rashness, justice into folly, temperance into unrestrained excess, and sincere piety into degraded superstition. Prudence stands in the same relation to these virtues, and is as essential to their proper guidance as truth to honor, justice, and probity.

The Mason who rightly understands the nature of his obligations, and is diligent in the pursuit of his duties, will not fail to cultivate this chief of all virtues. He will make it a desideratum and study in life, as the paragon of perfection to his happiness.

Prudence, like wisdom, becomes matured by experience as we advance in life. The young and ardent mind, buoyed with hope and ambition, is generally governed more by impulse and zeal than by prudent considerations. It is only by experience that we learn to consider and control our acts and restrain our desires with prudential considerations governed by wisdom and experience.

Man is so constituted by nature that, in youth, zeal and ambition are his inspiring motives. He builds his expectations and anticipated hopes—too often not to be realized—upon extravagant and visionary schemes and plans, which at times runs into excessive folly, often disastrous and ruinous in their nature. Wise and salutary counsel may sometimes prevail, but experience is the school in which he must learn; and it often proves to be a severe instructor; yet the discipline must be endured.

> Prudence, thou vainly in our youth art sought;
> And, with age purchased, art too dearly bought;
> We're past the use of wit, for which we toil—
> Late fruit, and planted in too cold a soil.—*Dryden.*

But happy is he who in time may learn so to guide his bark through the rugged and turbulent billows of life's tempestuous ocean, that he may avoid its shoals and quicksands, and finally bring his vessel into the haven of safety. All must, more or less, sooner or later, undergo this system of discipline ere Prudence and wisdom are brought into play to exercise their salutary influence and desirable consideration; hence, man's life and best energies are too often consumed and wasted in vain and fruitless efforts.

All men are not created and endowed with faculties alike for equal positions in society; yet nature has endowed man with abilities for some position or other; and while some must necessarily rule and govern, others, of necessity, must occupy more humble positions. But this ought not to militate against the more humble; for whatever position man may be called to occupy, he is equally useful; and justice is due to every one, whatever his station or occupation may be, for he has his part to fill in the great drama of human life, and he will receive his recompense according to his abilities, if they are properly applied, as liberally as the more exalted.

If mankind could understand its true and relative positions in society, and be governed with contentment of mind, man's happiness would be greatly augmented thereby; for true worth secures its own reward; justice, though often tardy, is sure.

Prudence is the symbol illustrative of the virtues inherent in wisdom. It matters not whether they consist of Temperance, or Fortitude, or Justice, for whatever virtues are governed by these principles, are, to a greater or less extent, governed by Prudence. The man given to the use of excessive indulgence in intoxicating stimulants, or to any other unnatural indulgence whereby he debases his moral nature, certainly is not governed by Prudence. Inconsiderate rashness, unrestrained temper, either in word or action, is inconsistent with the laws governing Prudence. Injustice, fraud, or corruption, are neither wise nor prudent; for while they inflict injury on others, they may, in turn, rebound upon us.

Brotherly love is guided by Prudence, for the affections are strengthened or weakened, according to the merits of the object upon whom they are bestowed. Relief is governed by the same laws; you bestow your bounties according to the confidence you have in those soliciting your favors. Even the heavenly virtue of Charity is not exempt from its controlling influence, but is more or less directed by Prudence.

As a still further illustration of the extent of this virtue, we may show its intimate connection with many of our symbols. By the moral application of the Compasses we learn to circumscribe our passions and desires, and keep them within due bounds of moderation; so, by a due observance of the laws governed by Temperance, we regulate our appetites and inclinations, and keep them subject to such regulations as are consistent with and conducive to health and happiness. And this Prudence dictates.

By an adherence to the moral precepts as taught by the Plumb-line we learn to walk uprightly in the majesty and dignity of manhood; so Fortitude sustains us, endows us with that strength and courage, patience and endurance, resolution and firmness, essential to a steadfast, faithful, and consistent course in the duties and obligations of life.

By the Level we are taught the principles of equality— not, however, an indiscriminate equality, for that would be injurious and inharmonious in association with feeling or sentiment, and would produce discord and confusion. You could not expect to assimilate virtue and vice—the cultivated and intellectual with the depraved and ignorant—for they would be incongruous elements in their association. It is not rank or wealth, but true worth and merit that gives equality of association; and it is thus we meet on the level; so Prudence teaches us to weigh and consider all things—their fitness of adaptation, their proximity and assimilation— and judge between right and wrong.

And as the moral application of the Square teaches us to be governed by truth and virtue, so Justice requires of us to give unto every one what is proper and due, neither inclining to the right nor left, yielding not in that which would be to the injury or injustice of others.

Then, my brother, if Prudence, as chief of the cardinal virtues, comprehends so great a field, and flows out in such numerous channels, how much more does it require of your consideration, as it enters, more or less, into every other virtue, and acts as the governing principle thereof. It should be diligently cultivated by you as a safe and sure guide to happiness, with faith in God as the final arbiter and redeemer of your labors.

Prudence is one of the safeguards of our institution, and no principle can be held or more sacredly cherished for its security than the observance thereof. A prudent Mason will never make the institution a subject for controversy. He will never deviate from that line of duty which requires him to observe circumspection, that improper persons may not draw him into unprofitable argument. He will never solicit applications from any one, as this is most strictly forbidden by our laws and regulations. He will at all times exercise due prudence in the recommendation of those who may apply to him, and with the same judicious care closely scrutinize their pretensions and their fitness for the privileges sought to be obtained; and thus he preserves the purity of the institution, and feels safety in its permanency.

Let Prudence, then, be your guard of safety; let it be your watchword in the outer world; let it restrain you from speaking evil of a brother, whereby you may perhaps do him injustice, and injure the reputation of the Fraternity, and thereby do not act with that charity toward his failings which you ought to observe, and which constitutes one of the sublimest principles of true nobleness.

A man of considerate mind is more or less governed by Prudence. It is the standard by which he weighs things and accords to them such considerations as matured judgment dictates. He reasons upon all matters pertaining to his interests, investigates them thoroughly, and acts with judicious care in disposing of them. He is not hasty in forming conclusions, but, with moderation, judges of their importance and value. Governed by Prudence, he will award justice to others, as it dictates to him that injustice and wrong inflicted may redound to his own injury; thus he reasons upon it in its moral bearing.

Prudence is wisdom applied to practice; yet it differs from wisdom in that it implies caution and consideration, while wisdom is governed by experience and knowledge, and is the attribute of a matured mind. Wisdom is the ripened fruit, cultivated in our youth, and harvested in our manhood. It is the treasure we obtain through the vicissitudes we experience, and consummation of that knowledge we gain by observation.

Prudence and Temperance bear a close affinity toward each other; they are, in a great measure, synonymous, being to a certain extent governed by the same laws. He who regulates his desires and actions by the rules governing Temperance, observes the dictates prescribed by Prudence, because they forbid the violation of the precepts inherent in Temperance, and impress him with their injurious effects. Hence, he who observes the requirements of Temperance will be governed by Prudence, and refrain from that which redounds in injury to himself or to others.

JUSTICE.

JUSTICE is that standard or boundary of right, which enables us to render to every man his just due without distinction. This virtue is not only consistent with divine and human law, but is the very cement and support of civil society; and, as justice in a great measure constitutes the real good man, so should it be the invariable practice of every Mason never to deviate from the minutest principles thereof.—*Craftsman.*

JUSTICE is that principle which dictates to us to do right in all things. Neither incline to the right nor left, but yield to every man whatever belongs to him. The demands of Justice are stern. It is the test of our action, and although, like truth, it may be perverted, yet it will, in time, prevail, and hypocrisy and deceit sink in contempt and disgrace. To be just is not a privilege but a duty. It claims no reward save the approval of a pure conscience, and this will overbalance all that may be gained by fraud.

> Justice must be from violence exempt:
> But fraud's her only object of contempt.
> Fraud in the fox, force in the lion dwells,
> But justice, both from the human heart expels;
> But he's the greatest monster, without doubt,
> Who is a wolf within, a sheep without.—*Dunham.*

> Who painted justice blind did not declare
> What magistrates should be, but what they are;
> Not so much cause they the rich and poor should weigh
> In their just scales alike; but because they,
> Now blind with bribes, are grown so week in sight
> They'll sooner feel a cause than see it right.—*Heath.*

Justice is that principle of right which requires of us to be just and honorable in our dealings and transactions one with another; render to every one what is his just due. Defraud not your neighbor; take no undue advantage of him, under any circumstances whatever; neither allow him, through his own want of knowledge, to suffer injury, to your profit or gain, for in so doing, in either case, you are culpable of inflicting wrong, and thereby you defraud Justice, which all honorable men, who invariably regard their moral obligations, will avoid.

> All are not just because they do no wrong:
> But he who will not wrong me when he may,
> He is the truly just.—*Cumberland.*

Justice also requires, for the interest and well-being of society, that punishments be inflicted for violations and offenses committed against such rules and regulations as are required for its well-being and security, but always in accordance with the nature and extent of the offense committed.

All associations of men have certain rules and regulations for self-government, and any violation of these is attended by that punishment Justice requires as adequate to the offense, and this is in accordance with Divine, as well as moral law, for God requires that we should be just, and for every offense we commit, whether it be of a divine or moral nature, we are accountable.

The justice of God consists in the perfection of that wisdom whereby he is infinitely righteous and just in all his transactions, proceedings, and dealings with his creatures. As our Supreme governor, he prescribes laws, equal and just, for our good, and dispenses equitable rewards and punishments as our superior judge. A violation of any of his laws, divine or moral meets its corresponding punishment, and this Justice requires.

> Man is unjust, but God is just, and finally
> Justice triumphs.—*Longfellow.*

Justice teaches us to honor, reverence, and respect those who are our superiors, to love those who are our benefactors, and always make honorable reparation wherever we have done injury or wrong, and this the just man will not fail to do, for it adds strength and value to his character.

As a further illustration of this virtue, we have again applied to the Divine oracles, from whence we have selected a few quotations demonstrative of God's divine justice, and what he requires of man at his hands, that he should also be just.

"And David reigned over all Israel; and David executed judgment and justice unto all his people."—2 Sam. viii: 15.

"Doth God pervert judgment? or doth the Almighty pervert justice?"—Job viii: 3.

"Defend the poor and fatherless, do justice to the afflicted and needy."—Ps. lxxxii: 3.

"Thou shall not oppress a hired servant that is poor and needy, whether he be of thy brethren, or of thy strangers that are in thy land, within thy gates."— Deut. xxiv: 14.

"Ye shall do no unrighteousness in judgment: thou shall not respect the person of the poor, nor honor the person of the mighty: but in righteousness shall thou judge thy neighbor."—Lev. xix: 15.

"And thou, Ezra, after the wisdom of thy God, that is in thy hand, set magistrates and judges, which may judge all the people that are beyond the river, all such as know the laws of thy God; and teach ye them that know them not."—Ezra vii: 25.

"Honor all men. Love the brotherhood. Fear God. Honor the king."—1 Peter ii: 17.

"To receive the instruction of wisdom, justice, and judgment, and equity."—Prov. i: 3.

"By me kings reign, and princes decree justice."— Prov. viii: 15.

"Thus said the Lord, keep ye judgment, and do justice: for my salvation is near to come, and my righteousness to be revealed."—Isa. lvi: 1.

From the foregoing quotations, we clearly see what God requires at the hands of man, and what his dealings will be with those who are unjust. From them we also perceive that God is no respecter of persons. No worldly distinctions will be recognized before his tribunal of justice, but all will be dealt with according to their just deserts.

Thus we see what God's dealings will be with man, the justice he will mete out to all, either in rewards for their good deeds, or punishments for their evil doings. How important, then, for us to understand our true position, and act according to his divine will, and have the approving conscience of being just and upright in all things.

Justice sums up the four cardinal virtues, which, as Masons, it is our highest duty to inculcate and practice, for our individual interest, the domestic and social happiness of those immediately dependent upon us, the well-being of society at large, and the great duty we owe to God, from whom we derive our being and every blessing and comfort surrounding us, and who will augment those blessings as we conform to, and live in obedience to, his divine will.

The principles of temperance demand justice in all their requirements, and a disregard of any of these virtues subjects us to the pains, sufferings, and anguish incurred thereby, in the violation of any of them. And this is just. God's moral law has so ordained it, and man can not set the consequences aside.

Fortitude is equally persistent in her demands, and a disregard of any of the principles inherent therein might be attended with corresponding evils. Our acts should be tested by the scales of justice. It should be the principle upon which our fortitude is based. Many of the dangers and difficulties incident to life would often be attended with serious consequences if not guarded against and resisted by Fortitude.

Prudence, although we claim for her a paramount consideration, yet, without Justice, we could not exercise the full requirements of her virtues. All our powers of logic, reasoning, deliberating, judging, disposing, and concluding are founded upon the principles of Divine truth and Justice; and without a proper appreciation of the value of Justice, we could not fully realize the distinction between right and wrong, and would often fall into serious difficulties and troubles.

Be ever just and true, in all your dealings and transactions with one another. Exercise the virtues called into play by Temperance, Fortitude, Prudence, and Justice, and you will be strongly fortified to battle successfully against the adversities of life. Remembering that you are constantly treading the CHECKERED GROUND FLOOR, which is a monitor to remind you of the uncertainties of human events, and that Justice should ever attend you on all occasions.

Hence, as Masons good and true, let Faith, Hope, and Charity, Brotherly Love, Relief, and Truth, lead you to the performance of good works. Have the principles of Temperance, Fortitude, Prudence and Justice, firmly and consistently established within you, cultivated with assiduity and zeal, sustained with the nourishment drawn from the word of Divine light, and you will give indubitable evidence that you have faithfully applied the moral teaching of the various emblems so often illustrated for your edification. You will then stand as a pillar in the temple, endowed with wisdom, sustained by strength, and ornamented with the graces which give beauty to character, and add luster to its dignity. Your virtues as jewels, will be the ornaments to embellish your life with joy and peaceful happiness as the reward due to one well-spent; and when the Grand Master of heaven and earth sooner or later calls you home from earthly labors, as the perfect ashler, you will be fitted and prepared to obey the summons, properly adjusted for the celestial temple, and partake of that heavenly refreshment as a compensation for labors well and faithfully performed while here below. Such, my brethren, will be the happy fruits to be realized and enjoyed as the reward of a virtuous and an upright life; a life devoted to good works and dedicated to God, the highest merit of excellence attainable to man.

If man would learn to be governed by consistency and act with fidelity to his engagements, he would thereby escape many of the unpleasant controversies he often encounters, and he would be enabled to accomplish much which he otherwise fails to do, through a want of system and promptness. His inconsistencies are also often attended with vexations, disappointments, and which may at times be of serious detriment to others; hence, promptness in all engagements should be strictly adhered to. It gives stability to character, and establishes reliability for veracity.

Justice demands promptness of us in our engagements, as well as fair and honorable dealings in our transactions. There ought strictly to be no difference, for although we do not commit fraud by withholding from others what is justly their due, yet we are unfaithful to our engagements. And thus far we are unjust—morally inconsistent to the promises we make, and thereby we violate a principle of Justice.

To be just and true to our engagements, prompt in the discharge of our duties, will not only secure to us confidence and respect, but it will establish our reputation for truth. And this is the fundamental principle upon which we maintain our integrity. Truth is the primary principle taught us upon the threshold of our institution. Our declarations are made in truth, and upon it is our acceptance. It is the first consideration to which the mind is directed, and attends us through all the several stages of progress we make. The revelation of Truth—Divine Truth—is our great light and guide, and Justice demands that we should be truthful in whatever is required of us.

TEMPERANCE, FORTITUDE, PRUDENCE, AND JUSTICE.

Temperance—a restraint upon the passions, just,
Whether of gourmand appetites to satiate,
Or licentious passions of lust to gratify—
Natural to brute—unholy, impure in man.

Fortitude—a noble purpose, steadfast and sure:
When, in uprightness, man pursues an even course,
With justice, honor, and integrity his aim,
He walks enrobed, in virtue's panoply arrayed.

Prudence—a virtue fair, circumspect in design,
Things, equal or unjust in merit or in worth,
Thereon doth reason, consider, reflect, and weigh,
With consideration, in scales of equal poise.

Justice is the correct standard of right and wrong,
Yet oft perverted by corruption foul, and fraud.
When, for base purposes, filthy lucre to gain,
Justice is injustice in her awards to man.

Temperance, Fortitude, Prudence, and Justice—
The cardinal virtues observed to be by man ;
Who, when, obedience to their precepts, he yields,
He honors God, and glorifies His holy name.

Be Temperate with the body and the mind;
Corrupting passions, firm with Fortitude resist;
Prudence and circumspection in your ways observe,
And Justice will most surely meed you your reward.

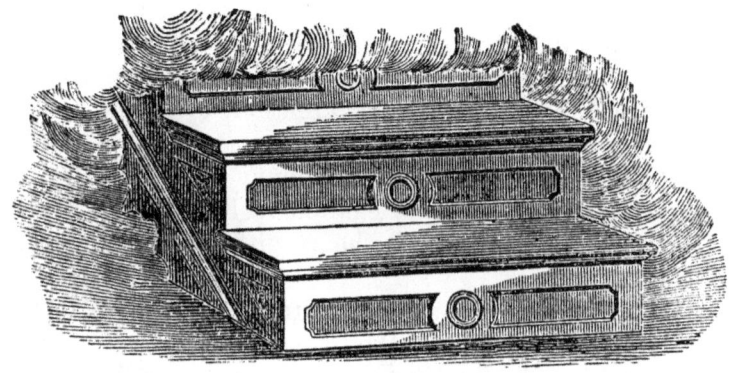

THE FELLOW-CRAFT'S DEGREE.

THIS is the second degree in Ancient Craft Masonry, and, while it partakes in part of the moral instructions as elucidated in the degree of Entered Apprentice, it opens out to us new pursuits, and introduces us into the field of intellectual research and investigation. The various arts and sciences are here illustrated, and to which the mind is particularly directed and impressed with their importance and usefulness for man's purposes. The human faculties are also considered in this degree, and their value and importance to us, as the rational and intelligent portion of creation, beautifully illustrated, for the Great Creator has bestowed upon man a mind—the intellectual power—whereby be understands and reasons according to the faculties with which he is endowed, and discriminates between good and evil, right and wrong. Here we are taught to apply ourselves, and improve the mind for a more extended degree of usefulness. The various subjects presented for our consideration are well calculated to develop our intellectual faculties, and direct them into every branch of useful study for the advancement of human skill and the development of our mental powers. It is a field wherein the intelligent Mason may display and exercise his powers to their utmost capacity, whether it be in the pursuit of the arts, or of the sciences, and particularly the more sublime study of astronomy, which comprehends a knowledge of the great works of creation, gives us more clear conceptions of the vast machinery of the universe, and inspires the mind with its sublimity, grandeur, and magnificence. It produces within us an awe of exalted feeling and reverence for their Great Author, and fills the heart with overflowing gratitude and inspiring love.

While Masons are enjoined to cultivate the moral virtues so beautifully symbolized by the various implements of the operative, and by which they are impressively taught to regulate their lives agreeably to the rules of justice, truth, integrity, and honor, so they are taught to cultivate and improve the mind by the various useful subjects presented in this degree for their consideration ; for it is by a combination of our physical and mental powers in their application that we fully develop our usefulness, to fill the destiny for which we are created.

It is not expected that we can all arrive at that degree of eminence as to become skillful and proficient Masters in every department, for our capacities may not be adapted and destined to that end; but that we should apply ourselves with diligence and strive to attain that fund of knowledge essential to a respectable position in society, which establishes within us a character for industry and usefulness, and is commendable.

When we consider the animal creation, that it is subject to man, how deeply we should be impressed with our superiority, and properly regard our responsibility. The brute creation is governed by instinct only, but man by reason and observation; and be realizes this fact of his superiority as he advances in the scale of enlightened intelligence; and the more enlightened, the more powerful the conviction impresses itself upon him; and the better he understands himself, the more consistent and useful he may be, and the nearer he approximates to the designs of his Creator.

It is in the rational use of our faculties that our superiority manifests itself; and a proper exercise of our five senses affords as a more full enjoyment of the bestowments of life in our social relations, a more extensive degree of usefulness in the proper direction of our several powers, a more consistent consideration of our duties toward each other, and a higher degree of love and reverence to God.

While the degree of Entered Apprentice is particularly devoted to inculcate the sublime principles and duties of morality and virtue, and a due reverence to Deity—all beautifully symbolized and portrayed by hieroglyphical illustrations to more indelibly impress the mind with the important necessity of conforming to, and living in obedience to their precepts—it is therefore well adapted as an introductory to the Second, or Fellow-Craft Degree, which introduces us into a higher field of study for intellectual improvement. It is proper that the mind be suitably trained for this stage of advancement by the symbolic instruction it receives of the moral virtues and duties, in order to prepare it for the better reception and greater enjoyment of the subjects here presented for its consideration.

As the infant learns to crawl before it attempts to walk, and hears the voice and lisps before it can articulate, so should the infant mind of the novitiate learn, and be well instructed in the sublime principles of truth and virtue before it can be properly prepared for the more advanced study and pursuit of intellectual improvement. Every step we progress opens new subjects for investigation more elevating in their themes, and more exalting to our higher natures, are presented—all tending to develop our mental powers. We emerge from darkness to light—from knowledge to wisdom—ere we attain to vigorous maturity.

When we traverse the ground-flour and behold the various emblems of useful instruction which surround us on every side, we are deeply imbued with our own infirmities and entire dependence; we feel ourselves divested of every principle of ostentatious pride and self-emulation, and truly realize our own insufficiency. It produces within us that state of feeling which makes us desirous to obtain light and knowledge, through which we make ourselves useful in the performance of good works. It impresses the mind with a spirit of meekness and humility, and inspires it with benevolent affections and glowing love to Deity, causes us to feel that a dependence on him is our only sure and safe reliance—our only true source of happiness.

Such is the nature of the first degree in Masonry, and the incipient steps preparatory thereto. It is the embryo state and birth of our Masonic creation, and dawns upon the mind as a world in miniature. We gaze upon its beauties with a bewildered admiration and love of devotion; we feel the tender emotions of affection flowing forth in genial streams of love and charity.

Such are the themes that impress the reflecting mind; and when properly considered and duly observed, are well calculated to open the channels of affection for more enlarged benevolence and usefulness, and intellectual advancement in the attainment of knowledge and human happiness, which is the great aim and desire that we should seek to attain.

How beautiful is the arrangement, and how well adapted for our advancement to the higher stages of our profession, prepared to enter into that field of exploration where the human intellect is brought into active operation to examine, investigate, and reason upon the nature of things in general, and maturely consider their adaptation and affinities, to study the anatomy of our own natures, and truly understand their real value and importance.

These are Just and proper considerations for a Fellow-Craft, and, when truly and properly considered, will have their due influences.

Fellow of the Craft. This expression conveys the ides that the Fellow-Crafts were composed of bands of workmen who were skilled in the art of handicraft. They were devoted to the culture of the arts, and were employed in the preparing, fitting, and shaping the material used in the construction of the Temple, while the Entered Apprentices, as bearers of burdens, were engaged in the quarries hewing out the rude material for the hands of the Fellow-Crafts, by whose art it was transformed and properly prepared for use, under the superintendence of a skillful master.

Being artisans, their services required a greater degree of skill and knowledge than that of the apprentices. In their capacity was combined both mental ability and ingenuity, as well as the application to manual labor in the execution of their work; and before their work was permitted to pass and be applied to use, it was required to undergo the inspection of the superintending overseer, who pronounced upon its fitness for that purpose.

In the Fellow-Craft was combined both intellectual application and physical ability. Application of the mind was essential to his branch of employment; hence, the Fellow-Craft, in the pursuit of his occupation, was of necessity required to employ the mental powers in the advancement of the arts. It was necessary, therefore, that he should be enlightened in mind for a skillful and intelligent display of his abilities; hence, the school of science was in his department; and as his skill and ingenuity developed and displayed itself in genius and ability, it prepared him for a more advanced stage of his profession, and thereby qualified him to rank among the masters.

The study of the arts and sciences are therefore fitly appropriate to the Fellow-Craft's Degree. The aspirant having wrought his term of service as Apprentice is in due time introduced into the inner chamber, devoted to the arts and sciences—the arcana for intellectual study and the cultivation of the mind—the mine of learning and investigation for the improvement and development of the human faculties. Here he is surrounded with all that is sublime in refinement and elegance—the highest themes for the exercise and display of the powers of the human mind are brought to his consideration, calling forth his admiring regard and his respectful appreciation of their importance.

Here, likewise, he enters into the unfathomable research of infinite wisdom, seeking truth; and, with venerated feelings and reverence, contemplates the great works of creative power, illuminates the mind with profitable instruction, partakes of the nourishment that infuses vigorous growth to the intellect, and endows it with all that is useful, elevating, and eminent in position.

Wide and extensive as the field of research is, yet the various subjects presented for our consideration are more or less within the reach of our capacities; and as we apply ourselves in the investigation of their natures and approximate knowledge of their purposes, we understand their phenomena and proper adaptation, and make them available to our use. They are all conducive to man's interests, useful to his purpose, essential to his comfort, and afford him the highest state of attainment to human happiness.

Its exhaustless themes bring into play and develop every energy and ability with which the human mind is endowed, and enlarges our sphere for usefulness; and although the indefatigable student may not be able to fully overcome and master the various subjects here illustrated to him, or cope with his more successful co-laborer, yet it should not deter him from a laudable desire and a diligent effort in the pursuit to gain knowledge; for in it consists his power, and it should be the goal of his ambition. True worth and merit lies in a proper application and use of our abilities, and diligence will most generally crown our efforts with success.

An industrious application, properly directed, will secure to the devotee a respectful consideration and esteem for his attainments. We are not all constituted with capacities equal or alike. Some will attain to eminence in one branch of usefulness, while others become equally so in another department; and yet all participate in a proportional share of pleasure and enjoyment. Whatever position man is adapted to occupy, a cheerful acquiescence therein and a faithful discharge of duty will produce an adequate share of contentment and satisfaction, and he essentially contributes his share in the affairs of human life—adds his mite to the store-house of knowledge.

Envious feelings are never cherished in noble and magnanimous minds. He who may not be able to soar aloft to eminence and stand distinguished for his wisdom and knowledge will not regard it derogatory to his character or attainments to receive instruction from the more enlarged and comprehensive mind.

It constitutes a beautiful feature in our system and theory that a respectful regard is awarded for true worth and merit. Some must, of necessity, govern, while others labor in humbler fields of usefulness, but all in harmony and union for the general good, and each receives his recompense according to his just merit.

Equality is one of the attributes of our institution. Industry is enjoined upon all to observe; and although we look to gain knowledge and wisdom from the more experienced, yet the humblest mind is useful in its sphere, and imparts its share of instruction.

Trials and difficulties should never be regarded as insurmountable; patience and perseverance will enable us to overcome seeming obstacles; diligence and close application will most generally crown our efforts with success. The vacillating mind, wavering and inconstant, has no fixed principles, and accomplishes nothing. Stability and steadiness of purpose secures the confidence and esteem of others, and establishes our character for consistency and regularity.

Here the Fellow-Craft has opened to him a school, an academy of the arts and sciences, into which he is introduced, and where he may exercise his intellectual powers of mind to their utmost capacity, investigate and study the various subjects presented for his consideration, examine and ascertain the relative bearings they may have toward each other, and their utility in general. The subjects here presented are all of interest to him; they are for his uses and purposes, and, in their practical application, for his improvement and advancement. They tend to ameliorate his condition and augment his happiness, and a correct knowledge of them affords rational enjoyments, as well as intellectual improvement. They enable man more fully to enjoy the privileges bestowed upon him by his Creator, and give him a more correct understanding of the operations of nature and her laws—without a knowledge of which he is ignorant of the purposes of his creation, and can not properly appreciate his being.

The improvement of the mind, by the acquisition of knowledge, when properly directed, not only tends to advance man's happiness, but gives him more clear conceptions of Deity; and this principle has been taught by the good and virtuous in all ages of the world.

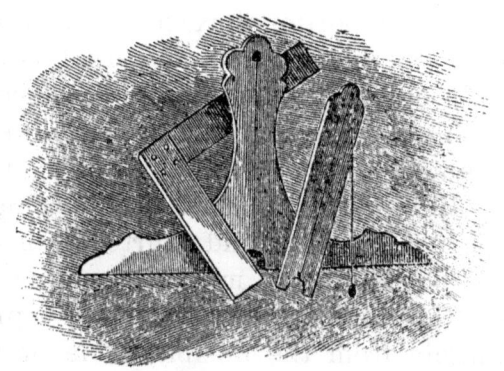

LECTURE XIV.

THE WORKING TOOLS OF A FELLOW-CRAFT.

THE *Plumb* is an instrument made use of by *operative* masons to raise perpendiculars; the *Square*, to square their work; and the *Level*, to lay horizontals; but we, as Free and Accepted Masons, are taught to make use of them for more noble and glorious purposes. The *Plumb* admonishes as to walk uprightly in our several stations before God and man, squaring our actions by the *square* of virtue, and remembering that we are traveling upon the *level* of time to "that undiscovered country, from whose bourn no traveler returns." —*Craftsman*.

THE PLUMB, SQUARE, AND LEVEL.—Our attention is again called to the consideration of these implements. In their present connection they are presented as the working tools of a Fellow-Craft, and here their significance in their moral application is more fully illustrated.

The Fellow-Craft, in his operative capacity, was employed in preparing, shaping, and adjusting the material used for building the temple; hence, these instruments were most appropriate to his purpose. By their application he was enabled to ascertain the fitness of his work:

by the Square, its proportional exactness; by the Plumb, its uprightness; and by the Level, its proper adjustment.

The moral lessons intended to be inculcated and impressed upon the mind by these instruments are justice, uprightness, and equality: justice, in being truthful and honorable in all things; uprightness, in being consistent with principle and purpose; and courteous in according to others what is justly due to merit or position. And, for a further illustration of the importance of these principles, we may draw largely from the inexhaustible mine of Divine light and truth—a jewel of inestimable value, and in which all others are absorbed.

"I know also, my God, that thou triest the heart, and hast pleasure in uprightness. As for me, in the uprightness of my heart I have willingly offered all these things."—1 Chron. xxix: 17.

"Let integrity and uprightness preserve me, for I wait on thee."—Ps. xxv: 21.

"Teach me to do thy will, for thou art my God: thy Spirit is good; lead me into the land of uprightness."— Ps. cxliii: 10.

"Better is the poor that walk in his uprightness, than he that is perverse in his ways, though he be rich." —Prov. xxviii: 6.

"The way of the just is uprightness; thou dost weigh the path of the just."—Isaiah xxvi: 7.

Rectitude and integrity are embellishments that adorn man's character and beautify his daily walks in life. As Masons, the plumb-line of rectitude should be ever present to our view, for by a continual recurrence thereto, we become disciplined and trained to a steady application of its precepts. Rectitude gives honor to man, and integrity establishes stability of character for consistency to correct principles.

The PLUMB admonishes us to walk uprightly, neither inclining to the right nor left, but to hold the scales of justice in equal poise. By its moral application we learn to avoid all kinds of double dealings, both in conversation and in action. It points from earth to heaven, and necessarily leads the mind to contemplations of the future, and directs it in the true path that leads to immortality. Adhering to the moral precepts of the Plumb, we honor our profession, secure the respect and esteem of the brotherhood, and wear our jewel with becoming dignity.

To walk uprightly before God and man is the duty of a Mason; and he who adheres to this maxim will neither be an enthusiast nor a persecutor; he will neither yield to innovations, nor be unfaithful to his trust, but will be true and firm in his allegiance, steadfast and faithful to our laws and constitutions, and, in all the duties required of him, be honest and just, free from avarice or selfishness, injustice or wrong, malice or revenge; but, consistent in the virtue of uprightness, he will in all things be governed by justice. To be an upright man, act justly, and have charity, are excellent and commendable virtues, and add luster to the Masonic character; and he who lives in obedience thereto will fully conform to all our other requirements.

By the moral application of the SQUARE we learn to square our actions and transact our dealings with justice to all men, making our conduct commendable by being just and equitable in all things; and by a faithful adherence to its moral precepts, our actions and doings will be honorable, our behavior will be regular and uniform, not inducing us to aspire to things beyond our reach, or pretending to those above our capacity, but learn with contentment to control ourselves and act in conformity to our abilities.

The intellectual qualities of men are various and diversified. Some will rise to eminence and position in one branch of pursuit, while others will excel and be equally eminent in another field. But man's attainments depend, in a great degree, upon application and study. Whatever occupation nature has adapted him for, proficiency can only be acquired by industrious habits and diligent perseverance in his pursuit.

> No work shall find acceptance in that day,
> When all disguises shall be rent away,
> That square not truly with the Scripture plan,
> Nor spring from love to God and love to man—*Cowper.*

"So David reigned over all Israel, and executed judgment and justice amongst all his people."—1 Chron. xviii: 10.

"Touching the Almighty, we can not find him out; he is excellent in power and in judgment, and in plenty of justice: he will not afflict."—Job xxxvii: 23.

"Defend the poor and fatherless; do justice to the afflicted and needy."—Ps. lxxxii: 3.

"Justice and judgment are the habitations of thy throne; mercy and truth shall go before thy face."— Ps. xxxix: 14.

"I have done justice and judgment; leave me not to mine oppressors."—Ps. cxix: 121.

"Thus said the Lord, Keep ye justice and judgment, for my salvation is near to come, and my righteousness to be revealed."—Isaiah lvi: 1.

"Thus said the Lord of Hosts, the God of Israel, As yet they shall use this speech in the land of Judah and the cities thereof, when I shall bring again their captivity. The Lord bless thee, O habitation of justice and mountain of holiness!"—Isaiah xxxi: 23.

"Thus said the Lord God, Let it suffice you, O princes of Israel; remove violence and spoil, and execute judgment and justice; take away your exactions from my people, said the Lord God."—Ezra xlv: 9.

Here we have an abundant evidence of that justice God requires at our hands; here we truly and forcibly learn the necessity of being just and upright to all and in all things. We are taught this, not only by the moral application of the Masonic jewel, but by that greater jewel of Divine light and truth, from whence we draw our precepts, and there also learn that justice is an attribute of Deity, whom we are taught to love and reverence as our Great Grand Master of heaven and earth, and in whose presence we should walk uprightly, and in obedience to his behests, if we desire his approval of our work.

To be just men and true is required of us as Masons; hence, let us ever endeavor to govern our actions by the square of truth and justice, so as to fully meet the requirements exacted from us, and in due time we shall receive the awards that await us as just and faithful

Craftsmen, having with diligence labored faithfully in the service of our Master's interest.

By the application of the LEVEL we learn the great lesson of equality among all men, according to merit, worth, and capacity for association. From its moral application we learn to disregard no one on account of their inferiority or want of ability, but to be charitable in our feelings, kind and liberal in our dispositions, and exert our influence for usefulness.

All men at birth and in the grave are on the level. Hence, when we meet in the lodge, we meet on the broad principle of fraternal equality. The checkered ground-floor upon which we tread reminds us of the varied uncertainties and fickleness of worldly greatness. To-day the smiles of fortune are upon us, and our paths are strewn with flowers of joy and happiness; to-morrow her withering frowns depress and surround us with cares and sorrows. We have nothing to boast of, for when the summons of the Great Leveler of time arrives, we must yield a prompt obedience to the mandate. Wealth, honor, rank, or title, can not offer an apology for us; no release or delay can prolong our stay; the summons is inexorable; our mother earth claims our mortal remains. Her bosom is the bed upon which they must rest. No distinction is made among her children, but all must repose alike in her domain— the king and the beggar are all on the level of equality in her embrace.

How beautiful the thought! How happily the illustration accords with the principles upon which we, as Masons, are taught to meet. No worldly considerations of wealth or rank to give preference or precedence, but all on the ground-floor of just equality are alike. The badge which distinguishes us is the symbol of an honest, virtuous, and pure heart—a heart that should glow with love and gratitude to God, beat in unison with the virtues of brotherly love and enjoy a charity broad and liberal in extent. Thus mother earth is prefigurative of the principles inculcated by the moral application of the level.

"Let my sentence come forth from thy presence; let thy eyes behold the things that are equal."—Ps. xvii: 2.

"To whom then will ye liken me, or shall I be equal? said the Holy One."—Isaiah xlii: 25.

"Yet ye say, the way of the Lord is not equal. Hear now, O house of Israel; is not my way equal? are not your ways unequal?"—Ezek. xviii: 25.

Man should not pride himself upon his birth or his worldly wealth. It is of but little consideration of what parents he is born—whether high or low, rich or poor—provided he be a man of merit. The lowest station in life often attains to the most exalted eminence of worth; and some of the most enlarged minds and greatest benefactors of humanity have sprung from the most humble sources, while others, under the most favorable circumstances, have fallen lowest in fortune's weal, and their favored advantages have been attended with unhappy and unfavorable results.

Neither should man pride himself upon his worldly honors; they are too often vain and illusory in their hopes, often fail in their designs, and create envy and intemperance of feeling, and, sooner or later, must pass sway and molder with the dust. Neither should he be over-covetous of his riches, for they, likewise, are uncertain dependencies, and can not gratify the desires and wants they create—often more imaginary than real—and too frequently fail in their anticipated hopes.

Let true worth and merit, however humble their possessor may be, receive their just awards, and this will beget love and respect, true and sincere friendship, secure confidence, and endear man more closely to his fellow-man. Avoid envy, which is as a cankering worm to the conscience, and destroys peace and happiness. Contentment of mind is a treasure above riches, and he who possesses this, enjoys a treasure which may truly be envied; for such is the frame of the human mind in its construction that when absorbed in the mere pursuit of the accumulation of worldly gain, that it becomes calloused and insensible to the finer feelings of an affectionate heart. Man, however, is required to be industrious, but that industry should always flow in the channels whereby he may benefit his fellow-beings as well as himself; and he who pursues this course, guided by prudence, will provide well for himself and those dependent upon him—avarice will find no abode in such a heart.

The Level teaches us that we are all descended from one common stock, partake of the same nature, have the same faith and the same hope, which places us naturally upon the level, one with one another, and that we ought not to divest ourselves of the feelings of humanity, and through distinctions necessarily make a subordination among our fellow-men. Eminence of station is desirable, and when honorably and praiseworthily obtained is commendable, and should always receive a corresponding degree of respect and consideration. Guided by such principles, those who truly merit eminence will not treat, or cause others to be treated with superciliousness, on account of their more humble position, but will regard their less favored fellow-beings with proper consideration. It is incompatible with an enlarged and liberal mind exalted by true worth and merit to be imbued with a narrow and contracted feeling of selfishness and hauteur; they are incongruities, not harmonious in action or sentiment. No nobleness of mind is or can be governed or controlled by such inconsistent and contracted influences. Magnanimous principles should therefore be cultivated, as they enlarge the mind and give a more liberal scope to our better qualities, imbue us with generous sentiments, and thereby adapt us for the more social enjoyments and relations due toward each other, and which we should be careful to observe.

To be magnanimous in mind and sentiment constitutes true nobleness of character, and is the standard a Mason should seek to attain; and he who labors in the Masonic fold, guided by this exalted feeling, will be an ornament in the temple—a pillar of wisdom, endowed with strength, and radiant with beauty—strength that will give force and power to his labors; and beauty that will be based upon intrinsic worth and value, such as ought to distinguish a true Mason, whose light shines forth in his daily walks, and whose works manifest themselves in acts of goodness and labors well and faithfully performed.

THE PLUMB, SQUARE, AND LEVEL.

Of rectitude, the Plumb a symbol is;
Not right nor left, but just and true it stands—
A Mason's guide: to walk thereby he ought,
Erect, in God's similitude—upright.

Your actions by the rule of justice square,
If approved you desire them to be;
To your brother share what is just and due,
And to all mankind equally be true.

To meet on the Level—the Mason's creed
Should and ever ought so in love to be,
As brothers good and true in union do,
With friendship's cords drawn in fraternity.

The Plumb, Square, and Level, instruments are
For the practical operatives' use,
But we, as Speculative Masons, are
To use them for their moral lessons taught.

SYMBOLS OF THE TERRESTRIAL AND CELESTIAL SPHERES.

LECTURE XV.

THE GLOBES AND PILLARS.

Seek him that make the seven stars and Orion, and turn the shadow of death into the morning, and make the day dark with night; that calleth for the waters of the sea, and poureth them out upon the face of the earth; the Lord is his name.—Amos v: 8.

THE GLOBES.—These emblems are here presented for our consideration. They are the maps upon which are delineated the external appearance of the earth and all things that pertain to the celestial spheres.

By their use we learn to distinguish the various parts of the earth, gain a knowledge of the planetary system and its various motions.

By the use of the Terrestrial Globe we are enabled to distinguish and describe the various countries delineated thereon, trace their boundaries and extent—also to study the oceans, rivers, and lakes—and thereby obtain correct ideas of the planet we inhabit, understand its revolutions, demonstrate its rotundity, and gain geographical knowledge.

In the use of this Globe is comprehended the study of the science of geography, the application of which gives us a knowledge of the earth, particularly of the divisions of its surface.

Knowledge of the principles of geography conveys to the mind correct ideas of the extent of oceans and seas, of the altitude of mountains, of the course and length of rivers, as well as of the several countries and their localities. And it is as essentially necessary to the science of navigation, as it is to possess knowledge of the country we traverse; it enables the mariner upon the broad ocean to track out his way with safety, upon his voyage to distant continents.

By the use of this Globe we also obtain knowledge of the various climates which affect the inhabitants of the earth, and thus influence their ways, customs, and manners. We also gain knowledge of the variety of animals, plants, minerals, and resources of the planet we inhabit, carry on our traffic and commerce with different nations, extend the boundaries of civilization and of friendly relations and intercourse with distant nations. Without knowledge of geography we would form a very limited idea of the extent of the world, its resources and developments; our usefulness would be confined within the compass of very narrow limits, and the energies of man but feebly developed. It encourages adventures, stimulates a spirit of energy and enterprise, opens out to us unexplored regions for research—all of which tend more fully to develop the latent energies of our nature, and bring us into more active and general usefulness.

By the use of the Celestial Globe we are directed to the study of astronomy, which discovers to us the magnitude and distance of the stars and planets—their rapidity and motion in their cycles in boundless space, measures their distances, ascertains their proximity, comprehends their extent, calculate the time and duration of comets and eclipses, and all things relating to the heavenly bodies, and the phenomena of the ebbing and flowing of the tides.

A practical knowledge of the science of astronomy gives us a most comprehensive view of the great works of creation, carries the mind into the boundless mazes of unfathomable research, and fills us with love and reverence for Deity.

The study of astronomy is the most sublime the human mind can be engaged in. It enlarges it with feelings of elevated gratitude, induces man to encourage the study of geography and navigation, to explore the sphere he inhabits, trace out the various inhabitants thereof, and search out its unfathomable resources for his usefulness and the advancement of his race.

The interests of agriculture and navigation require that we should have some knowledge of astronomy. It was a science pursued at a very early period of the world, particularly by the Egyptians, Babylonians, and the Phoenicians. The Babylonians were well skilled therein, and the Temple of Belus had apartments devoted exclusively to the study of astronomy, whereby they endeavored to foretell coming events, which they predicted through their knowledge of the celestial bodies. Their application of this science was more particularly devoted to the consideration of events connected with their present or future interests. Such was the case with most of the early nations who engaged in and encouraged the study of this science. It was denominated the science of astrology, and was held particularly sacred to the priests and hierophants who administered in the sacrifices and religious ceremonies.

It was by the study of the heavenly bodies and application of their knowledge that the early navigators pursued their voyages, and were guided in their course through the trackless ocean. Our seasons, years, months, and time are regulated thereby. It is also through the science of astronomy that we derive knowledge of the motions of the planet we inhabit.

In the early periods of the world the earth was supposed to be a flat surface, surrounded by extensive bodies of water, beyond which all was in a chaotic state; but as science began to develop itself, and the art of navigation emboldened man to venture abroad upon trackless oceans, he became convinced of its rotundity.

When the great navigator, Christopher Columbus, first laid his plans of discovery before the court of Ferdinand and Isabella, his schemes were regarded as visionary. But his perseverance was unabating; and, when fitted out with a small fleet of three vessels to embark upon his hazardous and apparently uncertain adventures, high mass was celebrated for his safe return. Even mutiny among his crew manifested itself; but he plead forbearance, and his perseverance was favored in discovering a continent inhabited by a race of beings, of whose origin, even in our present enlightened state, we have no certain knowledge, and yet among whom we have more recently discovered traces of our Fraternity.

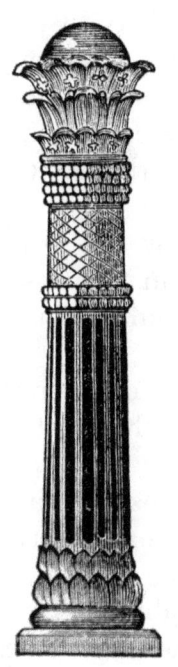 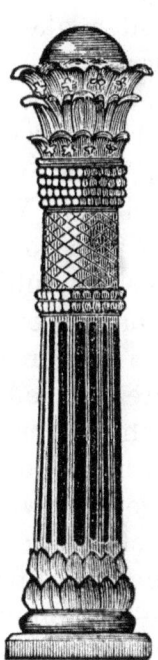

THE TWO PILLARS.

THESE refer to the two pillars set up in the porch in front of the Temple. In 1st Kings, seventh chapter, embraced within verses 15 to 22, we have a full and minute description of these pillars. Here they are described as being eighteen cubits in height, surmounted with chapiters, one and each of five cubits, which would give to each pillar, with its chapiter combined, twenty-three cubits—the two pillars, including the chapiters, forty-six cubits in all.

In 2d Chronicles, third chapter, verses 15 to 17, they are referred to as being thirty-five cubits in height, and the chapiters placed on top of them, each, as five cubits in height. In this instance the pillars are referred to collectively, and the chapiters eaclr as being five cubits. This would make them, combined, forty-five cubits—a discrepancy in the two accounts we have of them. Yet this discrepancy may be accounted for in this wise: These pillars may have been set upon a base of half a cubit, which would give them, according to the account in the book of Kings, eighteen cubits. Yet, when spoken of in the book of Chronicles in a collective capacity, they are said to have been thirty-five cubits in height; and in this instance the base may have been omitted. If so, it would account for this apparent discrepancy.

They are also referred to in Jeremiah, chapter 52, verses 21, 22, where the prophet portrays the destruction of Jerusalem by Nebuchadnezzar, by whom they were carried away, together with all the holy vessels and sacred treasures of the Temple. The prophet here describes them as being each eighteen cubits in height, and the chapiters of brass — one on each — were five cubits in height. This would give their combined measurement forty-six cubits, which agrees with the account we have of them in the book of Kings. And as these two statements agree, we can only account for the discrepancy, as given in Chronicles, upon the supposition that the base was not enumerated in their height. It is one of those things which would give rise to a caviling mind, but would have no weight with a considerate one.

In our rituals we have heard them referred to as being thirty and five cubits in height, with chapiters of five cubits, which conveys the idea that they are each forty cubits in height, including the chapiters—a very inconsiderable degree of altitude in proportion to their circumference, not consistent with the rules of architecture, and which certainly gives a very erroneous impression. We have been, thus far, minute in giving a statement concerning these pillars, in order to explain this seeming inconsistency regarding their height. It would be far better to describe them according to the account given in the book of Kings, as it would be a more consistent statement of them.

We have never been able to fully understand the propriety of placing the Globes upon the summits of these pillars. We cannot see the propriety in their association, unless it be to convey the idea of the universality of our institution, and that its principles are coextensive therewith.

These pillars were undoubtedly placed in front of the Temple to commemorate some event, particularly in reference to the children of Israel, already transpired, or of the designs of Providence in coming events. The only reason we have been able to conceive of for the Globes being placed there is that the terrestrial sphere was to remind them of their journey from the land of Goshen to the land of promise, and that the celestial sphere was their directing guide.

In Exodus, chapter 13, verses 21, 22, we are informed that the Lord went before them in a pillar of cloud by day, to lead them the way; and by night in a pillar of fire, to give them light, to go by day and night. This pillar of cloud which appeared unto the children of Israel in a flame of fire by night was not visible to the Egyptian hosts. To them it was a scene of bewilderment and an obstruction to their progress; for in Exodus, chapter 14, verses 19, 20, we are informed that the angel of God, which went before the camp of Israel, removed and went behind them; "and the pillar of cloud went from before their face, and stood behind them; and it came between the camp of the Egyptians and the camp of Israel; and it was a cloud of darkness to them, but it was light by night to these; so that the one came not near the other all the night."

Now, this pillar of cloud, while it was a guide to the children of Israel in their journeying through the wilderness, was also an obstacle to the Egyptians, and hindered their progress in the pursuit of them. It possessed two remarkable natures: to the hosts of Israel it was a pillar of cloud by day, and assumed the appearance of a pillar of fire by night. It went before and behind them, and stood between the two camps. In the day-time it preceded the hosts of Israel, and at night it stood between the camps, as darkness to the Egyptians, and reflecting rays of light to the Israelites; and when they were encamped, it rested above the ark. It was constantly with them as a visible manifestation of the Divine presence, and attended them on their journeying to the Promised Land.

This pillar represented two remarkable phenomena—darkness and light. It was symbolical of both natures. The outer world was enshrouded in benighted darkness and superstitious idolatry. The essence of pure religion and knowledge of the true God was obscured, and man worshiped the creation of his own hands. But the Divine light was preserved by Noah, and cherished by a chosen few, and transmitted through the patriarchs and prophets to David and to Solomon, whom the Lord had chosen to build the house, and which he dedicated to the Most High God; and before the porch of the Temple, at the east entrance thereof, he placed the two pillars.

God had communicated the plan of the Temple to David, and had permitted him to make preparation therefor, but designed that the house should be erected by Solomon, whose reign should be one of peace and prosperity, and whom he also blessed with great wisdom and knowledge. And when he had finished the house and all the holy vessels, agreeably to the designs communicated from on high, he solemnly dedicated it to God, the Divine Architect; and the Divine favor was again manifested in a flame of fire from heaven, which consumed the sacrifices; and the light continued to be visible in the Most Holy of Holies, resting upon the ark, overshadowed by the outstretched wings of the two cherubim, and, as such, remained with the children of Israel while true to God.

Hence, was a knowledge of the true God preserved by a chosen few through a successive period of ages; and, as a remembrance of these events, and of God's superabounding care, two pillars were erected and placed in the porch in front of the Temple.

It was a custom also that prevailed with the early nations of the world to erect pillars in commemoration of some particular event. In Gen. xxviii: 18, 19, in the vision of Jacob's ladder, we are informed that he took the stone that he had put up for his pillows and set it up for a pillar; and he sanctified it by pouring oil upon the top of it— "And this stone which I have set for a pillar shall be God's house."

So, also, the children of Israel, when they passed over the Jordan, the waters parted, and they passed over on dry land; and to commemorate this miraculous event, Joshua commanded that twelve stones should be brought up out of the bed of the river, and of which he erected a pillar as a memorial to perpetuate a remembrance thereof for future generations.

The Scriptures refer to numerous instances where pillars were erected to perpetuate some event of the miraculous interposition and favor of God.

Whatever else may have been the design and real object of these two pillars, we are unable to say. They could not have been placed in front of the Temple as mere ornaments without some meaning—some purpose of interest to the children of Israel, to remind them of some particular event that might help keep them constantly mindful of their duty to God — the past trials they had endured while in Egyptian bondage, and their forty years' wandering through the wilderness, their final entrance into the land of promise; their prosperity and happiness while obedient to God's Divine law. But they were also, doubtlessly, significant of some coming event, as well as of the past.

"And he set the pillars in the porch of the temple, and he set up the right pillar, and called the name thereof Jachin; and he set up the left pillar, and called the name thereof Boaz." — 1st Kings vii: 21. Boaz, according to the Hebrew, denotes strength, and Jachin signifies to establish. "In strength God will establish." These expressions are significant of a meaning. What can they refer to, if not to the fact that, through the lineage of the house of Judah, in due time, that God would manifest himself to the world, and a sacrifice of atonement be made, whereby we should become purified from the transgression and fall of our first parents? Are these two emblems, then, not susceptible of such interpretation? and do they not convey such impressions to the reflecting mind?

Through Noah, Abraham, Boaz, and David and Solomon, to Zerubbabel, who rebuilt the Temple, and in whom both branches of the house of David met and continued through that descent to the advent of the Promised One, and which promise was made on the fall of our first parents, when God pronounced the doom of the serpent: "It shall bruise thy heel, and thou shalt bruise its head."

But the caviling disposition will say that those pillars were carried away. Yes; and the Temple was destroyed, and God's chosen people were scattered abroad upon the face of the earth, because they disregarded the warning voice of his prophets, polluted the sanctuary, fell into idolatrous worship, departed from his just and righteous ways, and obscured the Divine light; but through the strength of the Lion of the tribe of Judah, will be restored again.

And Nebuchadnezzar, the proud monarch of Chaldea, who, in the pride and arrogance of his heart, to show his defiance of the God of Israel, set up a huge brazen image, before whom he commanded all to fall down and worship, under a threatened fiery ordeal as the penalty for non-compliance; and he who, in the vain imaginations of his heart, boasted and said, "Is this not great Babylon which I have builded," was, for his pride and arrogance, humbled to dwell with the beasts of the field; and his body was wet with the dews of heaven; and the mighty Babylon, with its towering walls and embattled ramparts, has become a desolate waste.

"And he made the chapiters of molten brass, to set upon the top of the pillars; and the height of the one chapiter was five cubits, and the height of the other chapiter was five cubits." —1 Kings vii: 16.

"And nets of checkered work, and wreaths of chain-work, for the chapiters, which were upon the top of the pillars." — 1 Kings vii: 17.

"And the chapiters that were upon the top of the pillars were of lily-work." —1 Kings vii: 19.

"And the chapiters upon the two pillars had pomegranates also above, over against the belly, which was by the net-work." —1 Kings vii: 20.

These pillars, as placed in our temple, afford us most happy and pleasing subjects for contemplation. Some of the most delightful themes for the reflecting and thinking mind are brought to our consideration, and afford us agreeable enjoyment, such as the pure in mind delight to dwell upon.

The net-work most beautifully illustrates to us the harmony that should ever exist in a brotherhood. It conveys to the mind the true principles of one of the tenets of our Order—Brotherly Love, entwined in sincere and undisguised friendship, devoid of dissimulation and hypocrisy. Kindness and affection are illustrated by this ornament of the chapter.

The lily-work is the emblem of purity and innocence. It conveys to the mind the necessity of a pure and virtuous life, the indwelling principles of loveliness and purity. It reminded the high priest of the necessity of clean and unspotted garments, a purifying of the mind and thoughts before entering the sanctuary, the HOLY of HOLIES, there to commune with the Shekinah resting upon the ark, overshadowed by the outstretched wings of the cherubim; so is the badge of a Mason an emblem of purity to remind him of similar observances.

The pomegranate reminds us of God's constant care and goodness toward his creatures; that his gifts are bountifully bestowed upon us with a generous liberality for our good. Hence, it may be regarded as the emblem of plenty. Among the oriental nations it was chiefly esteemed for its nutritious qualities. It contains a superabundance of seed, and every particle of it is delightful to the sense of taste. The skirts of the high priests' robes were ornamented with small golden bells and the pomegranate. It was classed with grape of the vine and figs, olive oil and honey, as one of the principal recommendations and enjoyments of the promised land. It was one of the three kinds of fruit brought from the brook of Eschol by the men whom Moses sent to spy out the land, and was held in high esteem by the children of Israel.

A pillar is an irregular column. It is not confined to any particular order of architecture, and it may consist of one or more parts. It is most generally intended to commemorate some particular occasion or event, past or present, as a memorial to perpetuate the remembrance thereof. Such was the nature and design of the pillars referred to in the sacred Scriptures.

The plan and designs of the Temple were the emanations of Infinite wisdom, and through inspiration were communicated to David, and likewise to Solomon; and its outward courts and interior arrangements conformed to the Divine will. Its inward sanctuary was hallowed by the Invisible Being, who was pleased to communicate with the high priest within its Most Holy of Holies. Every thing pertaining to its arrangements was significant and typical in its meaning. The garments and robes of the high priest and the breastplate—all were equally so.

Before the high priest was permitted to enter the Temple, he was required to perform the necessary ablution of cleanliness and invest himself in pure and unstained garments. Once a year he entered the sanctum sanctorum, or Holy of Holies, and where the Divine oracle was pleased to communicate, and through him reveal his will and purpose. He was the medium of communication between the Divine Being and the people. Hence, the two Pillars being placed in the porch, at the entrance to the temple, reminded him of his sacred calling and duties, and by them the children of Israel were kept in continual remembrance of God's preserving care over them, and of the just observance of his laws, as required at their hands.

These Pillars are often represented in our lodge-rooms by two beautiful columns of the Corinthian order of architecture, but which certainly do not convey a very correct idea of them, bearing no semblance to them whatever. Neither do they exemplify the import nor meaning those Pillars were intended to convey, but leave a very erroneous impression upon the mind of a reflecting brother. And the illustration and uses of them, as delineated, is equally inconsistent. They were placed in front of the Temple, but certainly not for such purposes as we hear described.

Every thing within the interior of our lodge-rooms has its meaning and purpose, intended for our edification. Our symbols are illustrative of the various virtues, and of the moral duties we owe to ourselves and toward each other. Particular localities are assigned to our officers, our altars, and lights, and a satisfactory reason is given for every particular form and ceremony connected therewith. Our outward courts, or ante-rooms, have their accessible and appropriate localities. It is here where the candidate is required to undergo the necessary preparation previous to his admission into the inner department of our temple— properly prepared to receive that light and knowledge he seeks and desires to attain.

How beautiful and appropriate is the analogy! It is

a type of the Temple. It has its outward courts and its inward sanctuary, and he who does not fully conform to its outward requirements, in spirit as well as in form, is not truly worthy of access to the inward departments. Divested of all that is offensive, pure and sincere in mind and purpose, and a desire for light and knowledge, a cheerful and willing obedience to just and reasonable requirements, are the purifying elements necessary to the reception of sound truths.

These Pillars ought therefore to be in conformity with the description we have of them in the first book of Kings, in order that they convey to the mind of the Fellow-Craft correct impressions; otherwise, they do not serve the purpose intended, and are not in harmony with our other emblems, and do not give a clear and comprehensive understanding of their real import and meaning. They are to us as symbols, and properly understood they convey some of the most beautiful thoughts for contemplation that the human mind is capable of enjoying.

Whatever the original purpose or design of these Pillars, whether to commemorate some past or coming event, we can only, at best, conjecture; but, placed in our lodges, they are beautiful ornaments, replete with profitable instruction.

LECTURE XVI.

THE ORDERS OF ARCHITECTURE, AND THE FIVE SENSES OF HUMAN NATURE.

By *order* in architecture, is meant a system of all the members, proportions and ornaments of columns and pilasters; or it is the regular arrangement of the projecting parts of a building, which, united with those of a column, form a beautiful, perfect, and complete whole. From the first formation of society, order in architecture may be traced. When the rigor of the seasons obliged men to contrive shelter from the inclemency of the weather, we learn that they first planted trees on end, and then laid others across to support a covering. The bands which connected those trees at top and bottom are said to have given rise to the idea of the base and capital of pillars; and from this simple hint originally preceded the more improved art of architecture.

The five orders are thus classed: the *Tuscan, Doric, Ionic, Corinthian,* and *Composite.*

THE TUSCAN

Is the most simple and solid of the five orders. It was invented in Tuscany, whence it derived its name. Its column is seven diameters high, and its capital, base, and entablature have but few moldings. The simplicity of the construction of this column renders it eligible where ornament would be superfluous.

THE DORIC,

Is the most plain and natural, is the most ancient, and was invented by the Greeks. Its column is eight diameters high, and has seldom any ornaments on base or capital, except moldings—though the frieze is distinguished by tryglyphs and metopes and tryglyphs compose the ornaments of the frieze. The solid composition of this order gives it a preference in structures where strength and a noble simplicity are chiefly required.

The Doric is the best proportioned of all the orders. The several parts of which it is composed are founded on the natural position of solid bodies. In its first invention it was more simple than in its present state. In after-times, when it began to be adorned, it gained the name of Doric, for when it was constructed in its primitive and simple form the name of Tuscan was conferred on it. Hence, the Tuscan precedes the Doric in rank, on account of its resemblance to that pillar in its original state.

THE IONIC

Is a kind of mean proportion between the more solid and delicate orders. Its column is nine diameters high, its capital is adorned with volutes, and its cornice has dentals. There is both delicacy and ingenuity displayed in this pillar, the invention of which is attributed to the Ionians, as the famous temple of Diana at Ephesus was of this order. It is said to have been formed after the model of an agreeable young woman, of an elegant shape, dressed in her hair, as a contrast to the Doric order, which was formed after that of a strong, robust man.

THE CORINTHIAN,

The richest of the five orders, is deemed a masterpiece of art. Its column is ten diameters high, and its capital is adorned with two rows of leaves, and eight volutes, which sustain the abacus. The frieze is ornamented with various devices, the cornice with dentals and modillians. This order is used in stately and useful structures.

It was invented at Corinth by Callimachus, who is said to have taken the hint of the capital of this pillar from the following remarkable circumstance: Accidentally passing by the tomb of a young lady, he perceived a basket of toys, covered with a tile, place over an acanthus root, having been left there by her nurse. As the branches grew up, they encompassed the basket, till, arriving at the tile, they met with an obstruction, and bent downward. Callimachus, struck with the object, set about imitating the figure: the base of the capital be made to represent the basket, the abacus the tile, and the volutes the bending leaves.

THE COMPOSITE

Is compounded of the other orders, and was contrived by the Romans. Its capital has the two rows of leaves of the Corinthian, and the volutes of the Ionic. Its column has the quarter rounds, as the Tuscan and Doric orders, is ten diameters high, and its cornice has dentals or simple modillions. This pillar is found in buildings where strength, elegance, and beauty are displayed.

The ancient and original orders of architecture, revered by Masons, are no more than three—*Doric, Ionic,* and *Corinthian*—which were invented by the Greeks. To these the Romans have added two — the Tuscan, which they made plainer than the Doric, and the Composite which was more ornamental, if not more beautiful, than the Corinthian. The first three orders alone, however, show invention and particular character, and essentially differ from each other; the two others have nothing but what is borrowed, and differ only accidentally. The Tuscan is the Doric in its earliest state, and the Composite is the Corinthian enriched with the Ionic. To the Greeks, therefore, and not to the Romans, we are indebted for what is great, judicious, and distinct in architecture.—*Craftsman.*

THE foregoing is a brief illustration of the noble science of Architecture as comprehended in our rituals, and there presented for our consideration. In such a work it could not be expected that an elaborate research should be made into the origin and progress of this science as particularly pertaining to the intelligence and tastes of the different nations of the world. It is not required, and therefore not necessary to do so, for sufficient is given to demonstrate the value of its importance and its usefulness to society.

"And God saw every thing that was made, and behold, it was very good: and the evening and the morning was the sixth day."—Gen. i: 31.

Here we learn that the Almighty, as the Great Architect of the Created Universe, designed his work and executed it in six days—six periods of time; and he beheld his work, the production of unlimited power, founded in unfathomable wisdom, and he pronounced it good; and he hallowed the seventh day as a day of rest. And Masons are enjoined to observe the seventh day and hallow it as a day of rest, to be devoted to meditation, to contemplating the great works of creation, and with filial reverence, to worship their Great Author.

Architecture is the art or science of planning, devising, and drawing designs for the erection of various structures for man's uses and purposes. It is the art of building according to certain prescribed rules and proportions, consistent with harmony and order.

Among all the inventions of genius for man's usefulness, a display of taste for elegance and beauty, agreeable to our sense of observation, none can possibly surpass it. It combines both art and science, for while the former consists in the mechanical construction and the erection of an edifice, the latter is displayed in the inventive skill and ingenuity of the architect. It brings his mental powers into full play, and develops his resources of ingenuity and originality. It consists in the exercise and display of his talents for strength and durability, comfort and convenience, elegance and beauty, with an excellence of taste in the order and just proportions necessary to be observed in the several parts of a structure.

Every nation, period, and age where this science has been fostered and encouraged has had a style of Architecture peculiar to itself, and which has given it a marked distinction from others, and become characteristic of its people and national in its character; and the more the state of society advanced and progressed in refinement, the more was this noble science adapted to meet its wants, and made agreeable to its tastes.

As an art, it stands eminently superior—above and distant from every other. It is the superlative display of genius and excellence. Who does not behold a structure, reared with magnificent skill of elegance, clothed in classical beauty, towering aloft, without feelings of admiration and exalted pride? We admire the genius and enjoy a pride of admiration in our hearts. It is essentially the most dignified of all arts. It elevates the mind with inspired feelings of admiration, and makes man love his home and his country. It is not the invention of originality, like painting, sculpture, or engraving, but it is originality itself. It is the parent, while they are the offspring.

Being, of necessity, the first of all arts, it necessarily embraces within itself a general knowledge of philosophical principles and an approximity and adaptation of things in general as to their fitness and affinity. It has a dignity which no other art possesses, whether we consider it in its rude state, as occupied in the rearing of the simple hut, or in its more advanced and practical state of improved cultivation—whether it displays itself in the superiority of the gorgeous and magnificent abodes of palatial royalty, the grandeur of the forum, or in the sacred temple dedicated to religious worship —it is considered in either case as an art and science; and in every nation wherever organized society and civilization has existed, it has left some monument of its skill in this department.

The Egyptians and Babylonians were doubtless the earliest nations that directed their attention to the science of Architecture, and gave it a nationality. The

Egyptian style was distinguished more for its sameness in character, its massive and somber appearance, than for any agreeable aspect it presented to the eye. It was more the production of servile labor than of science; yet was imposing in appearance.

The Babylonian system of architecture, although it partook more or less of the Egyptian style, it was less gloomy in aspect, and presented a greater degree of variety and taste. Those stupendous banging gardens, constructed and supported by immense rows of columns, have been unparalleled for their grandeur in any age of the world

The Grecian Orders of Architecture, however, are more classical, and display a greater degree of refinement and elegance than that of any preceding nation. It was from them the Romans borrowed their style of Architecture; and although they attempted various improvements, and covered them profusely with ornaments, yet they presented no general utility or improvement. And it is to the Greeks mainly that we are indebted for all that is elegant and sublime in this most useful science,

The science of Architecture was carried to a high state of refinement and perfection by the Romans. They were lavish in their expenditures upon their public edifices and upon their private dwellings. Their triumphal arches were sculptured with designs illustrative of the victor's triumphs.

Sir Christopher Wren, the great master-spirit of Architecture, whose memory we, as Masons, have cause to revere, thus speaks of this noble science in this wise:

"Architecture has its uses, public buildings being the

ornaments of a country; it establishes a nation, draws people and commerce, makes the people love their native country, which passion is the origin of all great actions in a commonwealth.

"It aims at eternity, and therefore is the only thing incapable of modes and fashions in its principles (the orders), which are founded upon the experience of all ages, promoted by the vast treasures of all the great monarchs, and skill of the greatest artists and geometricians, every one emulating each other; and experiments in this kind being expensive, and errors incorrigible, is the reason that the principles of Architecture are now rather the study of antiquity than fancy."

Such is the glowing description passed upon this noble science by this truly great and noble brother, who for many years was Grand Master of the Fraternity in England, until the infirmities of advanced years prevented him from a further continuance in the discharge of his arduous duties. The memory of such a brother should always be cherished with grateful recollections.

These considerations are not presented to Masons in the expectation that they are to become practical architects and builders, but that they should be lovers and patrons of the arts and sciences, as they inculcate a system of order and stability when properly regarded. They infuse a principle of moral sublimity and an elevated sentiment within man, and lead the mind to contemplate the grandeur of the universe, and, like all our illustrations, are intended for our moral and intellectual edification, our advancement in the scale of happiness, and our mental enjoyments; they impress upon us the necessity of industrious habits—of employing our time in useful pursuits—whereby we become our own architects, and rear a moral temple to be endowed with all the virtues which give nobleness and eminence to our characters, and make us moral architects, reflecting the glory and honor of the Supreme Architect of the Universe. Such are the purposes intended to be conveyed by the illustrations of the Orders of Architecture; and true Masons, who properly regard and cherish these considerations, will be lovers of the arts and sciences, imbued with order and regularity in deportment, and, as such, be pillars, not only of ornament, but for utility, to beautify and support our noble order with becoming dignity.

Every Mason is an architect—a moral architect— and if he works agreeably to the rules as prescribed by the various implements presented for his moral guidance, and draws his designs from the virtues of a pure mind; he erects an edifice, based upon the foundation of truth, for all our plans and designs, whatever they may be, if governed by correct principles, and prompted by honorable motives, are founded upon truth—the only reliable basis upon which they can stand.

As the operative mason is governed by certain prescribed rules in the erection of an edifice, to secure strength and durability, so the speculative is likewise governed by certain prescribed rules, which govern his actions, and give permanency of stability to his character; and in this he is a moral architect.

OF THE FIVE SENSES OF HUMAN NATURE.

AN analysis of the human faculties is considered in the Fellow-Craft's Degree; they are the five external senses of our nature: *Hearing, Seeing, Feeling, Smelling, and Tasting.*

HEARING

Is that sense by which we distinguish sounds, and are capable of enjoying all the agreeable charms of music. By it we are enabled to enjoy the pleasures of society, and reciprocally to communicate to each other our thoughts and intentions, our purposes and desires; while thus our reason is capable of exerting its utmost power and energy.

The wise and beneficent Author of Nature intended, by the formation of this sense, that we should be social creatures, and receive the greatest and most important part of our knowledge by the information of others; for these purposes we are endowed with hearing, that, by a proper exertion of our natural powers, our happiness may be complete.

SEEING

Is that sense by which we distinguish objects, and in an instant of time, without change of place or situation, view armies in battle array, figures of the most stately structures, and all the agreeable variety displayed in the landscape of nature. By this we find our way in the pathless ocean, traverse the globe of earth, determine its figure and dimensions, and delineate any region or quarter of it. By it we measure the planetary orbs, and make new discoveries in the sphere of the fixed stars; nay, more: by it we perceive the tempers and dispositions, the passions and affections of our fellow-creatures, when they wish most to conceal them; so that, though the tongue may be taught to lie and dissemble, the countenance will display the hypocrisy to the discerning eye. In fine, the rays of light which administer to this sense are the most astonishing parts of animated creation, and render the eye a peculiar object of admiration.

Of all the faculties, sight is the noblest. The structure of the eye and its appurtenances evince the admirable contrivance of nature for performing all its various external and internal motions; while the variety displayed in the eyes of different animals, suited to their several ways of life, clearly demonstrates this organ to be the masterpiece of nature's work.

FEELING

Is that sense by which we distinguish the different qualities of bodies, such as heat and cold, hardness and softness, roughness and smoothness, figure, solidity, motion, and extension.

SMELLING

Is that sense by which we distinguish odors, the various kinds of which convey different impressions to the mind. Animal and vegetable bodies, and indeed most other bodies, while exposed to the air, continually send forth effluvia of vast subtlety, as well in a state of life and growth as in a state of fermentation and putrefaction. These effluvia, being drawn into the nostrils along with the air, are the means by which all bodies are smelled, hence it is evident that there is a manifest appearance of design in the great Creator's having planted the organ of smell in the inside of that canal through which the air continually passes in respiration.

TASTING

It enables us to make a proper distinction in the choice of our food. The organ of this sense guards the entrance of the alimentary canal, as that of smelling guards the entrance of the canal for respiration. From the situation of both these organs it is plain that they were intended by nature to distinguish wholesome food from that which is nauseous. Every thing that enters into the stomach must undergo the scrutiny of tasting; and by it we are capable of discerning the changes which the same body undergoes in the different compositions of art, cookery, chemistry, pharmacy, etc.

Smelling and tasting are inseparably connected; and it is by the unnatural kind of life men commonly lead in society that these senses are rendered less fit to perform their natural offices.

The proper use of these five senses enables us to form just and accurate notions of the operations of nature; and when we reflect on the objects with which our senses are gratified, we become conscious of them, and are enabled to attend to them, till they become familiar objects of thought.

On the mind all our knowledge must depend; what, therefore, can be a more proper subject for the investigation of Masons ? By anatomical dissection and observation we become acquainted with the body; but it is by the anatomy of the mind alone that we discover its powers and principles.

To sum up the whole of this transcendent measure of God's bounty to man, we shall add that *memory, imagination, taste, reasoning, moral perception* and all the active powers of the soul, present a vast and boundless field for philosophical disquisition, which far exceeds human inquiry, and are peculiar mysteries, known only to nature and nature's God, to whom we are all indebted for creation, preservation, and every blessing we enjoy.—*Craftsman.*

If it were within the narrow and confined limits of man's comprehension to conceive of what would be most conducive to his general welfare, his interest and well-being in life, he could not possibly arrive at any thing more desirable in the attainment of his happiness than the possession of the five senses pertaining to his human nature; for when guided by reason and matured judgment, they are the basis upon which are built his real enjoyments of life. They are so intimately connected in their relations as, in a great measure, to be dependent upon each other; for it is in the exercise of correct reasoning and a matured judgment that our senses are properly directed, and enabled to discharge their several functions agreeably to the purposes for which they were designed.

Our senses are mental and physical. Hearing and Seeing are the mediums through which these faculties operate upon the mind, while those of Feeling, Smelling, and Tasting affect our bodies, and convey the impressions produced through these organs. Infinite wisdom created and endowed man with all that is necessary and requisite to constitute true happiness, and afford him social enjoyment in all that is agreeable in the relations of life; and his failing to realize these, rests in the perversion of the privileges bestowed upon him.

Hearing is the faculty by which we distinguish sounds, Deprived of the exercise of this power, although we may be in the enjoyment of the sense of sight, yet we would be in constant danger of harm, as our organs of sight do not afford us the advantages of observing objects under all and every circumstance. It is, therefore, by the faculty of Hearing that we avoid and escape from dangers, as well by that of Seeing. These two organs act in perfect harmony, and are the natural safeguards to avoid dangers and escape harm. They are mutually dependent upon each other for our protection and preservation, and, while they perform these offices, they afford us an equal share of enjoyment or disappointment in our intercourse with our fellow-beings, and they likewise enable us to partake alike in surrounding objects, whether they are productive of pleasure or pain, so intimate is their connection with each other.

Feeling is the faculty affected by our sense of touch. By it we are enabled to distinguish the various qualities of bodies susceptible to this sense. It also affects us bodily, wherein we experience the changes and varieties of climate to which we are continually exposed, and likewise the sympathies that draw upon our affections. Deprived of the power of this faculty, we would be incapable of distinguishing the different qualities of bodies or substances, we could not realize changes to which we are continually exposed, and our sympathies would remain unmoved where pain or suffering was endured, either by ourselves or others. We are by nature so constituted that we feel pain to a greater or less degree, although endured by others; the sympathies of our affections are so allied that they, of necessity, produce it, and also create pleasure within us; whether these emanate through the medium of our own faculties, producing pleasure to ourselves, or we behold the enjoyment of it by others, or in the surrounding objects of nature, this faculty is equally affected by the others. We undergo pain when we hear the discordant clashing that inharmoniously greets the ear, or when we observe the fury of the raging elements that leave ruin and devastation in their trail.

Smelling and Tasting have, likewise, their functions to perform. If we were deprived of the faculty of Smelling we would not be able to enjoy those odors that are delightful and afford pleasure to this sense; and we would be equally incapable of avoiding those that are disagreeable and offensive to it. The sense of Taste is intimately connected with that of Smelling. Their alliance is inseparable, for whatever is agreeable to one, affords pleasure to the other.

The faculties of Smell and Taste are also useful to that of Sight, for whatever affords pleasure to them, produces pleasure to the organ of Sight. Infinite wisdom has, for prudential purposes, so constructed the arrangement of our senses as to be of mutual service; otherwise, we would be unable to distinguish that which is wholesome and productive of benefit to us from that which would result to our injury.

But we often vitiate and deprive our faculties of the faithful performance of their proper functions by the indulgence of inordinate desires and the gratification of improper passions. An unrestrained indulgence given to habits of sensual intemperance vitiates our sense of Taste, and lessens that of Smelling. A life given to the gratification of lustful passions is not only debasing to our natures, but is injurious to one of our most cheering gifts, the vision of Sight.

We delight in the enjoyment of those objects that are agreeable to our vision. They often charm the ear with pleasant sensations, and awaken the sympathies of our affections; and whatever is obnoxious to the organs of Smelling and Tasting, is equally offensive to those of Hearing, Seeing, and Feeling.

While the organs of Smelling and Tasting have their purposes to perform for our general good, those of Hearing, Seeing, and Feeling are held in particular regard by Masons, for it is through the exercise of them that we know and recognize a brother; that we are enabled to discern and learn his wants, afford him that aid and protection his circumstances may require at our hands. We hail the inspiring sound, and behold the welcome messenger with joy that brings gladness to the heart.

Our organs of vision are, without doubt, the most extensive in usefulness, and afford us the greatest amount of interest. By their use we distinguish the different shades and varieties of colors, we behold the cheerful countenance of a friend, and greet him with a joy of welcome; and by it we often discern the inward workings of the mind, we enjoy the beautiful scenery of nature, and behold her numerous works, from the most minute particle of inanimate or animate production to the greatest of created works. Such are the privileges derived from the use of the faculty of Sight.

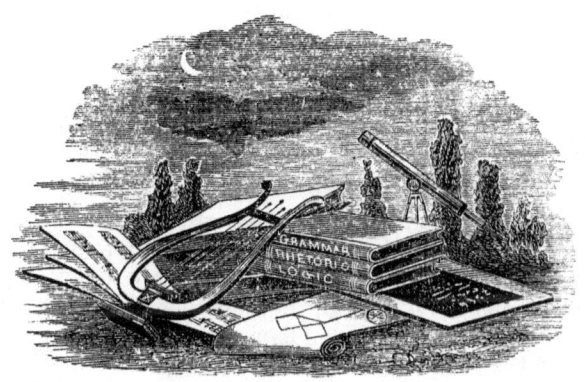

LECTURE XVII.

THE SEVEN LIBERAL ARTS AND SCIENCES.

THE seven liberal arts and sciences are illustrated is this section, which are *Grammar, Rhetoric, Logic, Arithmetic, Geometry, Music,* and *Astronomy*.

GRAMMAR.

Grammar teacher the proper arrangement of words, according to the idiom or dialect of any particular people; and that excellency of pronunciation which enables us to speak or write a language with accuracy, agreeably to reason and correct usage.

RHETORIC.

Rhetoric teaches us to speak copiously and fluently on any subject, not merely with propriety alone, but with all the advantage of force and elegance, wisely contriving to captivate the hearer by strength of argument and beauty of expression, whether it be to entreat and exhort, to admonish or approve.

LOGIC

Logic teaches us to guide our reason discretionally in the general knowledge of things, and directs our inquiries after truth. It consists of a regular train of argument, whence we infer, deduce, and conclude, according to certain premises laid down, admitted, or granted and in it are employed the faculties of conceiving , judging, reasoning, and disposing—all of which are naturally led on from one gradation to another, till the point in question is finally determined.

ARITHMETIC.

Arithmetic teaches the powers and properties of numbers, which is variously effected—by letters, tables, figures, and instruments. By this art, reasons and demonstrations are given for finding out any certain numbers whose relation or affinity to another is already known or discovered.

GEOMETRY.

Geometry treats of the powers and properties of magnitudes in general, where length, breadth, and thickness are considered, from a *point* to a *line*, from a line to a *superfices,* and from a superfices to a *solid.*

A point is a dimensionless figure, or an indivisible part of space.

A line is a point continued, and a figure of one capacity; namely, length.

A superfices is a figure of two dimensions; namely, length and breadth.

A solid is a figure of three dimensions; namely, length, breadth, and thickness.

By this science the architect is enabled to conduct his plans and execute his designs—the general to arrange his soldiers, the engineer to mark out ground for encampments, the geographer to give us the dimensions of the world and all things therein contained; to delineate the extent of seas, and specify the divisions of empires, kingdoms, and provinces; by it, also, the astronomer is enabled to make his observations, and to fix the duration of seasons, years, and cycles—in fine, geometry is the foundation of architecture and the root of mathematics.

MUSIC.

Music teaches the art of forming concords, so as to compose delightful harmony, by a mathematical and proportional arrangement of acute, grave, and mixed sounds. This art, by a series of experiments, is reduced to a demonstration with respect to tones and the intervals of sounds, inquires into the nature of concords and discords, and enables us to find out the proportion between them by numbers.

ASTRONOMY.

Astronomy is that divine art by which we are taught to read the wisdom, strength, and beauty of the Almighty Creator in those sacred pages, the celestial hemisphere. Assisted by astronomy, we can observe the motions, measure the distances, comprehend the magnitudes, and calculate the periods and eclipses of the heavenly bodies. By it we learn the use of the globes, the system of the world, and the preliminary law of nature. While we are employed in the study of this science, we must perceive unparalleled instances of wisdom and goodness, and, through the whole creation, trace the glorious Author by his works,—*Craftsman.*

HERE we are presented with a brief illustration of the subjects designated under the denomination of the seven Liberal Arts and Sciences, which are defined to be Grammar, Rhetoric, Logic, Arithmetic, Geometry, Music, and Astronomy.

Some of these subjects are more or less connected with those preceding them, and have, to some extent, already been referred to; but here they are brought to our special consideration. They are all of importance to us in our relations and intercourse with each other, and a knowledge of them gives us position in society, according to our attainments.

The culture of them refines the sensibilities of our natures, gives dignity and eminence to our characters, secures respectability, and advances our usefulness; they are accomplishments for utility, as well as embellishments of refinement and elegance, and make our association desirable of attainment, and our acquirements beneficial to others, while the influence they secure to us tends to augment our happiness and advance our interests. Devoid of these useful branches of education, we are but poorly qualified to assume a respectable position in society and acquit ourselves with becoming propriety; hence, a reasonable possession of them is desirable, and ought to be obtained.

Grammar is defined to be an art by which we connect our ideas and words, agreeably to certain rules and principles peculiar to the proper construction of the language or idiom of any particular nation or people. It is the art through which we convey our thoughts, intentions, and desires, either by oral conversation or epistolary communication, consistent to a proper connection of words and sentences.

It consists in the systematic arrangement of words, their affinity and bearing to each other, as words in every language have a relative connection and bearing in their import, which must be observed in the formation of sentences, to convey a correct meaning of our ideas; hence, this accomplishment is necessary to a grammatical style of writing and a proper use of words in our conversation. Nothing grates so inharmoniously upon a sensitive and refined ear as vulgar solecism and incongruous pronunciation. They are offensive, and betoken an uncultivated state of mind.

Rhetoric is defined to be the science of oratory. It is the artistic skill and genius of a cultivated mind that man brings into play when he desires to captivate and draw the hearer by the glowing beauty and elegance of language—the power of mind and fluency of speech, which enables him to illustrate and embellish his subject with highly-wrought and diversified expression of ideas, conveyed by action and gesture, as well as the illustrated beauty of language. It captivates the ear, wins upon the affections, and insensibly draws upon the passions. It is the gushing eloquence of a fertile imagination, fruitful in the conception of ideas, that sways us with its influence, enthralls us with its power, and leads us captive to its will.

It is that beauty of diction through which our thoughts and ideas flow in streams of eloquence, clothed in garbs of richness, radiant with beauty of thought and expression of sentiment—an ornament of superlative excellence, winning and persuasive in its power, captivating in its influence, and enlarges the mind in imaginations.

It is a faculty of rare genius, yet almost every individual possesses it to some extent. Upon some, nature seems to have been lavish in her bestowments of this accomplishment; and it is only such favored ones who rise to eminence in this gift. It becomes refined by culture, and improved by practice. The early Greeks and Romans paid particular attention to the culture of oratory; their youths were trained with great care, to be fitted for the forum and public declamation.

Action and gesture are necessary accomplishments and aids to oratory. They give force and power to words, and are the embellishments to an easy and graceful delivery. Effect can not be successfully obtained, unaccompanied by corresponding action and gesture, and these should be studied, in order to give ease and elegance in delivery. The force of persuasive power would, in a great measure, fall listless upon the ear, unaccompanied by suitable action and gesture. The Roman orators, previous to entering upon the rostrum, and in order to give grace and elegance in appearance, and more powerfully to impress their auditory, secure their attention, and work upon their affections, were robed in flowing garments, as these imparted an imposing dignity and gracefulness of appearance.

Logic is designated both as an art and science. In the investigation of principles upon which argument is conducted it is a science. In the faculty of reasoning, thinking, and analyzing upon correct and logical principles it is an art. Agreeably to the rules governing logic; we bring into play the faculties of reasoning, thinking, arguing and deducing upon certain premises laid down, admitted, or granted, investigate them in all their several bearings and ramifications, trace them through their various intricacies, until we finally arrive at a definite conclusion, and determine the subject in controversy. It is based upon the principles of truth and justice.

Logic is distinguished from Rhetoric, although allied and essential in association; for while the latter displays the oratorical powers of a fertile mind, with the embellishments in which it illustrates the ideas that charm the ear with its seductive influences, the former is based upon the substantial principles and investigations of truths, and exposes the fallacies and sophistries of errors. It brings into play the argumentative abilities, develops their skill and ingenuity in the research and investigation of primary objects, and traces out their origin. It is the anatomy of mind, that demonstrates man's reasoning powers, enables him to dissect his subject. Founded upon correct principles, it is the mine of exploration that leads to the origin of things in general, deduced upon fundamental principles and rational considerations.

While Grammar is an art, and is within the reach of almost every mind, even of ordinary capacity, and ought to be cultivated, in order to enable us to communicate and convey our thoughts and ideas in a proper manner, Rhetoric and Logic are gifts or bestowments of nature; and although all may not become proficient therein, yet they may be cultivated and supplied to a great extent. Where nature has left us deficient in these qualifications, a proper and systematic training of them will at least enable us to hold a respectable position, and acquit ourselves with credit, and we become improved by experience and time.

God endowed man with the faculty of reasoning, and, as he designed him to be a social being, he bestowed upon him the gift of speech, in the perfecting of which he calls to his aid Grammar, Rhetoric, and Logic. By the use of the first he rejects all impure expressions, and avoids solecism and improper pronunciations, purifies language, and clothes his ideas with elegance and refinement. By the second he seeks to beautify and adorn language, and convey his ideas with pleasing and agreeable expressions, and illustrates his conceptions with beauty of sentiment, winning and attractive to the affections. By the third he gives thoughtful consideration to objects presented to the mind where reflection and judgment are required to be exercised. Here he reasons, considers, weighs, and adjusts things, consistent with the principles of matured reflection, rejects or adopts as judgment and experience dictates, based upon the strength of logical argument founded on truth. All things have a primary consideration, and, in order to arrive at just and proper conclusions, we must trace them to their origin, through the force of reason and investigation.

Grammar, Rhetoric, and Logic are embellishments that give accomplishments and refinement to man; they impart ease and gracefulness of manners, and enable us to appear with respectability in society. They form a beautiful triad, dedicated to the culture, improvement, and beautifying of language.

Arithmetic is the science of numbers. It is the art of computation, by which we ascertain the aggregate sum of any given quantity of numbers, or reduce the same into fractional portions—all of which may be carried to an unlimited extent in magnitude, or reduced to the most minute fractions. It is of use to us in almost every requirement in life, and enters into the calculations and pursuits of our intercourse and relations with each other, however insignificant they may appear.

We measure our time, estimate the products of our labor, apportion our hours of repose, designate our appointments, numerate our hours, days, years, and seasons by the computation of numbers.

The Roman system of enumeration was by letters of the Roman character; and the use of these with mathematical signs are still retained in the solution of problems. The Arabic characters are used in all ordinary purposes of enumeration, and of which there are nine. These, with the use of the cipher, enable us to make calculations to any given quantity or amount in numbers.

As every stage of society is more or less engaged in a system of bartering, knowledge of the use of figures enters into all its several calculations—our losses and our gains, advantages and disadvantages—whether mentally or practically ascertained, are based upon our knowledge of the use of figures.

Geometry is the most primitive of all the sciences. It is the root and foundation of the mathematics, and enters into the science of Arithmetic and Algebra, where figures, signs, and symbols are used and made to represent numbers and quantities.

In the earliest periods of the world Geometry consisted in the simple use of measuring lands, and in the rude construction of such shelters as man's then present state required. Being of a pastoral nature, his wants were but few and simple; but as mankind began to multiply and spread upon the earth, the wants of society increased, and, in the formation of communities, this valuable science merged from its simple to more extensive usefulness to meet its required wants.

Geometry enters, more or less, into every department of man's requirements. It is essential to navigation, traversing the various parts of the earth, and every branch of usefulness, whether it be in the artisan or the mind of scientific investigation, exploration or research, the construction of language, the force of logical reasoning, or the arrangement of concord in sounds, all are based upon the science of Geometry.

Geometry, in connection with our institution, was essential to the operative mason and the architect, for by its rules they were enabled to measure their space, arrange their plans, and erect their edifices, agreeably to mathematical principles; so, in like manner, it enters into the principles of philosophical or speculative Masonry, for by the various implements of the operative mason we learn the division of our time and the proper application thereof, the duties and obligations inculcated in the moral instruction of our symbols, which teach us to erect a moral edifice agreeably to the rules presented thereby, laid upon the foundation of truth, honor, and justice, consecrated and dedicated to virtue and purity.

This science was taught by the sages and philosophers of old, who imparted their knowledge by symbols and figures. The center they represented by a point—Deity, from whom flows the virtues of love, purity, and holiness, circumscribed by eternity. It is a symbol beautifully illustrative of our lodges, in the center of which, upon our altar, rests the great light— the light of Divine truth—from whence radiates the precepts inculcating that brotherly love and charity, which should be as extensive as the bounds of our lodges, whose canopy is the starry-decked heaven, and whose limits are only circumscribed by the globe.

Music is the science of melody and harmony. It consists in a succession of sounds, which produce pleasant sensations to the ear, whether it proceed from the human voice or from the sound of instruments. The influence it often produces is wonderful in its effect. It has been known to calm the passions when under strong feelings of excitement. Its soothing influence has restored the distracted intellect, and given peace to the disturbed mind. There is in it an irresistible charm that softens the harshness of our natures and restrains our passion to moderation, as well as a powerful impetus that impels man, under its martial strains, to move forward on the battle-field and brave the cannon's mouth.

When Moses and the hosts of Israel had crossed the Red Sea, they sung a song of triumph to the Lord: "And Miriam the prophetess, the sister of Aaron, took a timbrel in her hand, and all the women went out after her with timbrels and with dances; and Miriam answered them, Sing ye to the Lord, for he hath triumphed gloriously."—Ex. iv: 20, 21.

"And the evil spirit departed from Saul, when David stood before him and played upon the harp, and he was refreshed and well."

Here we have the Scriptures, the record of Divine truth, as authority of the efficacy of Music: even David, called the Sweet Singer of Israel, in his moments of affliction and grief, sought consolation from the Lord in songs of praise, attuned to the sound of the harp.

Whatever produces melody and harmony, whether vocal or instrumental, affords a sensation of pleasure delightful to our feelings; and the better Music is known and understood, the more it will be valued, and the greater will be the desire to cultivate it.

The extent of encouragement given to the cultivation of the science of Music is a fair test of a refined and elegant state of society, and, from the pleasure it affords us, we naturally form a strong desire to possess knowledge of it. The elements of it are, more or less, within every human being. Upon some, however, nature has bestowed her favor largely with this gift, while others have received it in a less degree; but, with a will, they may, in a great measure, overcome and improve this deficiency.

Vocal Music is coeval with the creation of man. It is very reasonable to believe that our first parents, while in their state of paradisaical felicity, must have given expression of their love and gratitude in songs of praise as well as in communion with their Creator—joy and felicity, their companions, all nature in harmony, and in praise to the Being of their creation.

In all ages of the world Music has had her inspired votaries; but it is only in the past few centuries that it has attained to that degree of perfection as to be considered and ranked as a science, the perfection of which is yet in its infancy.

Astronomy signifies the law of the stars, and is applied to all that relates to the motion and theorems of the solar system, and of which the earth constitutes a part It is the science through which we gain a knowledge of the planets and their satellites—the stars and other bodies—that, in their several orbs, move through the field of boundless space.

It is through knowledge of Astronomy, and by the aid of mathematical calculations, that we learn the magnitude of the several celestial bodies, understand their motions, calculate their distances, comprehend their evolutions, define the period of eclipses, and the return of comets. A correct knowledge of this science depends mostly upon the observations we are enabled to make with the use of instruments constructed for that purpose.

The study of the celestial bodies has been cultivated from a very early period of the world among those nations who devoted attention thereto. The knowledge they gained from their observations was more particularly directed to the religious and political matters concerning their notion and dynasties than otherwise. It was supposed that their destinies were more or less under the influence of some of these bodies. The science was denominated astrology. The Greek nations, however, at more modern periods, purified and brought it to a high state of perfection as the science of Astronomy.

There is no branch of study that the human mind can be engaged in that is more sublime and more elevating in its pursuits than that of Astronomy. It creates within us inspired feelings, enlarges our affections, and gives us the most exalted conception of Deity. Contemplated as one great whole, the production of infinite wisdom, this science is the most beautiful monument of grandeur known to the human mind; it presents the noblest record of its intelligence. Man appears upon a small planet, almost imperceptible in the vast extent of the solar system—itself only an insensible point in the immensity of unbounded space. The sublime results and discoveries to which this science has led may console him for the limited period allotted to him here.

Truth and justice are the immutable laws upon which the Great Creator has founded his works; conceived in Infinite wisdom and Almighty power, they are as coextensive in duration.

Lamech was the descendant of Cain. We learn that he had two wives: the name of the one was Ada, and the name of the other was Zillah: "And Ada bare Jabal; and he was the father of such as dwell in tents, and of such as have cattle. And his brother's name was Jubal: he was the father of all such as handle the harp and organ. And Zillah also bare Tubal-cain, an instructor of every artificer in brass and iron."— Gen. iv: 20-22.

From this we learn that man, at a very early period of the world, turned his attention to the cultivation of the arts and sciences, as well as that of pastoral pursuits. Jubal, as the father of all such as handle the harp and organ, was the inventor of instruments for music, and Tubal-cain was the instructor of artificers that wrought in brass and iron, and from these primitive sources originated and descended the arts and sciences, which have been improved upon through succeeding ages and generations to their present advanced state of perfection. The attention of those engaged in pastoral pursuits was also at a very early period directed to the study of the heavenly bodies, through which they were enabled to tell the hours of night, as well as regulate those of the day by the sun, and from the simple observations of these shepherds preceded the science of astronomy.

The study of the arts and sciences should be cultivated by every rational being, however humble in life, not only for the advantages we may derive therefrom in point of position or pecuniary gain, but the mental enjoyments it affords us. A small portion of our time devoted thereto enables us to lay up a moderate fund of useful knowledge, which, if not practically employed, can at least be mentally enjoyed. Its tendency is to purify our minds, refine and elevate our natures, and make us useful members of society. Such are the moral advantages and benefits to be derived therefrom; hence, they are introduced into our rituals for our social enjoyment and intellectual advancement, and, as Masons, we should give them just and proper considerations.

OF THE MORAL ADVANTAGES OF GEOMETRY

GEOMETRY is the first and noblest of all sciences, and is the basis upon which the superstructure of Masonry is erected. By geometry we can explore the hidden arcana of nature, and trace them up through her intricate windings to her most concealed recesses. By it we are taught the power the wisdom, the omnipotence, and the unmeasured goodness of the Great Architect of all things. By it we are enabled to comprehend the nice arrangement of all its parts, and the wonderful propositions which connect together the stupendous machinery of the universe. By it we can climb above the canopy of the heavens, measure the distances of the most remote planets, detect in its passage a ray of light, and marshal into perfect order the multitudinous groups of worlds that are scattered over infinite space. By it we can rationally account for the return of the varied seasons of the year, and the rich and prodigal variety which each successive season displays for our health, our instruction, and our pleasure.

Worlds, and planets, and systems of surpassing magnitude are above and around us—all created by the same Divine Artist, all fashioned by the same Master hand, all conducted by the same unerring laws. A survey of nature and the observation of her beautiful proportions no doubt first influenced man to study symmetry and order. This world naturally gives rise to societies, and, in the course of time, to luxury, refinement, and every useful art. The designs of the architect at first were plain and simple, calculated only to administer to his immediate wants. Human ingenuity and experience, however, progressively improved upon these original plans until there have been produced monuments of art so finished in their execution, and so perfect in their structure, as to its the admiration of every age.

In imitation, then, of our ancient brothers, who were practical working *Masons,* the Fraternity of later days have also selected tools and implements of architecture, not in an operative, but in a symbolical and speculative sense, to imprint upon the mind wise and serious truths; and thus, through a succession of ages, have been transmitted, unimpaired, the sublime tenets of our institution.

The lapse of time, the ruthless hand of ignorance, and the devastations of war have lain waste and destroyed some of the most noble monuments of antiquity.

Even the Temple of Solomon, so spacious in its design, so majestic in its proportions, so magnificent in its execution, and constructed by the united exertions of so many celebrated artists, has not escaped the ravages of barbarous force; but the Order to which it gave a name still exists in all the harmony of its first formation, and it has gathered unto itself power and grandeur, and energy, and might, amid the desolate ruins of the temple FREEMASONRY STILL SURVIVES. It has existed where all things else of human origin have perished. The tempest of persecution has not injured it, the mutations of the world have not shaken it, the wing of Time has flapped over it in vain; through centuries of changes it has stood, changeless and serene.

And to the true and loyal brother it is a source of exulting promise to know that it will *continue to survive* so long as the *attentive ear* receives the sound from the *instructive tongue,* and the mysteries of the Order are lodged in the repository of *faithful breasts.—Craftsman.*

KNOWLEDGE is power, whether we regard it as being individually possessed, or in the aggregate numbers of society at large. It is the foundation of all well-regulated communities; and although many individuals of whom it is composed may possess but a very limited share, yet, in the aggregate, the general intelligence of the masses mark the degree of civilization to which society has advanced.

Knowledge is also desirable from other considerations; the value of it is incalculable; and we can not truly estimate the advantages to be derived therefrom. Independent of any outward benefits we may derive through it, the satisfaction and mental enjoyments it produces to its possessor is of infinitely greater value than all the external importance it can invest us with.

We may be surrounded with wealth, and regard it as the source and height of our happiness, and yet it may be the means of our misery, and entail upon us untold anguish and suffering. But not so with knowledge. Whoever heard tell of knowledge, directed by correct and virtuous principles, over producing misery or anguish? The possession of real knowledge produces contentment of mind, and affords a treasure of internal satisfaction that few would be found willing to exchange for the vain pomp of human vanity. Our wealth may become lost to us, and our honors fade into insignificance, but our knowledge will ever be steadfast.

The road to knowledge is mainly through the sciences, and requires the employment of mind and intellect — bestowments of Deity, that are elevating, and make man, when they are properly directed, God-like, Geometry is the most elementary of science, and the most important for the knowledge of truth it conveys to the mind, as the medium through which it develops its importance. Based upon the principles of truth, it inculcates rectitude of deportment, and implies a strict conformity to, and a faithful observance of, the precepts that are taught by the various implements morally symbolized for our guidance, and which must be complied with, as the rules governing our acts and walks in life, if we desire to be consistent to regularity and good order, and thus conform to the principles embraced in this science, whereby we become moral geometricians in the formation of our characters.

It is in its moral aspect that we desire to present these subjects and bring them to the consideration of Masons. As our illustrations are imparted by symbols, so should we consider and apply the principles governing science in a moral bearing.

Although we have heretofore referred to Geometry, under the designation of the Seven Liberal Arts and Sciences, yet it is here presented and considered under the moral advantages with which it imbues us. The letter G, the initial of Geometry, occupies a conspicuous place in our lodges. It is ever present to the view of a Mason as a symbol significant of a name that should be indelibly impressed upon the mind of every intelligent being—a name that we are taught to revere, and the sacredness of which ought never to be profaned.

THE MASTER MASON'S DEGREE.

THIS is the third degree, and the summit of ancient Craft Masonry. All that is sublime, impressive, and of real value in Masonic lore is summed up in this degree. Whatever the genius or fertility of the mind of man has produced in more modern times in inventing and augmenting the number of degrees in Masonry, nothing can add to or detract from this most sublime degree. All modern inventions of degrees are based upon it; and they may be illustrated with ornaments, but they can not surpass it in the important truth it reveals for the contemplation of the considerate mind.

The Entered Apprentice Degree unfolds to the initiate light and knowledge, through which are made known to him truths and principles that impress his mind with the necessity of his reliance being placed in God, inculcate the moral duties he is to observe, and impress him with the uncertainty of earthly dependence, and the important necessity of having faith, based upon truth, encouraging him to look forward with hope, when the joys of that faith would be rewarded with peace and happiness as the just awards for the toils of life.

His labors of servitude being faithfully performed, he is prepared for an introduction into the middle chamber, where the powers of his mind and intellect are to be brought into service for higher pursuits. It is here where he is brought to the consideration of those subjects which pertain mostly to the interest of his advancement in the scale of intelligence, whereby he becomes more fully prepared for the discharge of the duties which may devolve upon him in whatever station he may be required to act. It is here, likewise, that he prepares and qualifies himself to be advanced to the companionship of the Masters.

These are the necessary steps for advancement to the Master's Degree. The virtues and principles taught in the preceding degrees are essential qualifications preparatory to the reception of the truths revealed in this sublime degree of Master Mason, the ceremonies of which are most solemn and impressive, well calculated to imbue the mind with reflections of the future.

We learn from Sacred Scripture that, when God created man, he placed him in paradise, and surrounded him with all the felicity his earthly state required. Innocence, purity, and holiness were the enjoyments in which he participated. He was informed of the source of knowledge of good and evil, and endowed with a free-will agency, and the penalty of death was prescribed as the consequence that would attend his disobedience. But the weakness of his human nature could not withstand temptation; he yielded, and he fell, and died—died as to his communion with God and the felicity of paradise, and he became a wanderer upon the earth —cares, trials, labors, afflictions, sorrows, and mortal death were entailed upon him and his posterity as the consequence of his disobedience; but God did not forsake him in his forlorn and outcast state, but held out to him a glorious immortality—a restoration and an entrance into the celestial paradise. And this is his hope through faith in God's promise.

How beautifully is this illustrated upon the ground-floor of our Mystic Temple—emblem of human life! and how forcibly does it impress the mind with the uncertainties thereof, and direct it to that brilliant star in its center, as the hope of man's faith in that Being, who will never forsake him in the hour of need if his trust is firmly reposed in him. This emblem is an allegory replete with the most useful instructions. Coming as a wanderer from the outer world, duly prepared with a pare heart, and an honest and sincere desire for light and knowledge, we are received upon the ground-floor of the temple. Here we make our acknowledgments to Deity, traverse its apartments, consider the important lessons it imparts, learn the moral use of the various emblems presented to the mind, and apply them as we are taught, in obedience to the Master's instructions, and thereby prepare ourselves for an introduction into the middle chamber, whose apartments we traverse, and store the mind with useful information for our intellectual growth.

This apartment is for our mental employment. In it is possessed a fund of material profitable for information, which, if studied and properly applied, gives us an acquisition of knowledge that elevates the mind and suitably prepares us for more extensive usefulness to our own interest and happiness, while it conduces to the welfare of others. It prepares and fits us for the more exalted station of the Master's apartment—an eminence desirable to attain.

To this stage of advancement we can only arrive through industry, perseverance, and untiring application. To be admitted thereto, we ought to be well skilled in our abilities as workmen, possessed of all the qualifications necessary to a well-regulated life, fully imbued with the importance of what we have already acquired, for our admission to the rank and title of Master—the highest distinction of the Ancient Craft, and only bestowed upon the most meritorious and virtuous, such as were prepared and qualified in mind for the reception of its important truths.

This stage of our progress figuratively releases us from the toils and anxieties attendant upon labor. Having, in our days of strength, performed the allotted labors apportioned us, and, in our more mature years, having stored the mind with wisdom gained by experience, profitable to our advanced period in life, we enter upon that repose and quiet which is essential to age and to meditation, to which the declining years of life should at least be devoted.

If the Holy Scriptures, as our light and guide, teach us of man's mortality and his immortality, then are these truths inculcated in this degree of the Master Mason. Man dies, and his material part returns and mingles with the earth, but the immaterial part— the spirit—returns to God, who gave it.

The ceremonies of this degree are of the most solemn and impressive nature. They infuse within us a religious feeling; and no one can witness them without realizing the force of the truths inculcated in them. They produce reflections of a serious nature, and illustrate an example of pious duty, as well as unshrinking fidelity.

"Remember now thy Creator in the days of thy youth, while the evil days come not, nor the years draw nigh, when thou shalt say, I have no pleasure in them; while the sun, or the light or the moon, or the stars, be not darkened, nor the clouds return after the rain. In the day when the keepers of the house shall tremble, and the strong men shall bow themselves, and the grinders cease because they are few, and those that look out of the windows be darkened, and the doors shall be shut in the streets, when the sound of the grinding is low, and be shall rise up at the voice of the bird, and all the daughters of music shall be brought low; also when they shall be afraid of that which is high, and fears shall be in the way, and the almond tree shall flourish, and the grasshopper shall be a burden, and desire shall fail; because man goeth to his long home, and the mourners go about the streets; or ever the silver cord be loosed, or the golden bowl be broken, or the pitcher be broken at the fountain, or the wheel broken at the cistern. Then shall the dust return to the earth us it was; and the spirit shall return unto God, who gave it."— Ecclesiastes XII: 1–7.

LECTURE XVIII.

THE WORKING TOOL OF A MASTER MASON.

The TROWEL is an instrument made use of by operative masons to spread the cement which unites a building into one common mass; but we, as Free and Accepted Masons, are taught to make use of it for the more noble and glorious purpose of spreading the cement of *brotherly love* and affection—that cement which unites us into one sacred band, or society of friends and brothers, among whom no contention should ever exist but that noble contention, or, rather emulation, of who can best work and best agree.—*Craftsman.*

THE TROWEL is the working tool of a Master Mason, and with it are combined all the implements of Masonry, for it is to be presumed that the Master, during his servitude as Apprentice, and the skill he has exhibited and ability displayed as a Fellow-Craft, have fully enabled him to qualify himself with a familiarity of their use; for it is through a knowledge of their application in the several departments to which they are assigned that he prepares himself for the eminent position be occupies.

It is also to be presumed that he has with diligence applied and qualified himself in his mental capacity, to acquire such a degree of knowledge in the several branches of the arts and sciences as are necessary to be possessed by the master workman, who should be well experienced in all that pertains to the Craft. He should not only be familiar with the duties pertaining to his own station, but thoroughly understand the labors of the Apprentice, and possess the requisite knowledge of a skillful Fellow-Craft, to be fully qualified as a competent superintendent over their work. He plans and designs, as well as superintends, while they labor and execute their work agreeably to his directions.

The Entered Apprentice is assigned to labor on the ground-floor—figurative of the quarry—as the place appropriate to his unimproved and unprepared state. It is here where he learns to divest himself of those irregularities which surround and obscure his better qualities. The working tools assigned him are the most appropriate to his use, in their moral application, to prepare him for the duties of the Fellow-Craft.

All the implements of Masonry pertain to the Master, but more especially the TROWEL. By the operative its use is applied to spread the cement, whereby the several parts of a building become united and form a perfect whole; but with the speculative Mason its application is of a moral nature—the spreading of the cement of brotherly love and affection. It reminds him of the fraternal union and fellowship that should exist, of the duties and responsibilities that devolve upon him by precept and example, that the peace and harmony of the

Fraternity be not interrupted by discordant elements from irregularities of his own; that his deportment be consistent with equanimity and order, and prudence govern his actions, as the cement that strengthens our bond of union.

We represent the two Saints John in our lodges by two perpendicular lines—parallels—as emblems of rectitude, consistent in regularity and uniformity of course. These two eminent personages occupy a position in our lodges for their virtuous and exemplary lives; hence, the parallels comprehend the virtues for which they were distinguished, and, as such, are emblems illustrative for us to imitate their example. Governed by the precepts as illustrated by these parallels, we will be consistent in our duties, and live in obedience to Divine and moral law.

As our institution is not sectarian in its nature, we can, at least, all unite in emulating the noble precepts inculcated by these illustrious patrons of brotherly love and charity, which unite us in one great brotherhood, and is the cement of our union, the basis of our strength.

Brotherly love is the principle that operates upon the affections, imbues them with kindness, and causes them to flow in mutual sympathy of regard for each other's welfare; and the moral application of the Trowel spreads the cement which binds us in fellowship and endears us in our attachments.

Relief is the consideration we have for each other, whether it consists in administering to the wants of the needy or counseling and admonishing a brother. It is the cement by which we soothe and relieve the burdens of affliction, and sustain the sinking hope of those for whom it is our duty to consider, influence a wandering brother, and restore him to his proper position.

The plans and designs of the speculative Mason are drawn from the trestle-board of Divine Light. It is the unerring guide that directs him in the erection of a temporal edifice, based upon the foundation of truth, cemented in the virtues that give excellence to character and ornament man's life with purity and holiness.

The Master Mason, figuratively, is presumed to be endowed with that wisdom and knowledge he has gained through servitude in youth, and to which the vigor of his manhood has been devoted. Ripened by years of experience in labor and toil, he enters upon those duties for which his past services have qualified him. He should not only be the embodiment of wisdom and knowledge, but he should be equally so in the virtues of a correct and well-regulated life; his example should be one worthy of emulation; he should be ever zealous in the moral use of the working implement appropriate to his position, whereby he widely spreads the cement of brotherly harmony, and diffuses the wisdom and knowledge accumulated through time and experience.

Ability to instruct and govern is essential to the Master of a lodge, and he can only obtain these qualifications by a systematic training and close application, to familiarize himself with the duties of his station.

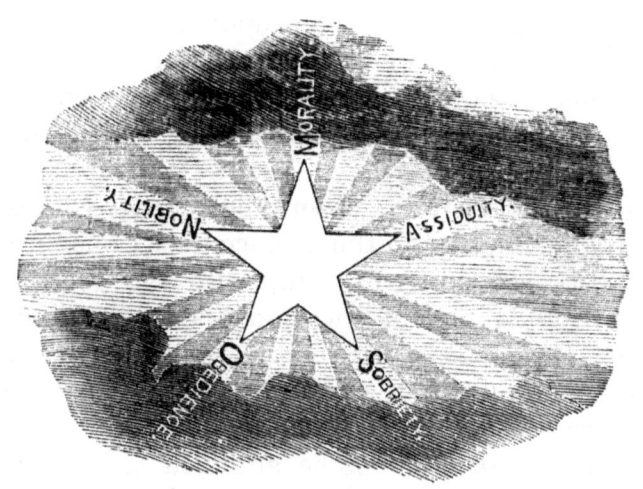

LECTURE XIX.

THE FIVE POINTS OF FELLOWSHIP.

MORALITY, ASSIDUITY, SOBRIETY, OBEDIENCE, AND NOBILITY are embraced within the sphere of this emblem, and radiate from its five points. It comprehends all the virtues taught in our esoteric schools— and not only the virtues, but our duty to God and to our fellow-beings, especially to those with whom we are allied in bonds of fraternal union.

Morality, Assiduity, Sobriety, Obedience, and Nobility are fundamental principles inherent in Masonry, and are the basis of the various virtues illustrated and portrayed by the symbols peculiar to our institution. They embrace that system of ethics which we are taught to cultivate and practice in our daily intercourse with each other in life; and, devoid of the virtues illustrated thereby, we can not fully meet the requirements enjoined upon us, nor can we be consistent to the obligations we have taken upon ourselves to observe; for we must be moral, assiduous, sober, and obedient, to possess nobleness of character; we must be exemplary, and live in conformity to the requirements of our duties as Masons.

Morality consists in the observance of those duties which we owe to one another in the performance of honorable and virtuous acts, refraining from injustice and wrong, abstain from the indulgence of vice, and shun its pernicious influences. Governed by this principle, we are careful and circumspect in our words and acts, respectful and decorous in our deportment.

The moral man will not be addicted and given to the baneful and pernicious practice of indulging in profane, immoral, and impure language — debased in thoughts, degrading and sensual in their nature—but in his deportment he will he distinguished by correct behavior, his thoughts and sentiments will be clothed with chasteness and purity, his mind will be elevated in its nature, and his character exemplary.

The man governed by morality shuns and abhors vice in all its forms; he walks in obedience to the Divine command, faithfully observing its just requirements, by which he refrains from the vices that tend to his degradation, and necessarily entail upon him the consequences resulting in a departure from right to wrong. His example is salutary, and his influence is diffused for good, and, like the genial rays of the sun, reflects luster upon his nature.

Morality embraces all that is pure, virtuous, and exemplary in life. It conduces to our present comfort and happiness, constitutes purity of mind, and its good influences, while enjoyed by the virtuous, are beneficial to others. Hence, the Mason who lives in obedience to the precepts as taught by this virtue will exemplify morality in all its requirements, and thus far dignify the moral temple with ornaments of beauty.

While our system of instruction inculcates the principles of morality, it also inculcates and enjoins those of religion; but not in a sectarian point of view, for Masonry does not interfere with the private opinions of its votaries, either religious or political, but it requires of us a full and unqualified belief in God as the Creator, Author, and Giver of all things for man's general benefit, and that his requirements are just and equitable. It enjoins love, reverence, and obedience to his Divine will, to regard him as the chief source of our happiness, and that we should ever be humble in our acknowledgments of gratitude to him.

Hence, the altar upon which rests our Great Light is presented to us as a symbol of devotion, whereby we are constantly reminded of our duty to God, our entire dependence upon him, and that we should ever seek his Divine aid and be guided thereby in all our undertakings in life, revere him as the chief source of the happiness and blessings we enjoy. His requirements are just and equitable; he exacts nothing from us that we can not fully comply with, and the Great Light is our unfaltering evidence of his will. Such are the requirements embraced in these principles, and of our duty to God, and they are symbolically exemplified in one of the points of Fellowship, and constitute the groundwork of an upright and consistent Mason who walks in obedience to his profession.

Assiduity is that principle which inculcates habits of application and industry, by which we are constantly engaged in the pursuit of some object. It infuses within us a spirit of energy and enterprise, the employment of our time, whether it be in the exercise and engagement of our intellectual or physical powers for the diffusion of usefulness, or as they may be otherwise applied; for we are so formed and constituted by nature that we can not be inactive or passive beings. Our minds and our energies, if not usefully and profitably engaged, will be diverted, and wander into vicious and injurious habits, our thoughts and sentiments become depraved, our natures degenerated, and we will lapse into indolence and uselessness, our light would be obscured, our pathway benighted, and thus far we would fail in the performance of our mission.

The assiduous man, when his physical or intellectual abilities are directed and flow into proper channels, guided by the moral principles of integrity, truth, and justice, becomes a useful member to society, and a valuable auxiliary in the field of active enterprise. His labors, whether intellectually or physically employed, are productive of good, and of which his fellow-beings are, to a greater or less extent, the recipients, proportionately enjoying their benefits as well as himself. So intimate are our associations in life, and so interwoven in each other's temporal interests is our welfare, that our example sheds its influence abroad, and becomes more or less diffused within the circumference of our sphere. And as we sow, so we shall reap; the spring is the seed-time of our youth, and the harvest the ingathering of our labors.

A man may be assiduous in the pursuit of improper desires and evil motives. In this he inevitably violates some moral law, and the penalty for the violation will be proportioned according to the extent of his digression; and he not only brings the infliction of his folly upon himself, but frequently is the instrument entailing suffering and misery upon others. How important is it, then, that our energies be properly directed for our good and welfare, as well as for the benefit and interests of others.

The principles inherent in Assiduity are enjoined upon Masons, but to be directed in proper channels. We are taught to be assiduous in the pursuit of some useful occupation, whereby we are enabled to make suitable provision for ourselves and those dependent upon us, to be industrious and useful members in society, to work diligently and live honorably. We are taught to be assiduous in the improvement of our intellectual faculties, in the cultivation of the mind, to garner the intellectual store-house with useful information, by which we more fully enjoy the blessings of life, and become more useful to our fellow-beings, more elevated in thought and sentiment, more pure and chaste in mind, have a higher and more exalted reverence for Deity, and live more in conformity to his will; become more fully confirmed in faith, grow stronger in hope, are more liberal and charitable toward others, more strongly cemented in the bonds of brotherly love, more active in dispensing the bestowments of relief, more securely established in the principles of truth, more faithfully observe the requirements of temperance, more steadfast in fortitude, circumspect in the exercise of prudence, and more equitable in the administering of justice. Such are the results that would flow from an assiduous life, whose energies are directed to useful and profitable pursuits. Its crowning joys will be contentment, peace and happiness, and honor to God.

The principles of Assiduity are beautifully symbolized by the Twenty-four-inch Gauge, which morally illustrates to us the necessity of a proper division of our time—how and to what purpose it should be given; and by it we learn that time should not be needlessly wasted, for time lost can not be restored again. It is the measure of man's probation on earth. It is loaned to us by God, and he will hold us accountable for the use of it; hence, an assiduous Mason will be active and useful; he will be an industrious laborer, faithful and prompt in the discharge of his duties—an efficient co-laborer in works of usefulness.

> Whether in pursuit of culture for the mind,
> Or in physical employ, my time is spent,
> My labors, with faithful energy and zeal,
> Shall them with prompt Assiduity pursue.

Sobriety. This principle embraces the several requirements comprehended in the cardinal virtue of temperance. It is not understood as merely abstaining from the indulgence of intemperance, the vice of which baneful effect lowers man, and sinks him below the grade of the brute, but it is in the general observance of a due and proper exercise of our passions, a temperate use and moderation in all things. Man becomes intemperate in the gratification of an unrestrained appetite—a gourmand—and thereby engenders disease in his system. By so doing, he departs from those laws of temperance, the observance of which are conducive to his health and comfort.

Sobriety does not consist in a melancholy, down-cast state of sadness, or a gloomy aspect, nor in an overheated imagination, or an inordinate enthusiasm, but it is calmness of mind freed from enthusiasm, uniform cheerfulness; a becoming and dignified degree of gravity, respectful in deportment, matured by judgment, free from passionate excitement or intemperate zeal. It is calmness, tempered with moderation—the exercise of prudence, governed by rational consideration—and wisdom, gained by experience.

Devoid of the virtues enjoined by the principles of Sobriety, man can not be said to be governed by those of prudence, Sobriety of deportment becomes matured as we advance in life. We can hardly expect, and it would be unreasonable to look for that degree of Sobriety in the youthful, gay, and volatile in life which we expect to find in the more matured and experienced years of manhood. They are the flowers of our youth, whose fragrant odors have ripened by the years of wisdom and experience, and are the solace of our advanced years. And who would wish to deprive youth of its hilarity, its joys and pleasures, when guided in proper paths. Youth must have its season of gayety, manhood its becoming and dignified sobriety. There is a time and season for all things; so says the Great Light; and this we also learn in our hours of labor and hours of refreshment and rest.

Sobriety will direct us in steadiness of purpose, while unrestrained zeal will often lead us into excessive folly. It will induce us to pause and reflect, while hasty impatience will often cause us to regret the imprudence of our inconsiderateness. It will produce calmness of mind, while uncontrolled passion will blindly lead us into turmoils and difficulties. Sobriety constitutes steadiness of purpose, dignified and becoming deportment, stability of character, serenity of mind, and secures us the respectful consideration of others.

The Mason who duly regards the principles of Sobriety will be cautious, prudent, and circumspect in his behavior; silence and secresy will be observed by him on all proper occasions, particularly when before the enemies of our Order. He will not permit himself to be drawn into injudicious or unnecessary arguments and controversies by those who may seek to do so, and thereby detract from his duty, and bring disrepute upon himself, to his own regret; for our institution often suffers more through the imprudence of its own members than through those who may, with evil intention, assail it; but, guarded and fortified with prudence, he will cautiously avoid all improper attacks that may be made through sinister designs and improper motives to lead him astray. It matters not in what his digression may consist, whether in the indulgence of profanity, intemperance, or any other vice, whatever it may be, he so far departs from his duty, is unfaithful and recreant to his trust, inconsistent to his profession, and inflicts a wound upon our time-honored institution.

A man's character is a tender thing, and a wound inflicted therein sinks deep into his spirits, even of a good and virtuous man; and nothing is so painful to a just and upright Mason as the wayward digressions of an erring brother. He feels the infliction caused by his derogation, and sorrows in his own heart for the erring one.

The virtues of Sobriety may be illustrated by the Lambskin, the badge of a Mason, the moral application of which is significant of purity and innocence—that purity of heart, guilelessness of conscience, and serenity of mind, which displays the better qualities of our nature, and imbues us with the necessity of leading a virtuous and upright life, which alone constitutes true happiness, the gem of man's hope and desires.

> Where virtue dwells within the heart,
> Sincerity the mind possess,
> And Sobriety is observed,
> There purity supremely reigns.

Obedience is a principle that is enjoined and required by the rules and regulations of our Order. It constitutes a cheerful and willing acquiescence in a faithful and prompt discharge of the several duties required to be performed; and unless a strict regard and adherence is paid thereto, confusion and discord would soon prevail, and our peace superseded by discordant elements. It is that spirit of proper subordination which constitutes the strength of our Mystic association, and gives harmony and order to the labors of the Craft. It is the cement which unites the brotherhood in ties of sincere affection. It is love, regard, and respect for our superiors—affability and courteousness toward one another. It is the ornament which beautifies our temple with the graces of loveliness, and makes it the resort of happiness and pleasure, concord and joy, and our labors effective.

Our ancient constitutions, while they require obedience to our laws, they also enjoin that a Mason should pay implicit obedience to the moral laws; that he should also be a peaceable subject to the laws of government under which he resides, pay a due deference of respect and obedience to the civil magistrates; that he should labor diligently and serve his Master faithfully.

Here is not only a direct injunction and requirement of obedience to the moral law, but it also requires obedience to the laws of government under which we live, and due respect to the civil magistrates. This principle is carried out in our own internal regulations, and strictly enforced. No impropriety or infringement of our rules committed by a Mason could possibly be regarded as a greater offense, and meet with a more summary condemnation, than a state of insubordination; and none surely could interrupt our harmony or produce greater confusion among the brotherhood than a spirit of contumacious disobedience.

Obedience does not derogate from character or dignity; but cheerful and willing Obedience to wholesome and proper regulations is conducive to our general good, beneficial to our prosperity, not only in our own internal regulations, but to the well-being of society in general; hence, Masons who are respectful and obedient to their own laws and regulations, are necessarily obedient to such laws and regulations as are conducive to the well-being of society at large. An obedient Mason will truly and faithfully observe the requirements exacted from him. He will not only observe and cultivate the excellent precepts of our institution, but will exemplify them in life. He will be a practical illustratration of fidelity, order and decorum.

Obedience is essential to good order; and, as the harmony and prosperity of our institution is founded upon a congruous system of rational morality, beautifully interwoven in harmonious union, consistent with order, it is therefore of the utmost importance for its well-being and prosperity that cheerful Obedience be yielded to all its just and reasonable requirements, as it exacts nothing that we can not consistently and faithfully perform. It requires that we should be faithful and prompt in the discharge of our duties, consistent and orderly in all things, for therein consists our strength. It is the vitality of our brotherhood, the bond of our union.

While the common Gavel is presented as one of the working tools of an Entered Apprentice, and its moral application intended to impress us with the necessity of divesting our minds and consciences of the vices and superfluities of human life, to free ourselves from the asperities and harshness of a rude and uncultivated nature, and thereby fit and adapt ourselves for the more advanced and improved state of society, so it is to us an emblem of Obedience. It is the Master's insignia of authority, by which he governs his lodge, and a Mason will always pay due respect and Obedience to its injunctions.

As the operative application of the gavel is to dress and prepare the rough ashler, to shape and fit it for the builder's use, so is its moral application intended to impress as with the necessity of divesting ourselves of the asperities and rudeness of our unsubdued and harsh natures, to improve and cultivate them by moral precepts, and thereby adapt and fit ourselves as useful members in the moral temple; and as it inculcates moral Obedience to man's better nature, so it inculcates Obedience and respect to our laws and requirements.

As the spirit of Obedience runs through the whole system of our institution, it constitutes one of its greatest safeguards, and is the fulcrum which supports it with strength and preserves it in its pristine purity.

Nobility consists in those traits of character which give eminence to man's position in society, whether they be of a religious or of a moral cast. The man imbued with a sense of his religious obligations, and leading a life of piety in conformity to its requirements, possesses a nobleness of character for his pious and self-denying life. It may be truly said of him that he is a living pillar in the temple, whose indwelling spirit is purity and holiness; whose sanctuary is the abode of Divine light, from whence flows incense of heavenly love.

And he who lives in obedience to the moral obligations,

possesses nobleness of worth for his virtuous and exemplary deportment.

Man is noble wherein he conforms to those principles of justice, honor, and integrity, which distinguish him in his intercourse with his fellow-men. A noble mind does not indulge in a selfish, vindictive, or unforgiving disposition, but is ever generous, magnanimous, and honorable in action and sentiment, free from unjust resentment or reproach, and, while forbearing and tolerant in disposition, is, with a corresponding degree of justice, ready to make honorable amends for any wrong or injury inflicted. A noble mind will never engage in vituperation or slander, but will rather vindicate the assailed from unjust attacks.

Hence, true Nobility consists in those traits of character which give eminence and elevation to the mind; candor and frankness distinguish it in its actions and sentiments; it is dignified in mien, and bears contempt of any thing that is dishonorable.

A conscientious observance of the reverence due to God, and a conformity to the requirements of morality, and an assiduous and proper employment of our time, are the duties required of us. A degree of becoming Sobriety and solemnity of deportment, with respectful considerations and a free and unrestrained Obedience, accorded with due cheerfulness, constitutes true nobleness in the character of man, and gives him commanding honor and secures him just respect.

These virtues should distinguish a just and upright Mason, as they are the qualifications that constitute true nobleness and worth, and, as such, are the principles he is taught to observe; and wherein he adheres to their maxims, so far he is consistent in the duties of his obligation, and stands forth as a worthy and honored son of light; and in whatever his derelictions may consist, he is deficient, and thus far derogates from the standard of what a Mason ought to be.

As the Five Points of Fellowship, are illustrative of these principles, we may enumerate in connection and association with them those of MODERATION, AFFABILITY, SINCERITY, OBSERVANCE, AND NEIGHBORLY. These are also subjects embraced within its scope, and are of equal value, and claim from us just considerations.

Moderation is that state of being whereby we keep ourselves within the bounds of proper restraint, and are governed by a just and equitable equilibrium in all things; not given to unrestrained excitement and violence of temper, or undue indulgence in the sordid gratification of our appetites and desires, but, governed by reason and prudence, conducive to our peace and comfort. By the exercise of this principle we preserve calmness of mind, steadiness of purpose, a reasonable forbearance and proper consideration in all things, and a just propriety in our words and actions.

Governed by Moderation, we are neither over elated by prosperity nor grievously depressed by adversity, but are prepared to meet the varied events of life, with becoming resignation. This virtue is beautifully illustrated by the checkered ground-floor of the temple, which reminds us of the precarious uncertainties of human life, and impresses on our minds with the necessity of our dependence upon God.

Affability consists in those social and agreeable qualities which distinguish us for our civilities and our courteous manner of respectful deportment toward others, whereby we render ourselves agreeable to society, cheerful and pleasant in our intercourse, and secure the affectionate regard and esteemed consideration of our fellow-beings—an attainment that is at all times desirable to secure.

By the exercise of this principle we cultivate those amenities in life which gives confidence and makes us accessible to others. By it we diffuse cheerfulness, and make the social relations of life desirable, strengthen the bonds of fraternal brotherhood, impart good counsel, admonition, and advice to the listening ear, and soothe the cares of a troubled mind; hence, Affability may, with consistent propriety, be illustrated by the tenets of our Order—Brotherly Love, Relief, and Truth.

Sincerity is that frank, candid, and honest purpose of the mind, which should actuate us in all our dealings and transactions with one another. It is that purity of mind, frankness of expression, artless simplicity which imparts confidence in man, undisguised by hypocrisy and deception. The sincere mind will always be guided by candor and frankness; truth will be the foundation of its actions, the ruling principle of its motives. It will secure love, respect, and esteem; it will win the confidence and regard of others, establish our characters for veracity, and give reposing assurance in our integrity.

No principle should be more strictly observed than

pure and undefiled sincerity; and the Mason actuated by this virtue will always be candid and frank; he will be ever ready to apprise a brother for his interest and welfare, admonish him of his shortcomings and failings, with kind considerations for his good. Sincerity is the offspring of pure affections, and is illustrated by the emblem of Fidelity, the token by which we confirm the sincerity of our professions and honest intentions of purpose. This emblem is the connecting link of the affections, which flow from one to the other when joined by its union.

Observance is that proper regard and principal consideration that should be adhered to in the performance of our duties to each other. It is the rule of our practice, and regard of our attention to laws and ceremonies, customs and habits, and a becoming obedience to order and decorum. The observant mind will be considerate, respectful, and attentive to surrounding circumstances, will pay a due deference of respect to superior position, and conform to just and reasonable requirements, adhere to the rules of propriety and decorum, and thereby avoid giving unnecessary offense.

The observance of moral law requires just and fair dealings between men, while the Divine law inculcates obedience to God, and leads us to the performance of pious duties—all conducive to our happiness, and assimilate us in characters to the Divine will.

The Mason who is observant of the precepts of our Order will be gentle in his demeanor, kind and affectionate in feeling, obedient to its injunctions, and sincere in his attachments; he will avoid immorality and vice, cultivate the principles of virtue, and live in obedience to its just and wholesome requirements.

Neighborly consists of social civility and friendly relations in our intercourse, terms of amity and good understanding, mutual respect and esteem, and agreeableness in association. It is that state of harmonious feeling that should exist for the mutual benefit and welfare of society; and, as social beings, we should be always ready and willing to render kind aid and assistance when needed, as we know not what circumstances may bring around us; the necessity of Neighborly attention, either received by ourselves, or extended to others, affords mutual protection and reciprocity of attachment.

While the principles of our institution require that we should live on terms of amity and good-fellowship with one another, whereby our bond of union becomes more matured and strengthened in friendship and fraternal attachment, it, at the same time, enjoins upon us, as a duty we owe to society, to carry out this principle toward others, for, by so doing, we extend the operations of our usefulness, enlarge the affections in offices of kindness, and thereby we silence the tongue of envy, and convince the world at large of the honesty of our purpose and the sincerity of our profession.

Thus far the emblem at the head of this subject illustrates the reverence we owe to our God, and the duties we owe to ourselves and to our fellow-beings, and, while it portrays these virtues, it is significant of still further elucidation.

By it we are reminded of the necessity of responding

to a brother's call in time of need, that we should be ever swift on foot to serve him in time of distress, lay aside selfish considerations, and be not indolent or tardy in giving a helping hand to a brother's wants; for timely aid, opportunely afforded, may be the means of his preservation and the strong hope of his salvation.

It also reminds us that we should ever consider a brother's interest and welfare in connection with our own; that we should be mindful of him in our supplications to Deity, remembering that we are all on a level before the Great Judge of all things, who does not regard worldly distinctions, but will reward us according to our labors.

It also enjoins upon us that we should be faithful and constant to a brother, whose repose of confidence may with safety be lodged in our breast with sacred security; that we may not betray him, whereby he may fall into dangers or be led into difficulties, but consider his welfare and interest, and befriend him with timely counsel and admonition.

It also requires of us that, with outstretched arms, we should be ever ready to support and sustain a sinking brother, render him that sustaining and needful aid his trials and adversities may require at our hands, ever remembering the frailties of our fallen natures, and that we too may require to be infolded in the supporting arms of a brother.

It also admonishes us that we should ever be ready to give good counsel, advice, and comfort to the listening ear of a brother; that we should vindicate his character from unjust aspersions, ever warn him of approaching dangers. Linked together, as we are, by ties of sincere affection, we can not, therefore, be indifferent to the obligations resting upon us.

Such are the various illustrations portrayed by the emblem representing the Five Points of Fellowship. Within its sphere is comprehended every virtue and duty which we are called upon to perform as social and rational beings placed here for each other's good. And it is not only in the performance of the various duties and obligations we owe to one another in life that we are reminded by it to exemplify—all of which are so forcibly and impressively conveyed to the mind by symbolic instruction, for the purpose of more deeply impressing it with the important lessons they convey. But it also impresses the mind with the duties we owe to God, the love and reverence we should always bear to him as our chief source of reliance; and without a pious observance of which we are not fully up to the standard of our duty.

We may possess all the virtues required by morality, live in the daily practice of them; yet, devoid of that filial duty, reverence and obedience due to the will of God, we would be, as an eminent apostle has described, without charity and love to God, as a sounding brass and tinkling cymbal.

Hence, Masons can not be too careful in the faithful observance of the duties they are called upon to perform both to God and man. Guard well the avenues that lead to vice; shun its ways, and walk in wisdom's path, that, when your labors on earth are closed, you may be called to partake of the refreshments of heaven.

The word Mason is comprised in the five points of the star, which is an emblem of fellowship. It also comprehends the title of our profession, and the letters of which it is composed also constitute the initials of the several virtues of morality illustrated by the five-pointed emblem, and which we are taught to inculcate as the precepts that should be the governing rules of our actions.

There is a degree of becoming dignity in the Masonic character, that many who enjoy the privilege do not seem to properly appreciate—a want of that moral honor and integrity which should distinguish a Mason; and it is a source of regret to those who truly estimate and place a proper appreciation and value upon our association—it lessens confidence and creates distrust in the mind, which often retards our usefulness. Properly appreciated, our institution comprehends and inculcates all that man can desire for his present state to constitute his happiness, and it directs him to seek the paths that will lead to his endless felicity. Its standard is the very highest grade of morality, and its religion undefiled purity and reverence to God.

LECTURE XX.

EMBLEMS OF CONSIDERATION.

THE THREE STEPS,

USUALLY delineated upon the Master's carpet, are emblematical of the three principal stages of human life—youth, manhood, and age. In youth, as Entered Apprentices, we ought industriously to occupy our minds in the attainment of useful knowledge; in manhood, as Fellow-Crafts, we should apply our knowledge to the discharge of our respective duties to God, our neighbors, and ourselves, so that in age, as Master Masons, we may enjoy the happy reflections consequent on a well-spent life, and die in the hope of a glorious immortality.

THE POT OF INCENSE

Is an emblem of a pure heart, which is always an acceptable sacrifice to Deity; and as this glows with fervent heat, so should our hearts continually glow with gratitude to the great and beneficent Author of our existence for the manifold blessings and comforts we enjoy.

THE BEE-HIVE

Is an emblem of industry, and recommends the practice of that virtue to all created beings, from the highest seraph in heaven to the lowest reptile of the dust. It teaches us that, as we came into the world rational and intelligent beings, so we should ever be industrious ones, never sitting down contented while our fellow-creatures around us are in want, when it is in our power to relieve them without inconvenience to ourselves.

When we take a survey of nature, we view man in his infancy, more helpless and indigent than the brute creation; he lies languishing for days, months, and years, totally incapable of providing sustenance for himself, of guarding against the attack of the wild beasts of the forest, or sheltering himself from the inclemencies of the weather.

It might have pleased the great Creator of heaven and earth to have made man independent of all other beings; but, as dependence is one of the strongest bonds of society, mankind were made dependent on each other for protection and security, as they thereby enjoy better opportunities of fulfilling the duties of reciprocal love and friendship. Thus was man formed for social and active life, the noblest part of the work of God; and he that will so demean himself as not to be endeavoring to add to the common stock of knowledge and understanding, may be deemed a *drone* in the *hive* of nature, a useless member of society, and unworthy of our protection as Masons.

THE BOOK OF CONSTITUTIONS,

Guarded by the Tyler's sword, reminds us that we should be ever watchful and guarded in our thoughts, words, and actions, particularly when before the enemies of Masonry, ever bearing in remembrance those truly Masonic virtues, *silence* and *circumspection*.

THE SWORD POINTING TO A NAKED HEART

Demonstrates that justice will, sooner or later, overtake us; and although our thoughts, words, and actions may be hidden from the eyes of man, yet that

ALL-SEEING EYE!

Whom the *sun, moon, and stars obey*, and under whose watchful care even comets perform their stupendous revolutions, beholds the inmost recesses of the human heart, and will reward us according to our works.

THE ANCHOR AND ARK

Are emblems of a well-grounded *hope* and a well-spent life. They are emblematical of that divine *ark* which safely bears us over this tempestuous sea of troubles, and that *anchor* which shall safely moor us in a peaceful harbor, where the wicked cease from troubling, and the weary shall find rest.

THE FORTY-SEVENTH PROBLEM OF EUCLID.

This was an invention of our ancient friend and brother, the great Pythagoras, who, in his travels through Asia, Africa, and Europe, was initiated into several orders of priesthood, and raised to the sublime degree of a Master Mason. This wise philosopher enriched his mind abundantly in a general knowledge of things, and more especially in geometry or masonry. On this subject he drew out many problems and theorems; and among the most distinguished he erected this, which, in the joy of his heart, he called *Eureka*—in the Grecian language signifying *I have found it*—and upon the discovery of which he is said to have sacrificed a hecatomb. It teaches Masons to be general lovers of the arts and sciences.

THE HOUR-GLASS

Is an emblem of human life. Behold! how swiftly the sands run, and how rapidly our lives are drawing to a close. We can not, without astonishment, behold the little particles which are contained in this machine; how they pass away almost imperceptibly; and yet, to our surprise, in the short space of an hour, they are all exhausted. Thus wastes man! To-day he puts forth the tender leaves of hope; to-morrow blossoms, and bears his blushing honors thick upon him; the next day comes a frost, which nips the shoot, and when he thinks his greatness still aspiring, he falls, like autumn leaves, to enrich our mother earth.

THE SCYTHE

Is an emblem of time, which cuts the brittle thread of life, and launches us into eternity. Behold! what havoc the scythe of time makes among the human race: if by chance we should escape the numerous evils incident to childhood and youth, and with health and vigor arrive at the years of manhood, yet, withal, we must soon be cut down by the all-devouring scythe of time, and be gathered into the land where our fathers have gone before us.

AT the head of this lecture stands a group of emblems, all illustrative of useful instructions to us, and which we have, from their nature, classified under the general term of consideration, as they are all mental in their application, and are therefore mainly for the consideration of the mind. They inculcate virtues and precepts, which should be the governing rules of our actions in life. We are all more or less influenced by objects that affect the senses of our natures, and we gain wisdom from the observations we make. Even the most minute object in nature affords some useful information, of value to us at some period in life, from whence we may glean profitable lessons of instruction.

The Great Creator has designed his works for man's benefit, his uses and his purposes, and for His own eternal glory and honor; and the greatest of all his works is man, whom he created erect, and endowed with mind and intellect. And this is the evidence of his superiority in the animated creation; hence man, when he digresses and departs from rectitude of character, and abuses his privileges, he degrades his nature and dishonors his creation.

The Three Steps delineated in the group are illustrative of the three periods pertaining to human life—youth, manhood, and age. They are also significant of the three symbolic degrees—Entered Apprentice. Fellow-Craft, and Master Mason—and impress the mind with the importance of these stations, the discipline we undergo to prepare and qualify ourselves for the privileges and honors that pertain to the rank of Masters.

The Pot of Incense, as an emblem of a pure heart, that should ever glow with fervent love and gratitude, reminds us of that devotion we should ever offer upon our altars when we make our acknowledgments and put forth our supplications with pure sincerity, which can only make them acceptable, as an incense ascending from the creature to the Creator. It also reminds us of the badge we should never desecrate, but ever honor it as the emblem of purity and innocence, as it is intended to remind us of the necessity of preserving a pure and spotless character. How warmly the heart glows with gratitude! how tenderly the sympathies flow in affection when governed by pure motives influenced by Divine love. It subdues the harshness of our natures, and makes us more gentle and kind in feeling.

THE BEE-HIVE is an emblem of industry; and from the industrious and busy little insect that inhabits this humble tenement we may learn a useful lesson. Ever active in unremitting industry, it gathers its store from the flowers of the field in their season of bloom, and stores it away in its cell, harvested for sustenance when its labors must cease from the chilling blasts of winter. What a provident lesson we may here learn! How beautifully is this also illustrated by the moral application of the Twenty-four-inch Gauge, by which we are taught the necessity of dividing our time, that a portion may be devoted to the pursuit of labor, whence we secure and make provision against casualties, and for the coming period of life when our active energies must cease and our declining years seek repose; for man can not always toil—the abilities become exhausted, and the powers of mind and body enfeebled.

THE BOOK OF CONSTITUTIONS, guarded by the Tyler's sword, signifies that we should be constantly faithful to our duty, and, as vigilant sentinels, be watchful that no unguarded moment of indolence may overtake us, whereby the enemies of our Order may, through our own injudicious attention, lead us into some false step, and thereby induce us to betray confidence that should ever be cherished with the strongest ties of sincere integrity. Fidelity is one of the most important jewels that a Mason can possess, and should be esteemed as the highest prize to enjoy. It is the guarantee of security he feels in the integrity of a brother, and the repose of confidence he with safety places in him.

As the elements of our institution are embraced in the book of Constitutions, so ought the virtues it inculcates be firmly implanted in our hearts as the repositories of pure and virtuous principles, upon which we build our characters for moral excellence.

THE SWORD POINTING TO THE NAKED HEART.—This emblem illustrates to us that no injustice or wrong can be committed which does not, at some period, meet a corresponding retribution; for although we may feel ourselves secure, and that our acts, in the confidence of our assurance, are unobserved by human eyes, yet we betray our deception, sooner or later, by some overt act, or in some unguarded moment of unexpected observation, and, when we least anticipate it, the pointed Sword will pierce the heart with remorse of guilt, and the retribution that justice demands bring disgrace and shame to our door.

THE ALL-SEEING EYE is the incomprehensible emblem that illustrates the constant presence and paternal watchfulness of that Invisible Being to whom alone is known every secret thought of the mind, and every act we perform, although unobserved by our fellow-beings; and before whom, as our final Judge, we must appear, and shall stand condemned or acquitted. We may, by our art, dissemble and deceive the human eye, but the All-seeing Eye is ever cognizant of our acts, and the inward workings of the heart are fully known to it. Omnipotent, Omnipresent, and Omniscient is that Being by whose fiat worlds innumerable were formed and brought into being, and by whose Almighty will they are sustained and move in their order.

THE ANCHOR AND ARK are the emblems of a well-grounded faith and hope—faith in God, who will bear us triumphantly through the trials and turmoils of life in the ark of security, if our reliance is steadfast and the faith of our hope is firmly placed in him. He will moor us in the harbor of safety, secured by the anchor of that hope we possess through faith, as the only reliable assurance of our permanent security.

Man ever looks forward. He builds his hopes upon the future, and his anticipations are more often disappointed than realized; but his genius still impels him onward; his frail bark is drifting upon the ocean of time, and he seeks to gain a harbor where he may cast his anchor, moored in safety. But he is a subject of time, wafted to and fro in its eventful uncertainties, until he is gathered in the ark of safety, secured by the anchor of Divine favor.

THE FORTY-SEVENTH PROBLEM OF EUCLID. This figure is illustrative of the mathematical genius. It pertains to the intellect, and develops its abilities for the advancement of the arts and sciences. By the use of mathematics we gain knowledge essential to surveying, navigation, planning and erecting structures agreeably to the laws regulating their strength and support. By it the astronomer makes his observations and calculations, wherein he defines the magnitudes of celestial bodies, and measures their distance. As arithmetic, geometry, and algebra are branches of mathematics, it enters more or less into all the affairs of life, although we may be ignorant of a knowledge of science.

THE HOUR-GLASS is the emblem of human life. It prefigures to us the flight of time, and impresses the mind with the short duration of man's earthly career; and as the sands therein diminish, so man's days roll on, and are numbered with the past. It is an emblem that should impress us with the necessity of a useful employment of our time, that we should sow in our youth, reap in our manhood, and enjoy the fruits of our labors in mature age. Although, in the order of Providence, we may not pass through these periods, yet our time should be well and profitably employed, as we know not its continuance. Even at the allotted period of three-score years and ten, our time is short in duration with eternity; the days and years imperceptibly pass away, the sands of life are run, and the frail tenement returns and mingles with the earth. And thus terminates man's earthly career.

THE SCYTHE is the emblem of time. Its approach is uncertain; it regards neither youth, manhood, or age, and its harvest is at all seasons. It often comes, without timely notice or warning, when we are least prepared or anticipate its near approach. Death reaps his harvest with the scythe of destruction, and wields it with an uncertainty to man, who can make no calculation how soon he may fall a victim to its power. No wealth, rank, or distinction of honor can stay his inexorable and devouring will or insatiable hunger for human life.

EMBLEMS OF MORTALITY.

"Let me die the death of the righteous, and let my last end be like his."— Num. XXIII: 10.

These constitute the last class of emblems pertaining to the Master Mason's Degree, and they are calculated to produce reflections and thoughts for meditations of a serious nature—reflections upon the past course and events of life, thoughts of approaching dissolution, the terrors of death, and the retribution that awaits us when summoned before the unbiased tribunal of eternal Justice. Not that our Judge is inexorable in his demands, but the overpowering of his mercy, his love, and his infinite goodness causes us to dread the presence of an indulgent parent, who has ever desired our happiness.

What can the poor finite creature do to offend the

Divine Majesty of heaven, infinite and eternal love? he only suffers the consequences of his own wrongdoings. This is the decree of the Divine and moral law, and can not be set aside; and the more we depart and the further we estray ourselves, and wander from the paths of rectitude and justice, the more anguish we endure in returning. We are of the heritage; and as the body returns to the earth, the spirit will also return from whence it came—although the probation may be long. If we wander far from our Father's house we can not return by a shorter way.

"Let us hear the conclusion of the whole matter: Fear God, and keep his commandments; for this is the whole duty of man."—Eccle. xii: 13.

IN MEMORIA.

The memory of the good and virtuous should ever be cherished with grateful remembrance, and their ashes safely deposited in the urn of mortality. And whatever the faults and frailties of an erring brother may have been, the broad mantle of a Mason's charity should cover them.

OUR SYMBOLS.

ENTERED APPRENTICE.

DEVOTIONAL.

THE ALTAR.

MY brother, do you before your ALTAB kneel,
In lowly meekness, humbly before your God,
And his forgiveness for your offenses ask—
His mercy and his forgiving pardon seek?

THE BOOK OF LIGHT.

My brother, do you the Book of Life peruse,
The light Divine, unerring guide to faith,
The rock whereupon, securely firm, you stand—
Your hope, your joy, realized through faith to be?

MORAL.

THE SQUARE.

My brother, have you the SQUARE of Truth applied
As the test whereby your actions to adjust,
With honor, justice, and probity to man,
As are by its moral application taught?

THE COMPASSES.

My brother, have you the COMPASSES applied
For the moral purposes they inculcate,
And thereby your passions and desires kept
Within the just bounds of prudence, circumscribed?

THE LAMB-SKIN.

My brother, have you the LAMB-SKIN worthily worn,
As most strictly given in charge that you should do,
Unsullied, untarnished, pure, as it should be,
By a brother who its purity reveres?

THE TWENTY-FOUR-INCH GAUGE.

My brother, do you the Rule and Gauge apply,
Thereby your time apportion, as taught to do,
For service required to be performed by you
Of labor, rest, service to God, and RELIEF?

THE GAVEL.

My brother, do you the GAVEL exercise
As its moral application symbolize,
Whereby the mind and conscience divested are
Of superfluities, freed from sin and vice?

THE VIRTUES.

FAITH.

My brother, have you FAITH in God's promise made—
Faith, as taught that you should ever have in him?
Your dependence for aid on him wholly place,
As your chief reliance for support in need.

HOPE.

My brother, have you confiding HOPE through faith—
Hope, as revealed through God's holy word to man—
Hope, in anticipation of blissful joy;
Realized to be through faith in him on high?

CHARITY.

My brother, have you CHARITY and Love—
Charity Divine—toward your fellow-man,
Such as you were in our Mystic Temple taught
As the virtue chief, possess'd to be by you?

THE JEWELS MORAL.

SQUARE.

My brother, are you governed by the SQUARE—
The Square of truth and justice in equity—
Consistent to the plumb-line of rectitude
And equality as by the Level taught?

LEVEL.

My brother, do you the principle observe
Of equality as by the LEVEL taught—
Regard your brother for his merited worth,
Cherish his interest and welfare with your own?

PLUMB.

My brother, do you, by the PLUMB, upright walk
In rectitude just, erect before your God,
As Masons true are, in duty, bound to do,
Who justly observe the precepts by it taught?

THE JEWELS OPERATIVE.

THE ROUGH ASHLER.

My brother, have you improved your allotted time
'Portioned to service as you were taught to do,
Or, like the ROUGH ASHLER, unimproved remain,
Unsuited and unfit for the builder's use?

THE PERFECT ASHLER.

My brother, have you improved your given time
In works of Brotherly Love, Relief, and Truth,
Thereby yourself suited to the temple's use,
As PERFECT ASHLER, squared and finished, is.

THE TRESTLE-BOARD.

My brother, have you from the Great Light designed
The TRESTLE-BOARD of your light and life divine,
And drawn there from your plan of life to pursue,
As the moral architect, you're taught to do.

THE TENETS.

BROTHERLY LOVE.

My brother, have you BROTHERLY LOVE in heart—
Brotherly Love, pure, in affection sincere,
Entwin'd with silken cords in angelic love,
Such as brother with brother entwined should be?

RELIEF.

My brother, do you relieve and kindly aid
Your afflicted brother when in time of need,
Seek out the orphan and the widow bereaved,
Aid and give RELIEF to their dependent wants?

TRUTH.

My brother, is TRUTH observed in all your deeds,
Your dealings, and your acts with your fellow-man,
With justice and equity, as it should be,
Free from deception by fraud corrupt or foul?

THE CARDINAL VIRTUES.

TEMPERANCE.

My brother, are the just rules of TEMPERANCE,
As required, adhered to and observed by you—
A proper restraint upon your passions placed,
From whence health, happiness, and peace ensue?

FORTITUDE.

My brother, are you strengthened by FORTITUDE
As the safeguard upon which you firmly stand,
The varied events and trials of life to meet
With steadfast firmness and constant courage true?

PRUDENCE.

My brother, are you by PRUDENCE guarded well
In all your acts, whether in word or deed—
So circumscrib'd as in lawful bounds to be,
Whereby invidious danger you avert?

JUSTICE.

My brother, is JUSTICE the standard of your acts
As founded upon the principles of Truth,
Conforming in rectitude and equity
Of Justice to all men, as is justly due?

FELLOW-CRAFT.

MORAL.

THE PLUMB.

My brother, does your work upright, erect, stand,
As when by the PLUMB-LINE prov'd it should be—
Perpendicular, not right nor left inclin'd,
But erect, as in the temple should be found?

THE SQUARE.

My brother, does your work to the SQUARE conform,
Just and exact, in all its proportions true,
Such as adapted is to the builder's use,
And with safety may be in the temple placed?

THE LEVEL.

My brother, does your work by the LEVEL lay
Horizontal to the plane, as it must do—
Tested by the Level, Square, and Plumb to be—
For foundation firmly laid to build upon?

MASTER MASON.

MORAL.

THE TROWEL.

My brother, do you the principles observe
As morally by the TROWEL symbolized,
Widely the cement of Brotherly Love to spread
In affection's bond of union firmly laid?

THE FIVE POINTS OF FELLOWSHIP.

My brother, are the precepts of fellowship
As within the FIVE POINTS thereof contained,
Conformed to and faithfully observed by you,
And their just requirements adhered thereto?

Are you swift on FOOT, in answer to the call,
Prompt in response for a brother's aid in need—
Surrounded by distress or overburdened grief,
Cheerfully, with speed, to give him kind relief?

Do you a brother's interest truly regard;
In connection seek his welfare with your own;
Mindful of him; when upon your bended KNEE
Your supplications offer in his behalf?

When brother repose confiding in you place,
Is the unbosomed secret securely safe—
No false, unkind betrayal lurking within
The BREAST, wherein confiding repose is plac'd?

Do you, with outstretched HAND, stand forth to sustain,
Give support and succoring aid in time of need,
Save a desponding brother with prompt relief,
And his troubled mind with balsam to peace restore?

Do you counsel to the LISTENING EAR impart;
With mildness advise, admonish, or reprove
A brother what his failings or his errors be,
As his merits or demerits may require?

EMBLEMS OF CONSIDERATION.

THE THREE STEPS.

Youth, Manhood, and Age, periods three in life,
Which to useful purposes applied should be—
Youth, as the spring-time of life, to be prepared
For the toils of Manhood and the repose of Age.

THE POT OF INCENSE.

Pure gratitude from the heart should ever flow,
As an incense of offering due to God
For benefits we daily receive from HIM,
Bestowed with gracious aid, with bounteous hand.

THE BEE-HIVE.

From industry learn the true value of time,
As we know not the needs the morrow may want,
Or what the uncertainties of life bring forth
In prosperity's or adversity's train.

THE BOOK OF CONSTITUTIONS.

Prudence should ever guide us watchful to be,
With circumspect deportment, in our ways;
Carefully our acts with caution due observe,
That through neither we're betrayed or led astray.

THE SWORD POINTING TO THE NAKED HEART.

Integrity, a principle of the heart,
Justice, with fairness of purpose, will observe,
The conscience preserve pure from a stain of fraud,
Not pierc'd with remorse of guilt or shame for wrong.

THE ALL-SEEING EYE.

Omniscience, the All-seeing Eye,
Ever watchful o'er creation's surrounding works,
Observant of man's acts, penetrates his thoughts,
And the inward workings of his heart reveals.

THE ANCHOR AND ARK.

A firm and steadfast reliance placed in God,
As the Ark of Safety o'er life's tempestuous toil,
Is the Anchor of Hope, encouraged through faith,
That secures happiness of Celestial life.

THE FORTY-SEVENTH PROBLEM OF EUCLID.

The foundation firmly laid we build upon,
Our work squarely by the right-angle place,
As by the rule of mathematics prescribed,
And our moral temple raise by plumb-line true.

THE HOUR-GLASS.

How swiftly the sands of life their course do run,
Heedlessly regarded in our daily walks!
Thoughtless of the moments in their rapid flight,
Onward we hurry, regardless of our time.

THE SCYTHE.

The hour has arrived, the summons to obey;
Time, the prime minister of death, hurriedly
Cuts the brittle, vital thread of mortal life,
And man falls a victim to the Scythe of Time.

MORTALITY.

The windows are darkened, and the doors are shut;
The silver cord loosened, the golden bowl broken,
The grinding not heard, the fountain ceased to flow,
And man goes to the grave—the spirit to God.

Stone Guild Publishing

Look for these and other great titles at:
http://www.stoneguildpublishing.com

Book of Ancient and Accepted Scottish Rite by Charles T. McClenachan
The Book of the Holy Graal by A. E. Waite
The Book of the Lodge by George Oliver
The Builders by Joseph Fort Newton
Chymical Marriage of Christian Rosencreutz translated by A. E. Waite
The Doctrine and Literature of the Kabalah by A. E. Waite
Fama Fraternitatis and Confession of the Rosicrucians by A. E. Waite
Freemasonry in the Holy Land by Robert Morris
The Freemason's Manual by Jeremiah How
The Freemason's Monitor by Daniel Sickels
The History of Freemasonry and Concordant Orders
The History of Initiation by George Oliver
Illustrations of the Symbols of Freemasonry by Jacob Ernst
The Kybalion by The Three Initiates
Low Twelve by Edward S. Ellis
The New Masonic Trestleboard by Charles W. Moore
Opinions on Speculative Masonry by James C. Odiorne
The Perfect Ceremonies of Craft Masonry
The Poetry of Freemasonry by Rob Morris
Real History of the Rosicrucians by A. E. Waite
The Symbolism of Freemasonry by Albert G. Mackey
Symbolism of the Three Degrees by Oliver Day Street
Taylor's Monitor by William M. Taylor
Taylor-Hamilton Monitor of Symbolic Masonry by Sam R. Hamilton
Three Hundred Masonic Odes and Poems by Rob Morris
True Masonic Chart or Hieroglyphic Monitor by Jeremy Cross

www.ingramcontent.com/pod-product-compliance
Lightning Source LLC
Chambersburg PA
CBHW072003150426
43194CB00008B/980